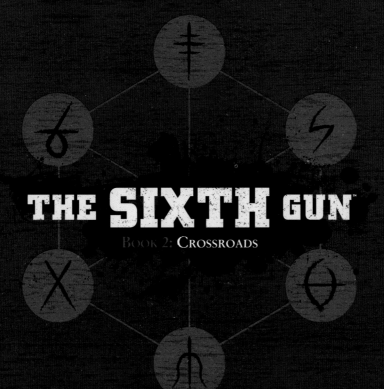

THE SIXTH GUN

BOOK 2: CROSSROADS

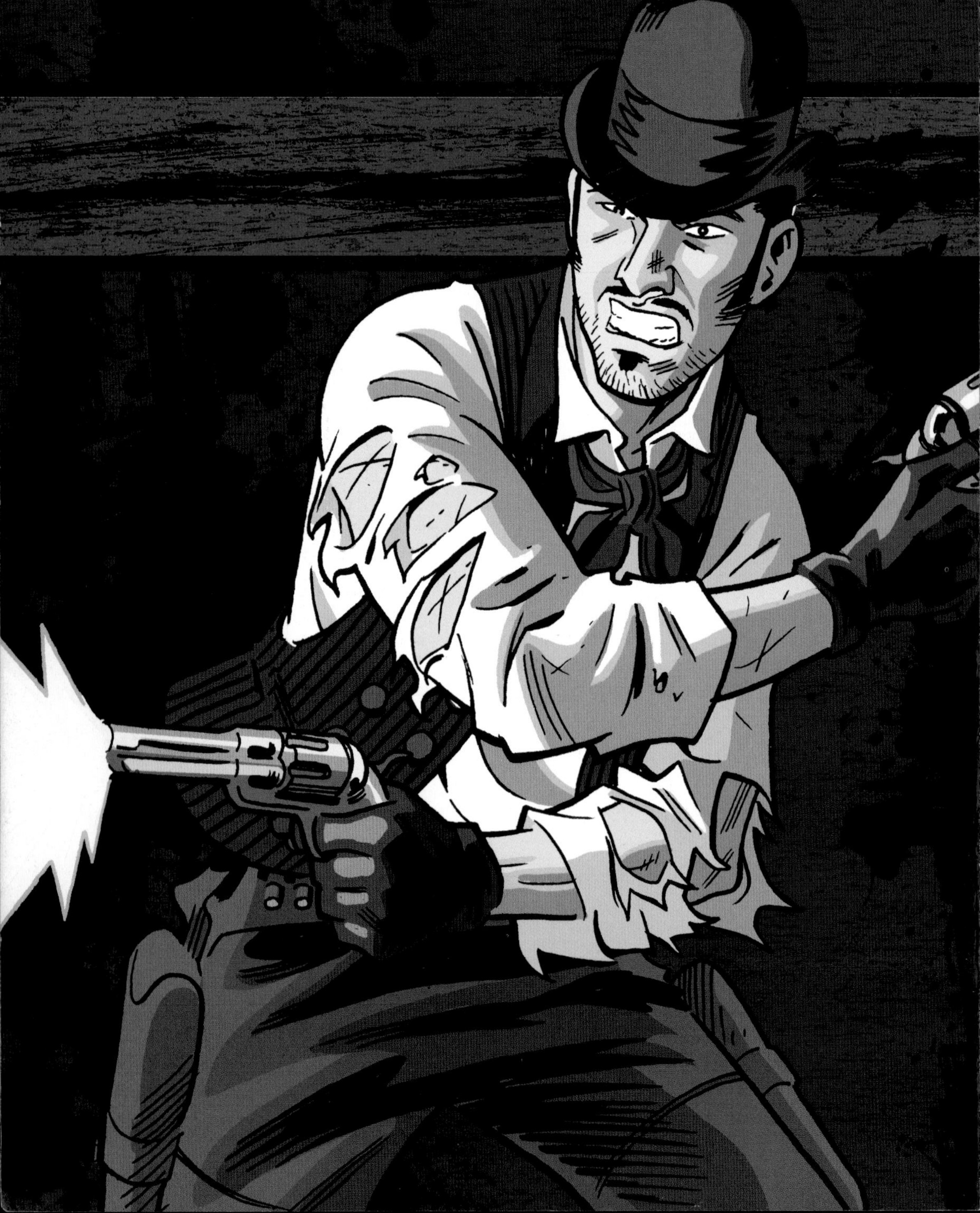

THE SIXTH GUN™

BOOK 2: CROSSROADS

WRITTEN BY
CULLEN BUNN

ILLUSTRATED & LETTERED BY
BRIAN HURTT

COLORS BY
BILL CRABTREE

EDITED BY
CHARLIE CHU

DESIGN BY
KEITH WOOD

ONI PRESS

AN ONI PRESS PUBLICATION

THE SIXTH GUN™
BY CULLEN BUNN & BRIAN HURTT

PUBLISHED BY ONI PRESS, INC.
JOE NOZEMACK *publisher*
JAMES LUCAS JONES *editor in chief*
CORY CASONI *marketing director*
KEITH WOOD *art director*
GEORGE ROHAC *operations director*
JILL BEATON *editor*
CHARLIE CHU *editor*
DOUGLAS E. SHERWOOD *production assistant*

THE SIXTH GUN, June 2011. Published by Oni Press, Inc. 1305 SE Martin Luther King Jr. Blvd., Suite A, Portland, OR 97214.

This volume collects issues #7-11 of the Oni Press series *The Sixth Gun*.

ONI PRESS, INC.
1305 SE MARTIN LUTHER KING JR. BLVD.
SUITE A
PORTLAND, OR 97214
USA

onipress.com
Become our fan on Facebook: facebook.com/onipress
Follow us on Twitter: @onipress
onipress.tumblr.com

cullenbunn.com • @cullenbunn
thehurttlocker.blogspot.com • @brihurtt
@crabtree_bill

First edition: June 2011
ISBN: 978-1-934964-67-5

10 9 8 7 6 5 4 3 2

Printed In U.S.A.

DRAKE SINCLAIR - A treasure hunter with a bleak past. He now holds four of the Six.

BECKY MONTCRIEF - A brave young woman who holds the Sixth Gun, a weapon that can divine the future.

GORD CANTRELL - A former prisoner who helped Drake and Becky at the battle of the Maw.

BILLJOHN O'HENRY - Drake's friend. Killed at the battle of the Maw and raised as a golem-like creature by the power of the guns.

GENERAL HUME - A murderer and a fiend, killed at the battle of the Maw. But he's been killed before.

CHAPTER ONE

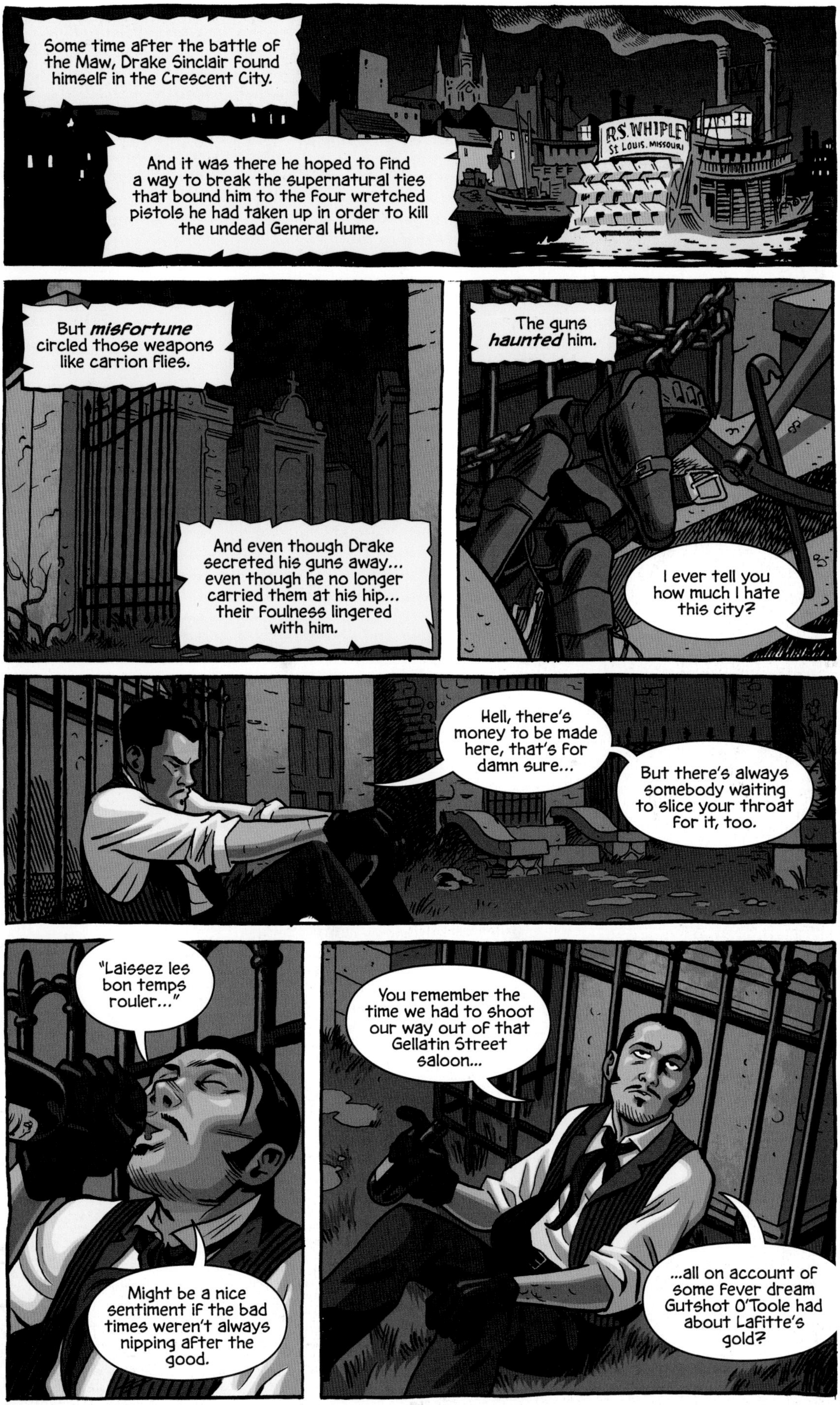
Some time after the battle of the Maw, Drake Sinclair found himself in the Crescent City.
And it was there he hoped to find a way to break the supernatural ties that bound him to the four wretched pistols he had taken up in order to kill the undead General Hume.
R.S. WHIPLEY
St LOUIS, MISSOURI
But *misfortune* circled those weapons like carrion flies.
And even though Drake secreted his guns away... even though he no longer carried them at his hip... their foulness lingered with him.
The guns *haunted* him.
I ever tell you how much I hate this city?
Hell, there's money to be made here, that's for damn sure...
But there's always somebody waiting to slice your throat for it, too.
"Laissez les bon temps rouler..."
Might be a nice sentiment if the bad times weren't always nipping after the good.
You remember the time we had to shoot our way out of that Gellatin Street saloon...
...all on account of some fever dream Gutshot O'Toole had about Lafitte's gold?

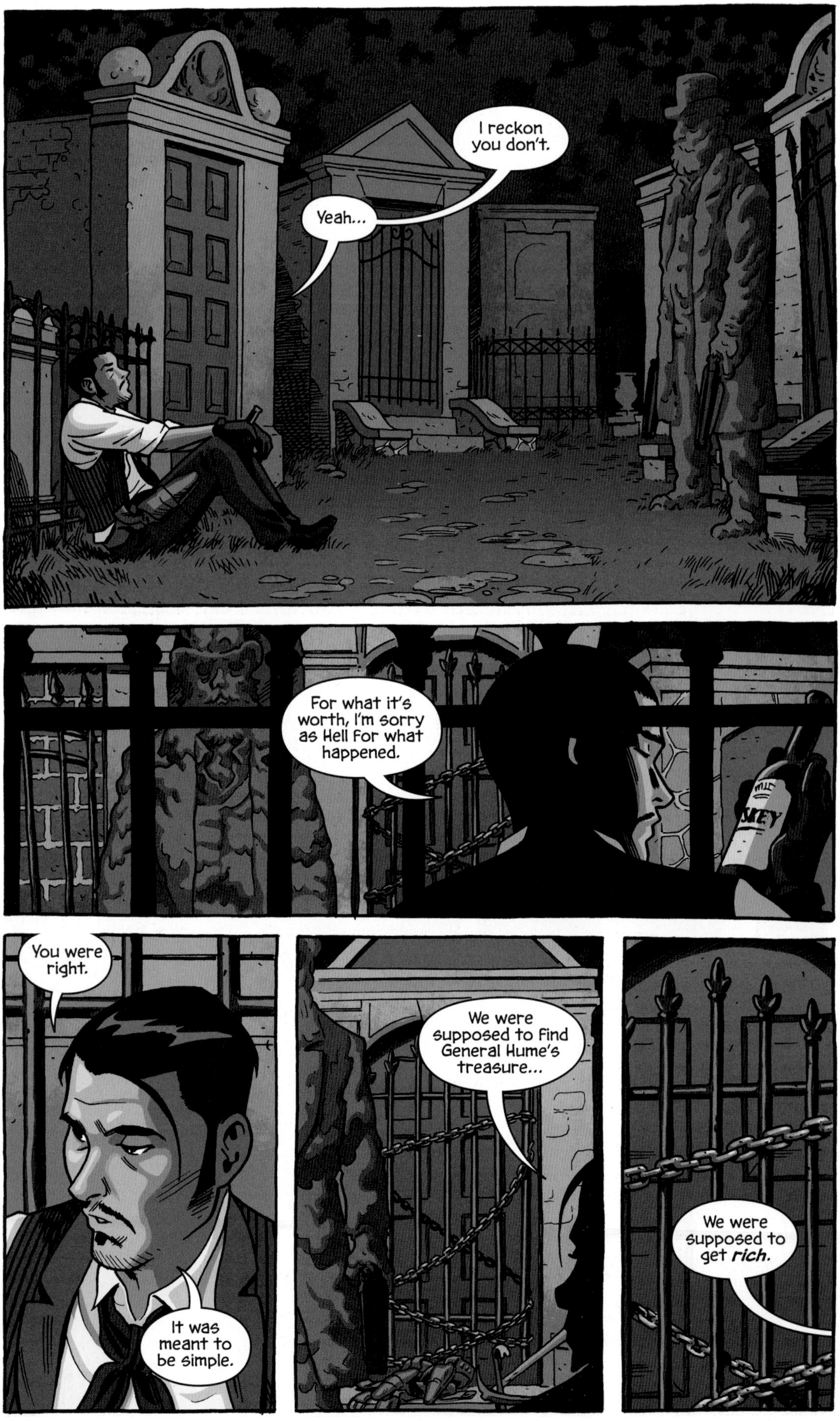

Yeah...
I reckon you don't.
For what it's worth, I'm sorry as Hell for what happened.
SKEY
You were right.
It was meant to be simple.
We were supposed to find General Hume's treasure...
We were supposed to get *rich*.

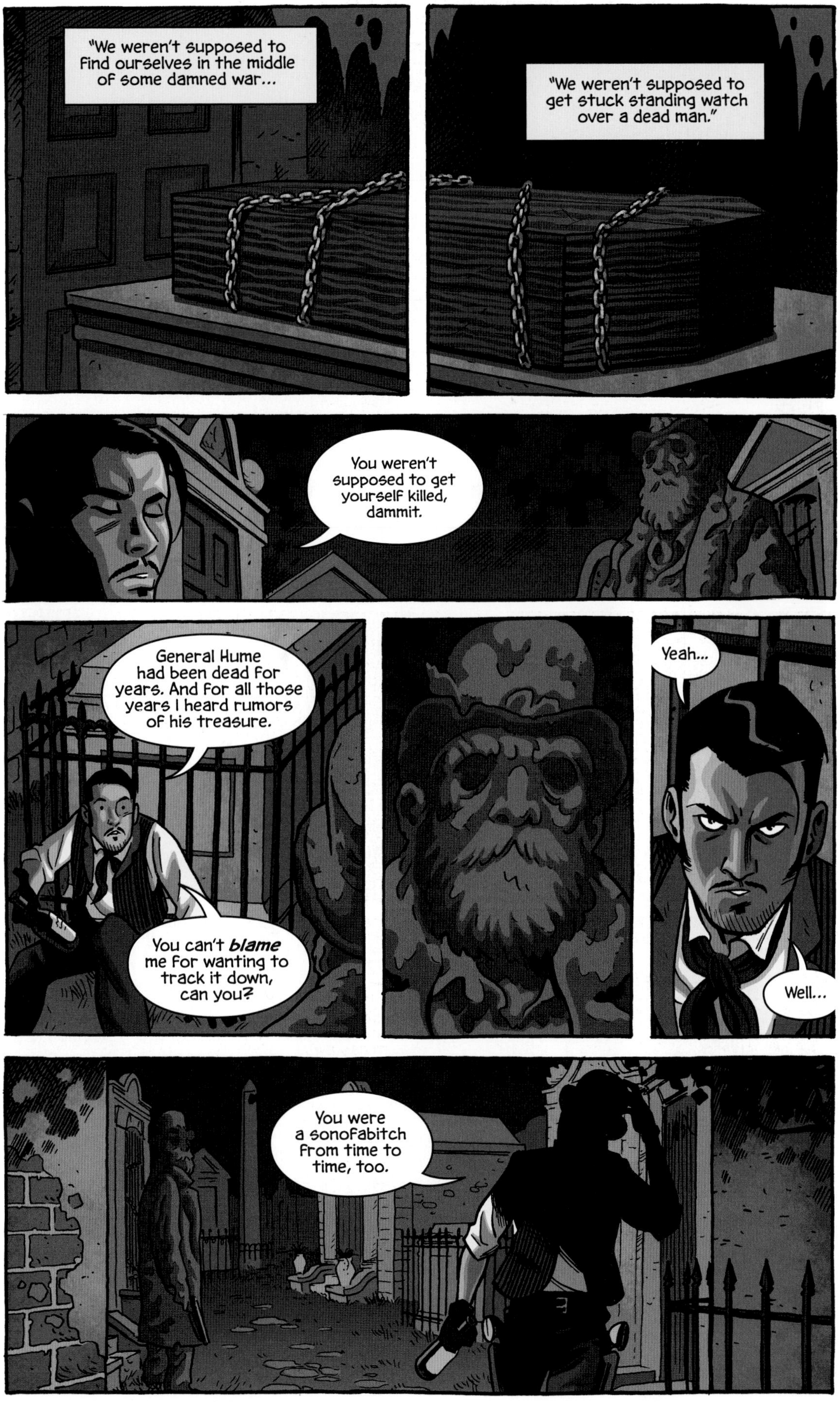
"We weren't supposed to find ourselves in the middle of some damned war...
"We weren't supposed to get stuck standing watch over a dead man."
You weren't supposed to get yourself killed, dammit.
General Hume had been dead for years. And for all those years I heard rumors of his treasure.
You can't *blame* me for wanting to track it down, can you?
Yeah...
Well...
You were a sonofabitch from time to time, too.

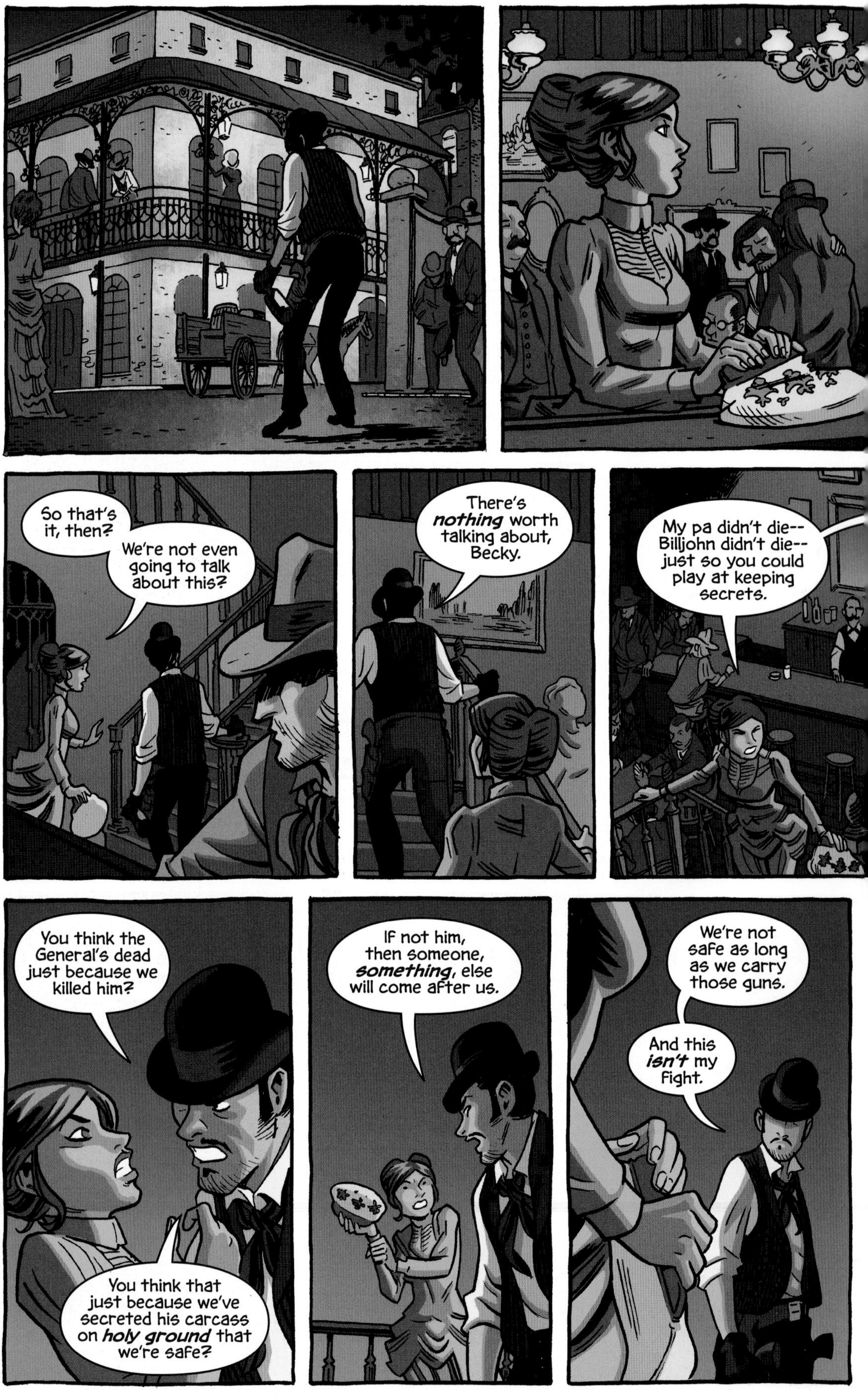
So that's it, then?
We're not even going to talk about this?
There's nothing worth talking about, Becky.
My pa didn't die-- Billjohn didn't die-- just so you could play at keeping secrets.
You think the General's dead just because we killed him?
You think that just because we've secreted his carcass on holy ground that we're safe?
If not him, then someone, something, else will come after us.
We're not safe as long as we carry those guns.
And this isn't my fight.

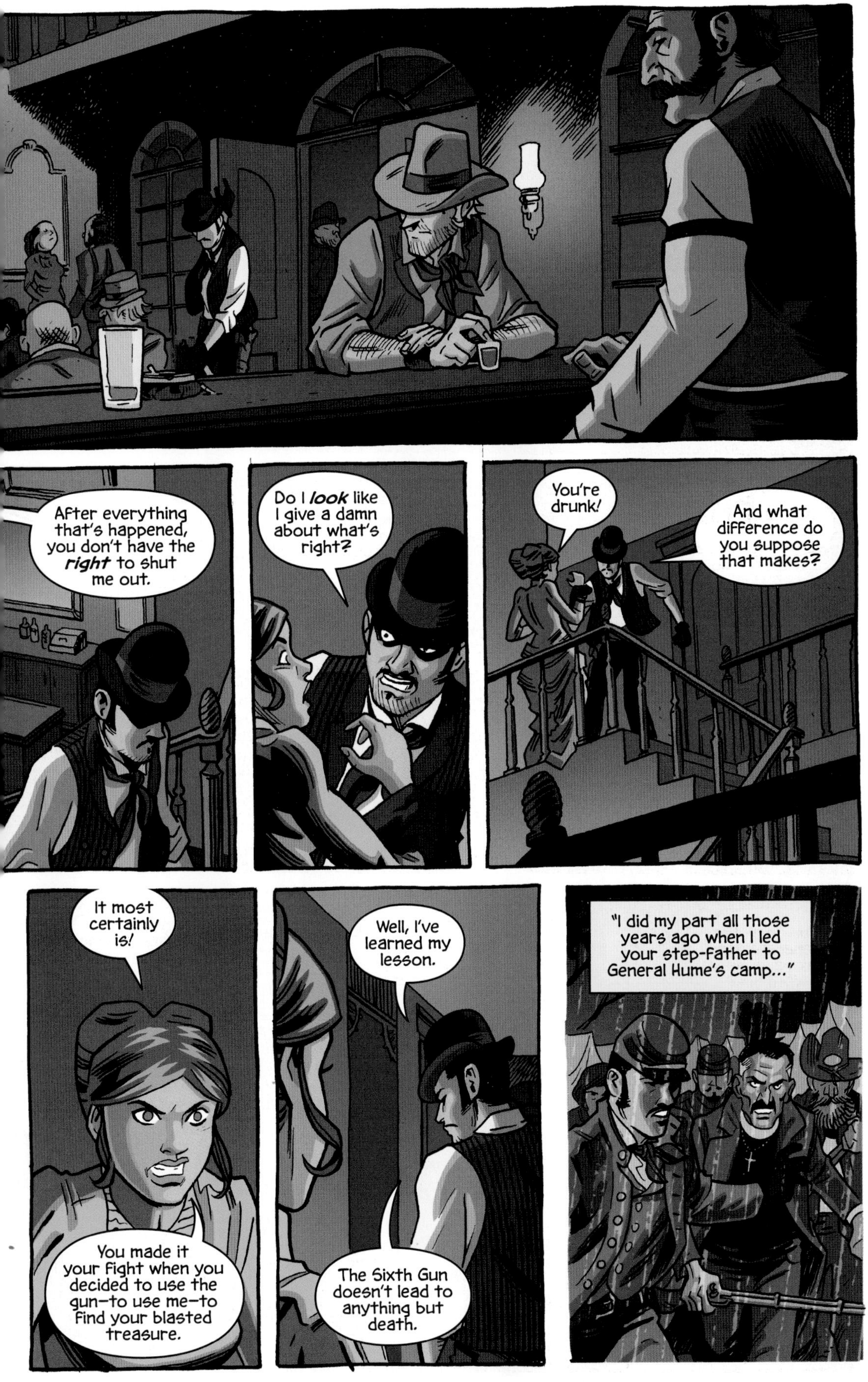
After everything that's happened, you don't have the *right* to shut me out.
Do I *look* like I give a damn about what's right?
You're drunk!
And what difference do you suppose that makes?
It most certainly is!
You made it your fight when you decided to use the gun—to use me—to find your blasted treasure.
Well, I've learned my lesson.
The Sixth Gun doesn't lead to anything but death.
"I did my part all those years ago when I led your step-father to General Hume's camp..."

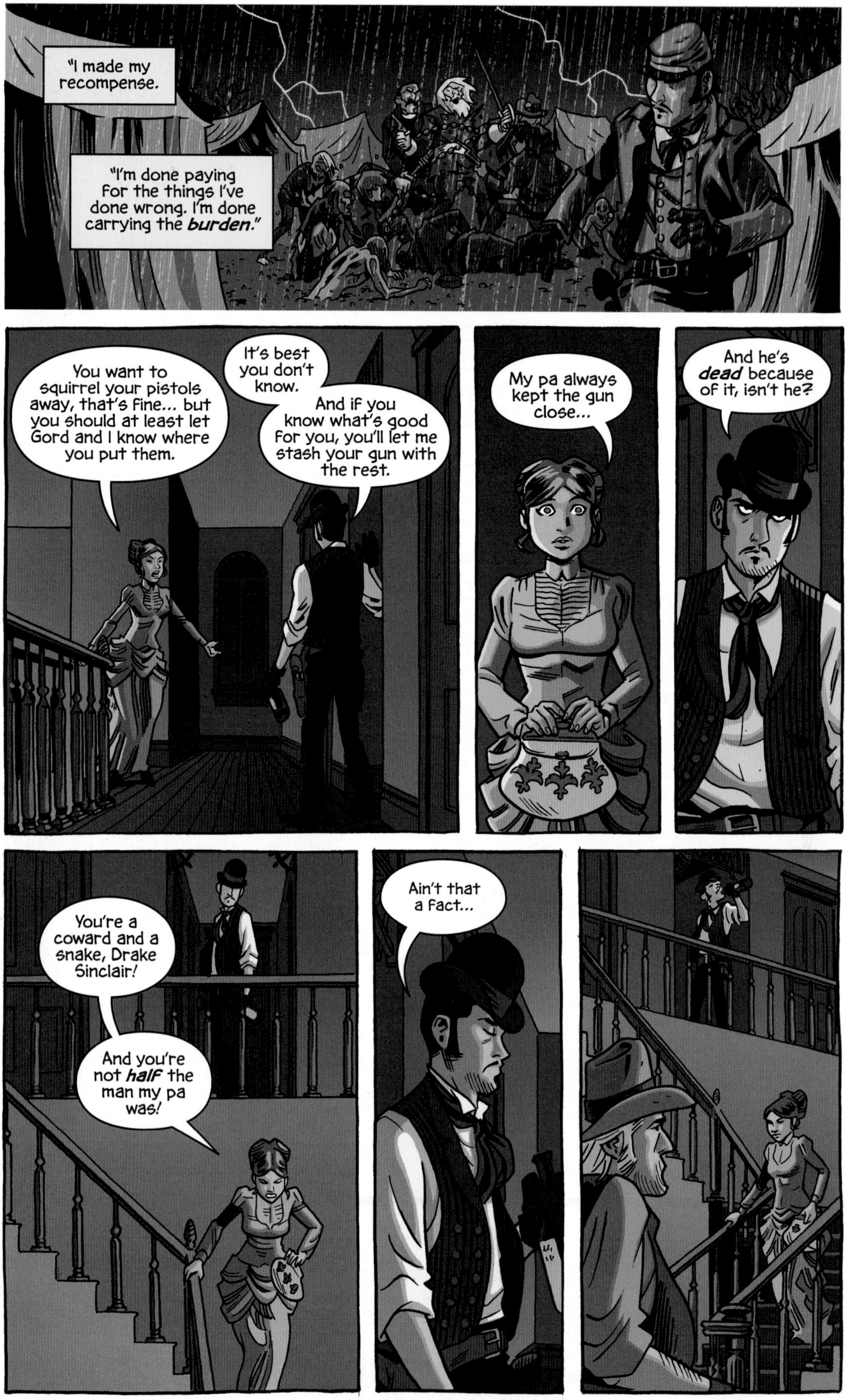
"I made my recompense.
"I'm done paying for the things I've done wrong. I'm done carrying the **burden**."
You want to squirrel your pistols away, that's fine... but you should at least let Gord and I know where you put them.
It's best you don't know.
And if you know what's good for you, you'll let me stash your gun with the rest.
My pa always kept the gun close...
And he's **dead** because of it, isn't he?
You're a coward and a snake, Drake Sinclair!
And you're not **half** the man my pa was!
Ain't that a fact...

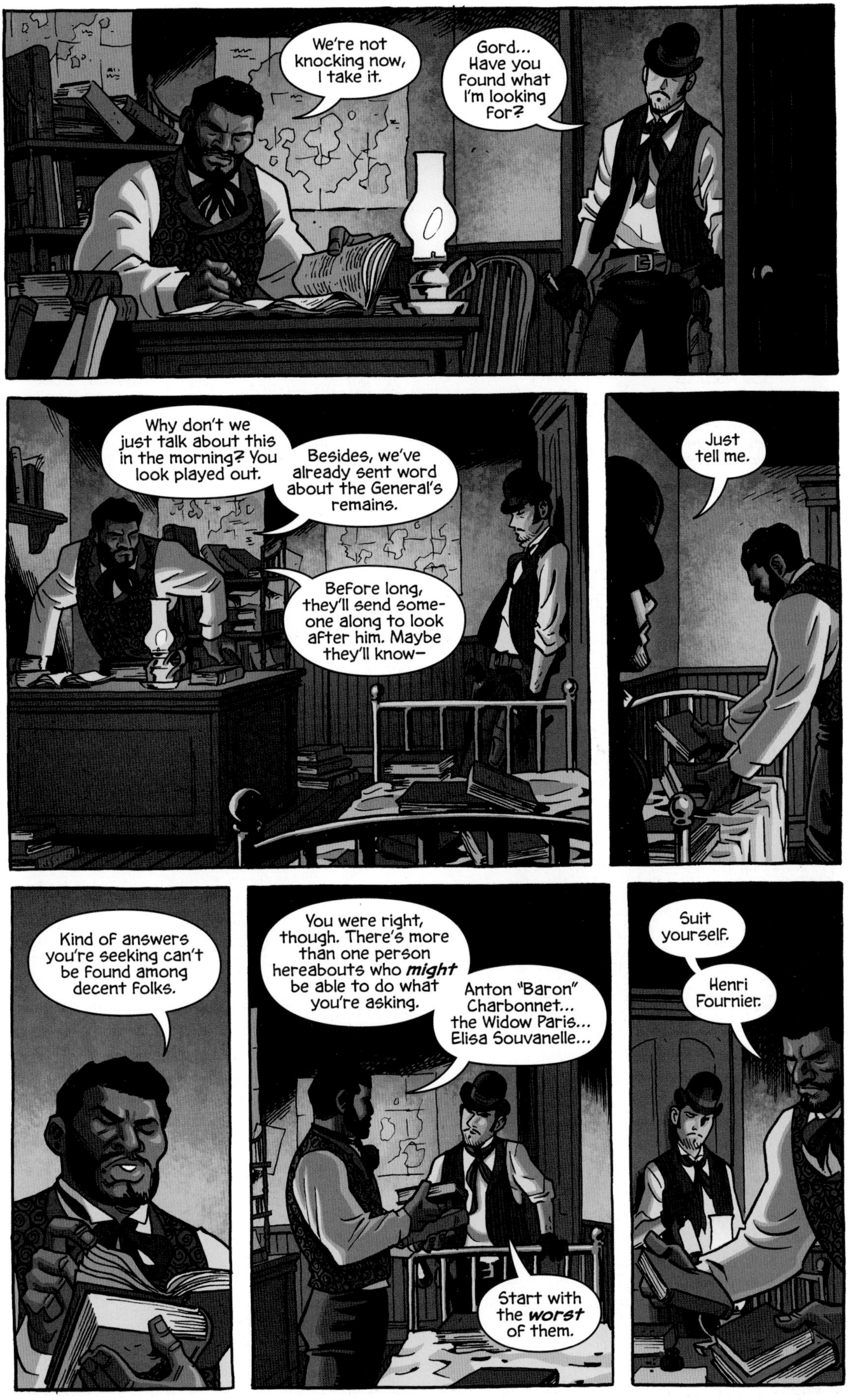
We're not knocking now, I take it.
Gord... Have you found what I'm looking for?
Why don't we just talk about this in the morning? You look played out.
Besides, we've already sent word about the General's remains.
Before long, they'll send some-one along to look after him. Maybe they'll know—
Just tell me.
Kind of answers you're seeking can't be found among decent folks.
You were right, though. There's more than one person hereabouts who *might* be able to do what you're asking.
Anton "Baron" Charbonnet... the Widow Paris... Elisa Souvanelle...
Start with the *worst* of them.
Suit yourself.
Henri Fournier.

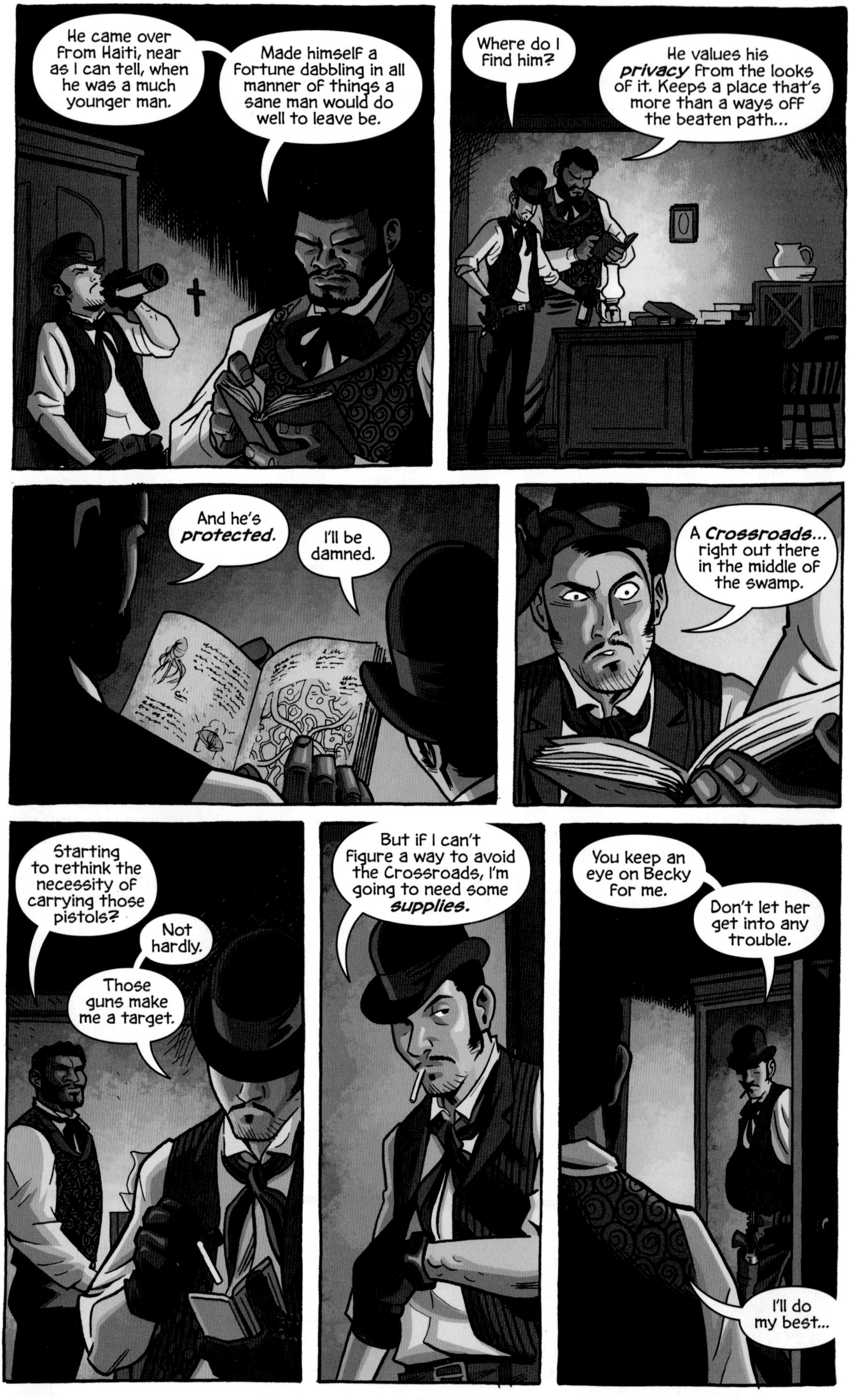
He came over from Haiti, near as I can tell, when he was a much younger man.
Made himself a fortune dabbling in all manner of things a sane man would do well to leave be.
Where do I find him?
He values his *privacy* from the looks of it. Keeps a place that's more than a ways off the beaten path...
And he's *protected.*
I'll be damned.
A *Crossroads...* right out there in the middle of the swamp.
Starting to rethink the necessity of carrying those pistols?
Not hardly.
Those guns make me a target.
But if I can't figure a way to avoid the Crossroads, I'm going to need some *supplies.*
You keep an eye on Becky for me.
Don't let her get into any trouble.
I'll do my best...

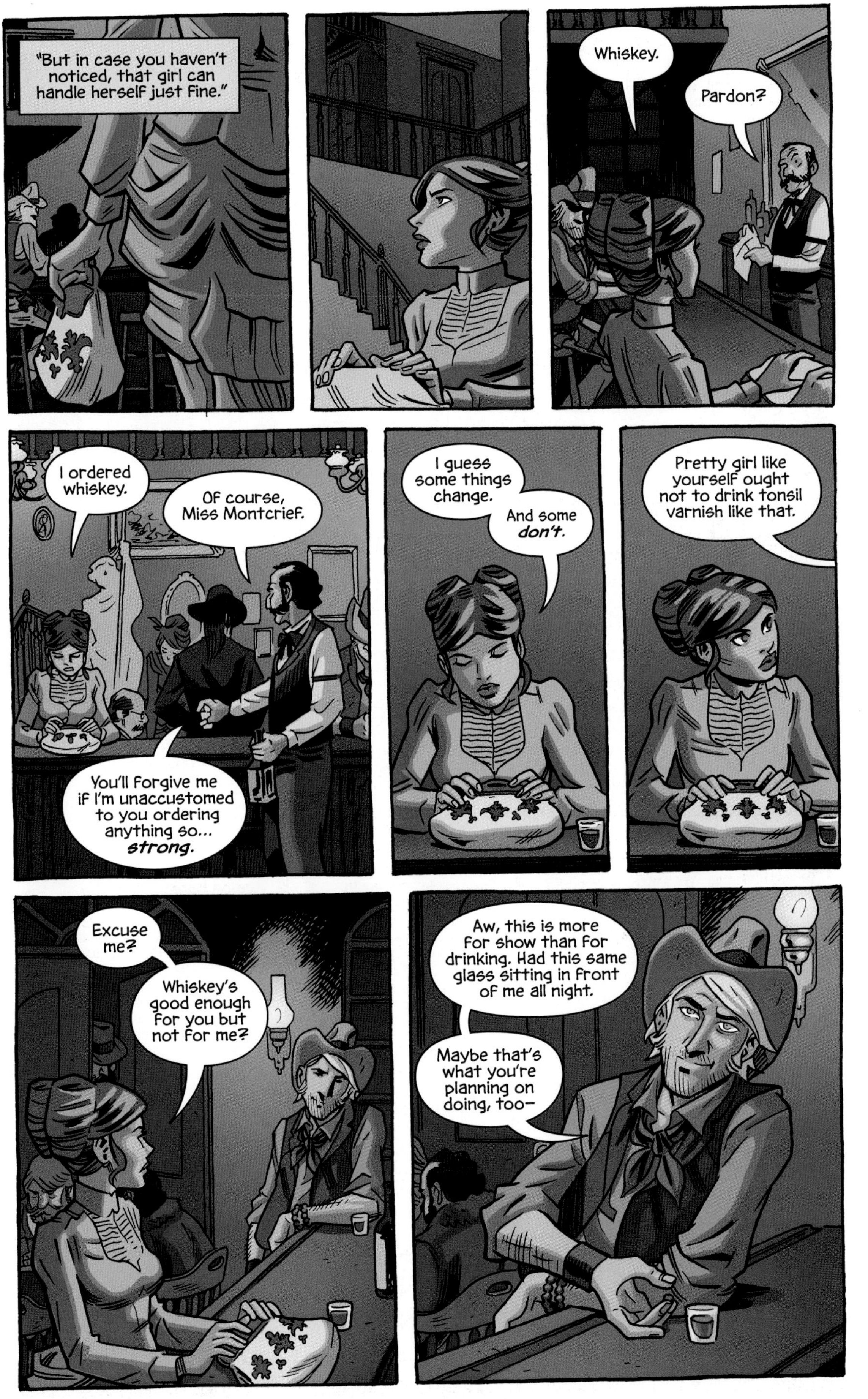
"But in case you haven't noticed, that girl can handle herself just fine."
Whiskey.
Pardon?
I ordered whiskey.
Of course, Miss Montcrief.
You'll forgive me if I'm unaccustomed to you ordering anything so... *strong*.
I guess some things change.
And some *don't*.
Pretty girl like yourself ought not to drink tonsil varnish like that.
Excuse me?
Whiskey's good enough for you but not for me?
Aw, this is more for show than for drinking. Had this same glass sitting in front of me all night.
Maybe that's what you're planning on doing, too—

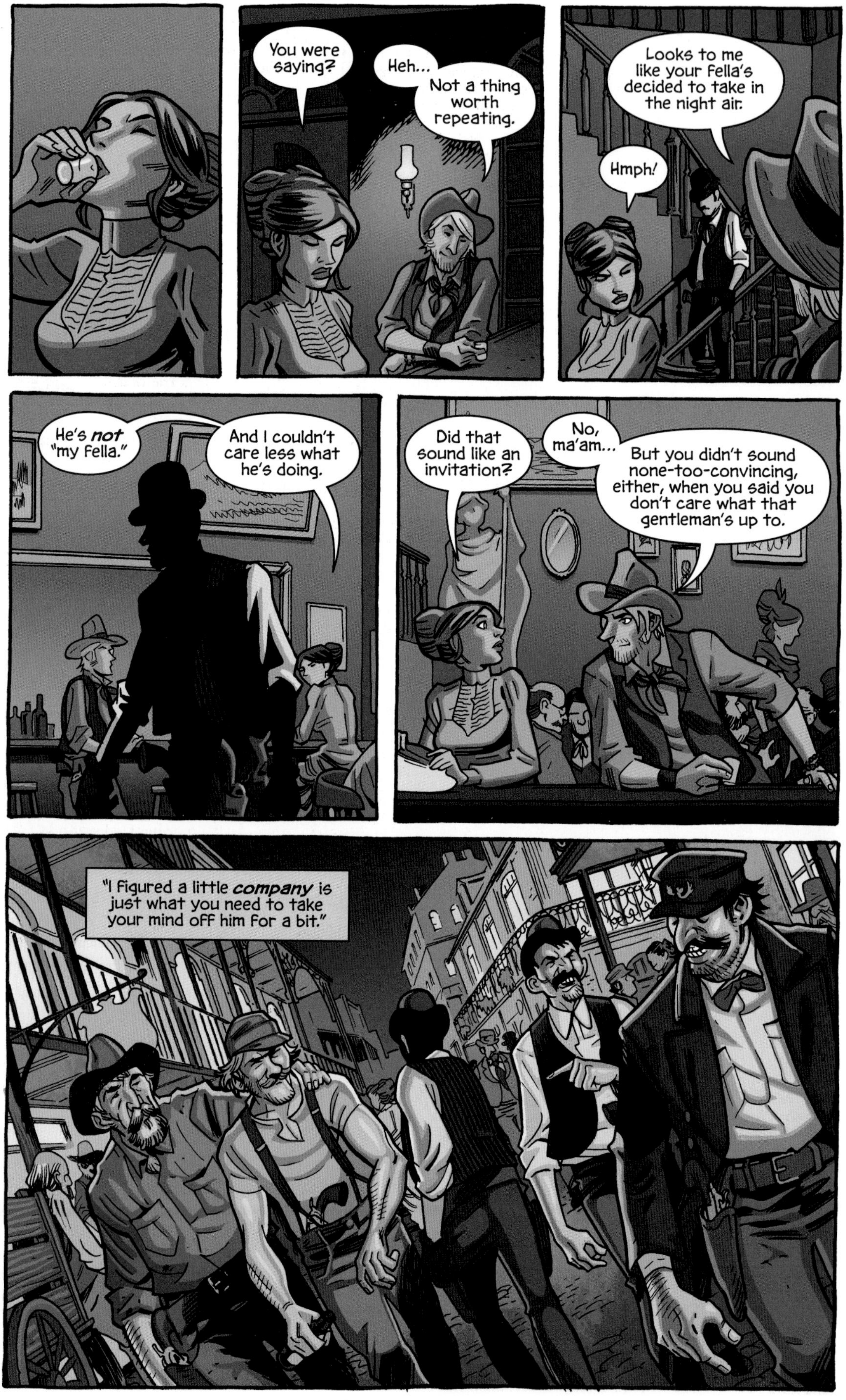
You were saying?
Heh...
Not a thing worth repeating.
Looks to me like your fella's decided to take in the night air.
Hmph!
He's *not* "my fella."
And I couldn't care less what he's doing.
Did that sound like an invitation?
No, ma'am...
But you didn't sound none-too-convincing, either, when you said you don't care what that gentleman's up to.
"I figured a little *company* is just what you need to take your mind off him for a bit."

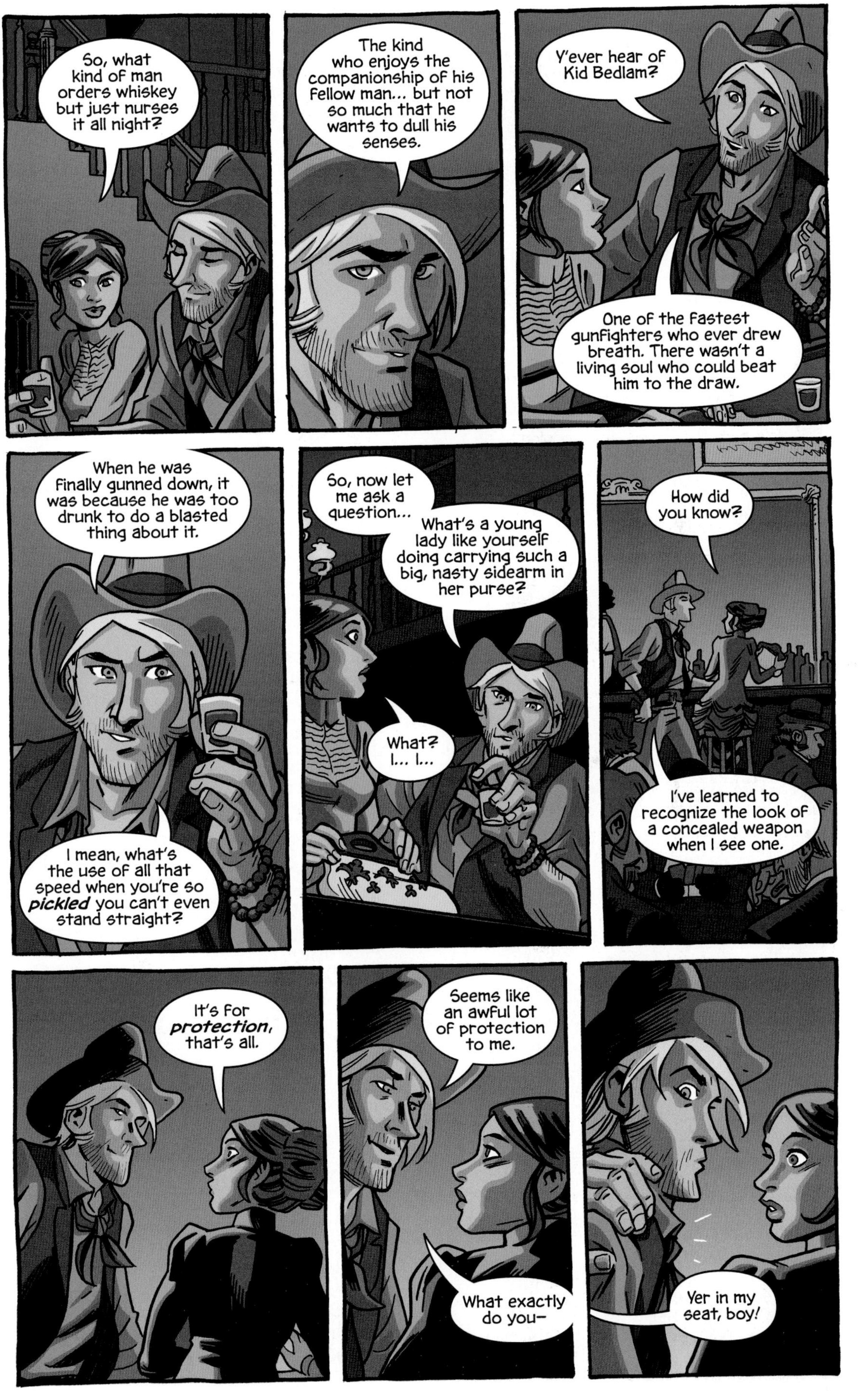
So, what kind of man orders whiskey but just nurses it all night?
The kind who enjoys the companionship of his fellow man... but not so much that he wants to dull his senses.
Y'ever hear of Kid Bedlam?
One of the fastest gunfighters who ever drew breath. There wasn't a living soul who could beat him to the draw.
When he was finally gunned down, it was because he was too drunk to do a blasted thing about it.
I mean, what's the use of all that speed when you're so *pickled* you can't even stand straight?
So, now let me ask a question...
What's a young lady like yourself doing carrying such a big, nasty sidearm in her purse?
What? I... I...
How did you know?
I've learned to recognize the look of a concealed weapon when I see one.
It's for *protection*, that's all.
Seems like an awful lot of protection to me.
What exactly do you–
Yer in my seat, boy!

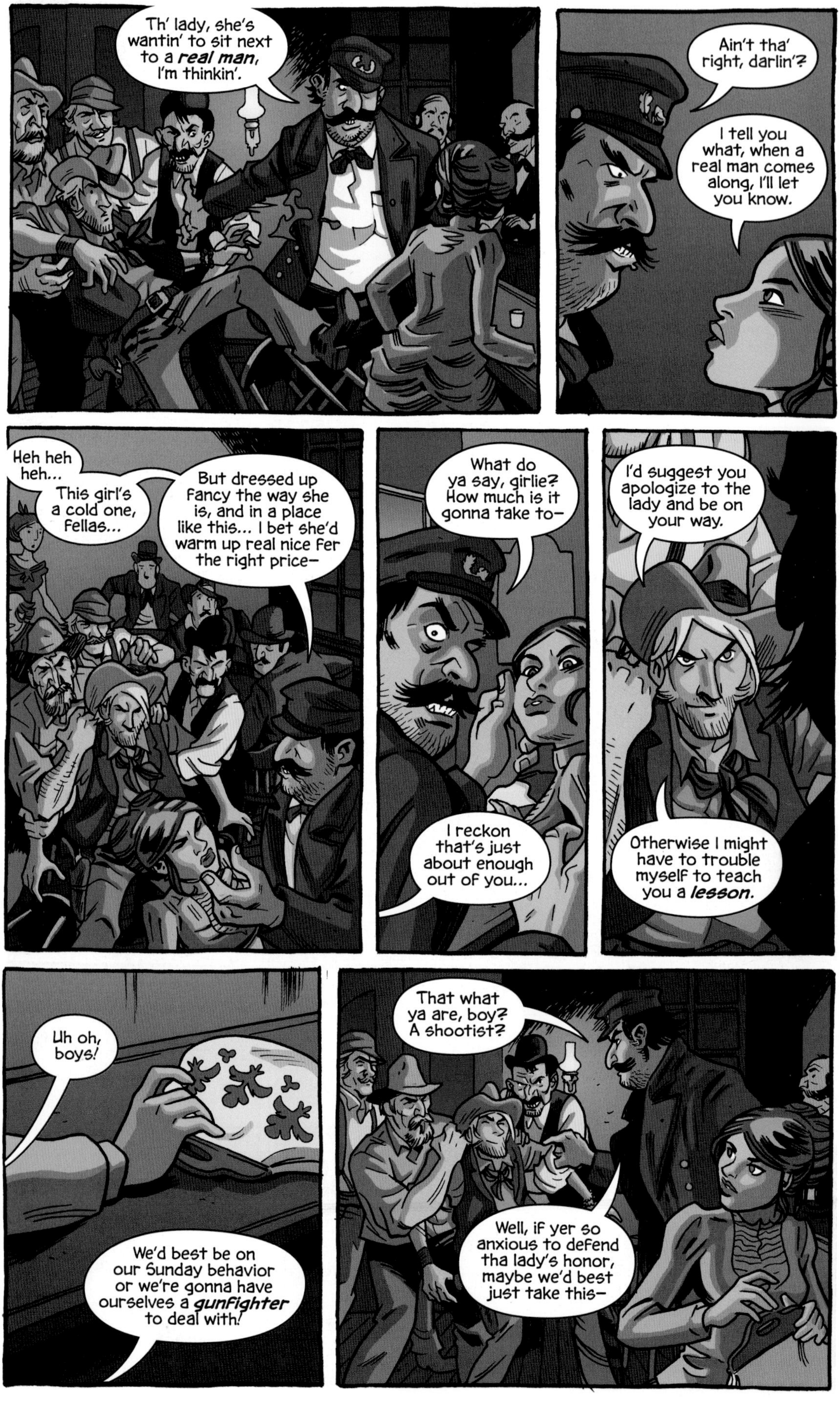
Th' lady, she's wantin' to sit next to a *real man,* I'm thinkin'.
Ain't tha' right, darlin'?
I tell you what, when a real man comes along, I'll let you know.
Heh heh heh...
This girl's a cold one, fellas...
But dressed up fancy the way she is, and in a place like this... I bet she'd warm up real nice fer the right price–
What do ya say, girlie? How much is it gonna take to–
I reckon that's just about enough out of you...
I'd suggest you apologize to the lady and be on your way.
Otherwise I might have to trouble myself to teach you a *lesson.*
Uh oh, boys!
We'd best be on our Sunday behavior or we're gonna have ourselves a *gunfighter* to deal with!
That what ya are, boy? A shootist?
Well, if yer so anxious to defend tha lady's honor, maybe we'd best just take this–

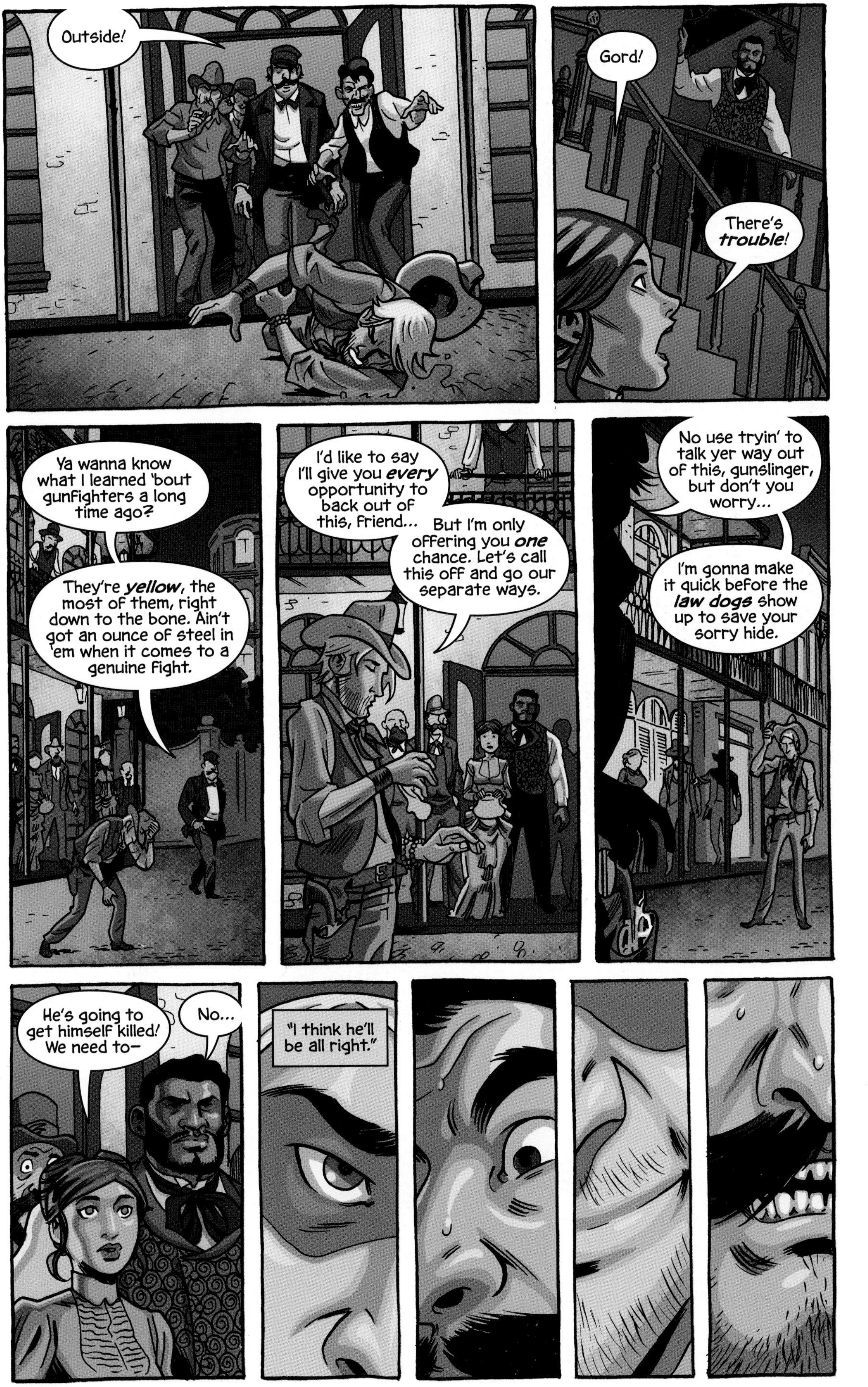
Outside!
Gord!
There's *trouble*!
Ya wanna know what I learned 'bout gunfighters a long time ago?
They're *yellow*, the most of them, right down to the bone. Ain't got an ounce of steel in 'em when it comes to a genuine fight.
I'd like to say I'll give you *every* opportunity to back out of this, friend...
But I'm only offering you *one* chance. Let's call this off and go our separate ways.
No use tryin' to talk yer way out of this, gunslinger, but don't you worry...
I'm gonna make it quick before the *law dogs* show up to save your sorry hide.
He's going to get himself killed! We need to—
No...
"I think he'll be all right."

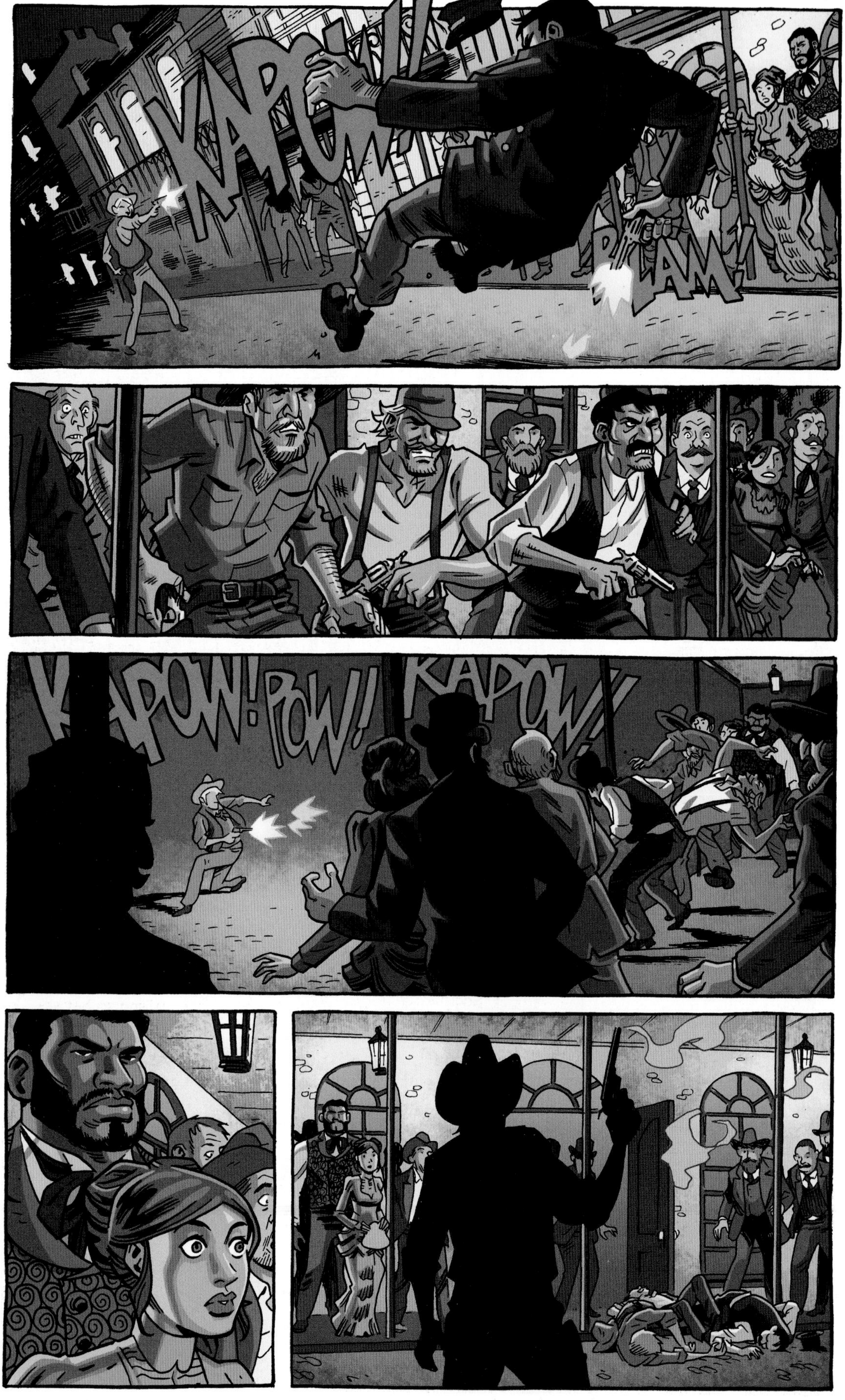
KAPOW!!
BLAM!!
KAPOW! POW!! KAPOW!!

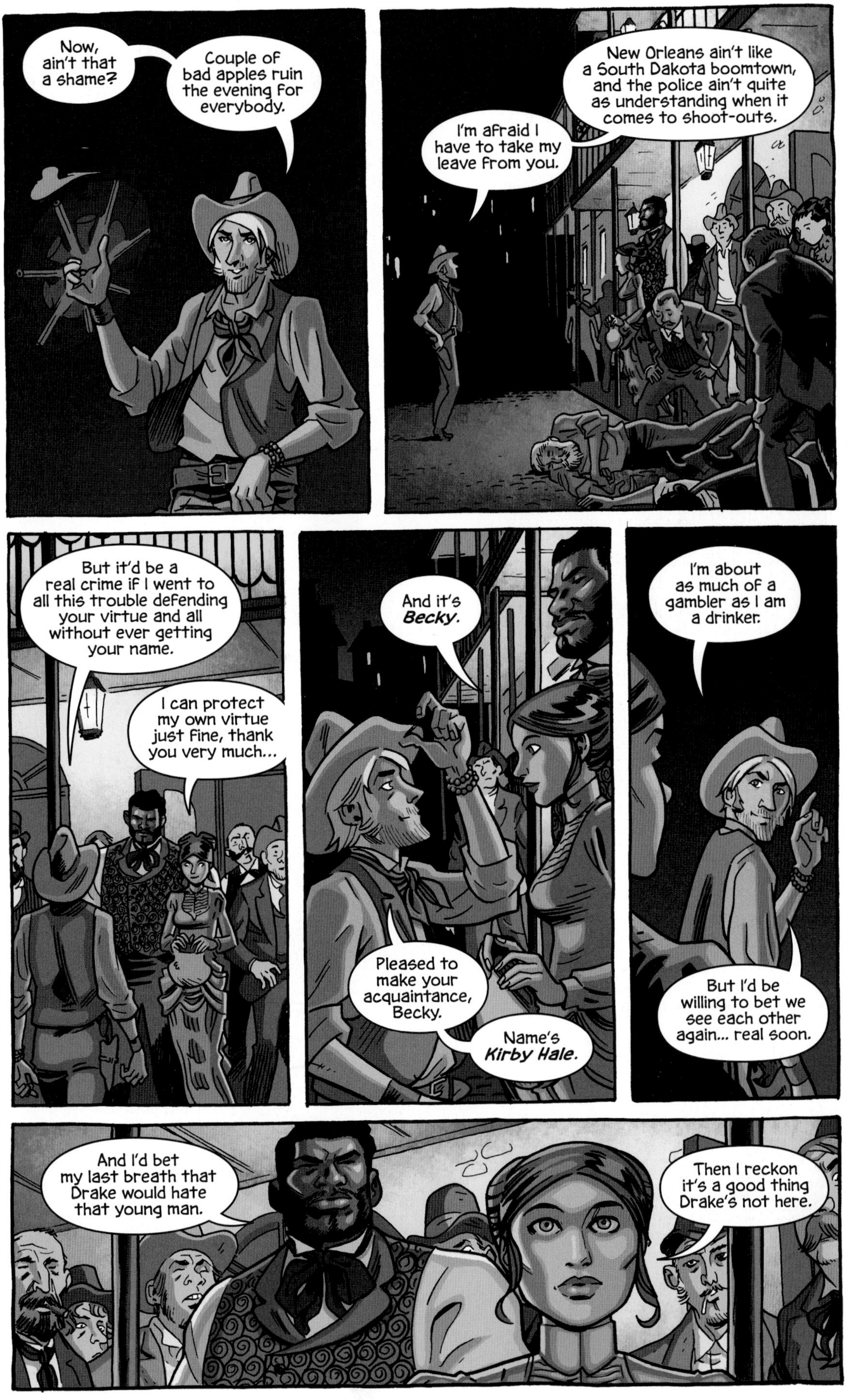
Now, ain't that a shame?
Couple of bad apples ruin the evening for everybody.
New Orleans ain't like a South Dakota boomtown, and the police ain't quite as understanding when it comes to shoot-outs.
I'm afraid I have to take my leave from you.
But it'd be a real crime if I went to all this trouble defending your virtue and all without ever getting your name.
I can protect my own virtue just fine, thank you very much...
And it's *Becky*.
Pleased to make your acquaintance, Becky.
Name's *Kirby Hale*.
I'm about as much of a gambler as I am a drinker.
But I'd be willing to bet we see each other again... real soon.
And I'd bet my last breath that Drake would hate that young man.
Then I reckon it's a good thing Drake's not here.

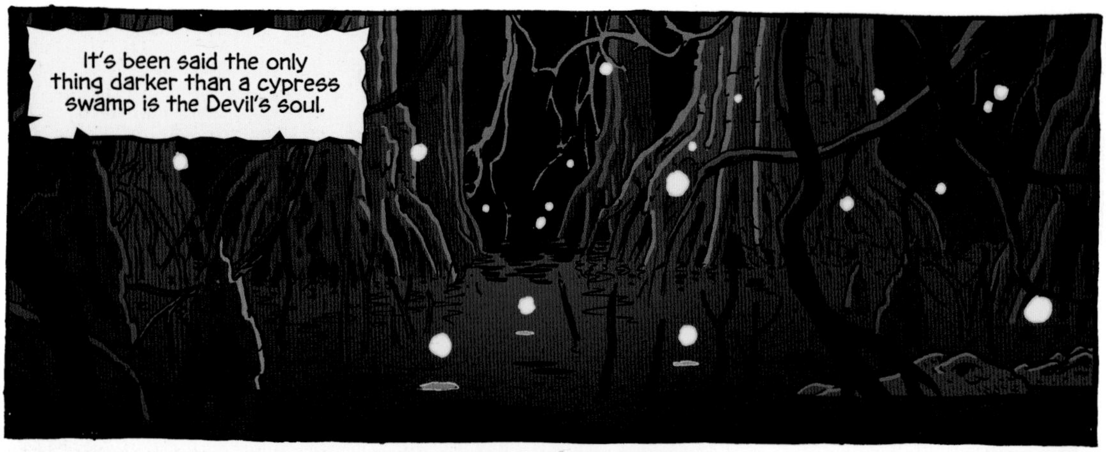
It's been said the only thing darker than a cypress swamp is the Devil's soul.

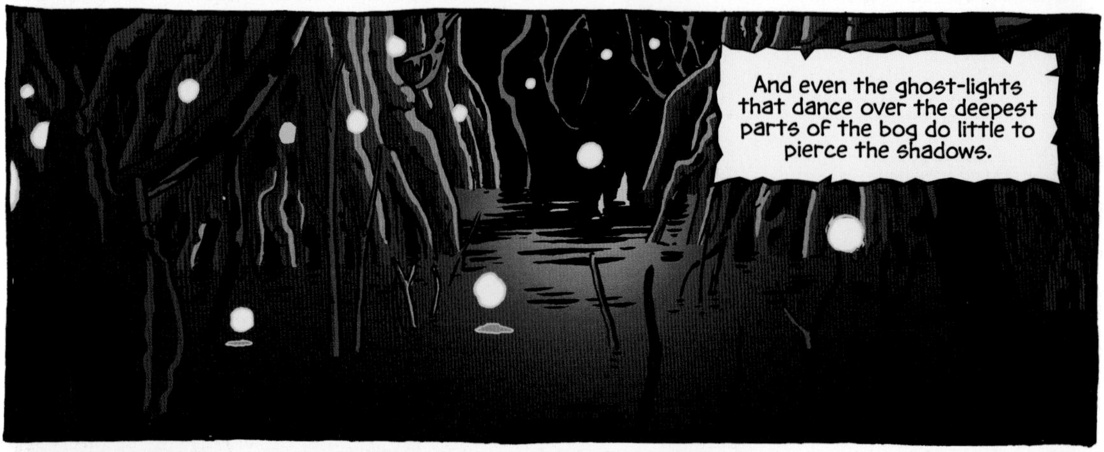
And even the ghost-lights that dance over the deepest parts of the bog do little to pierce the shadows.

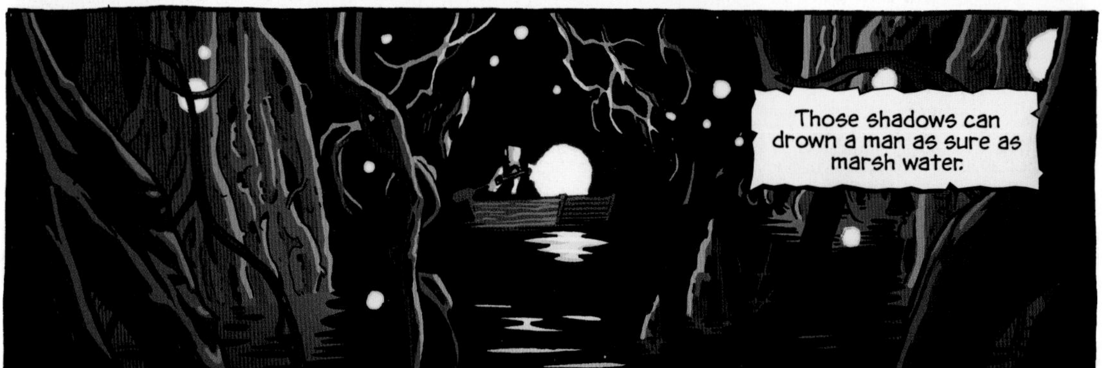
Those shadows can drown a man as sure as marsh water.

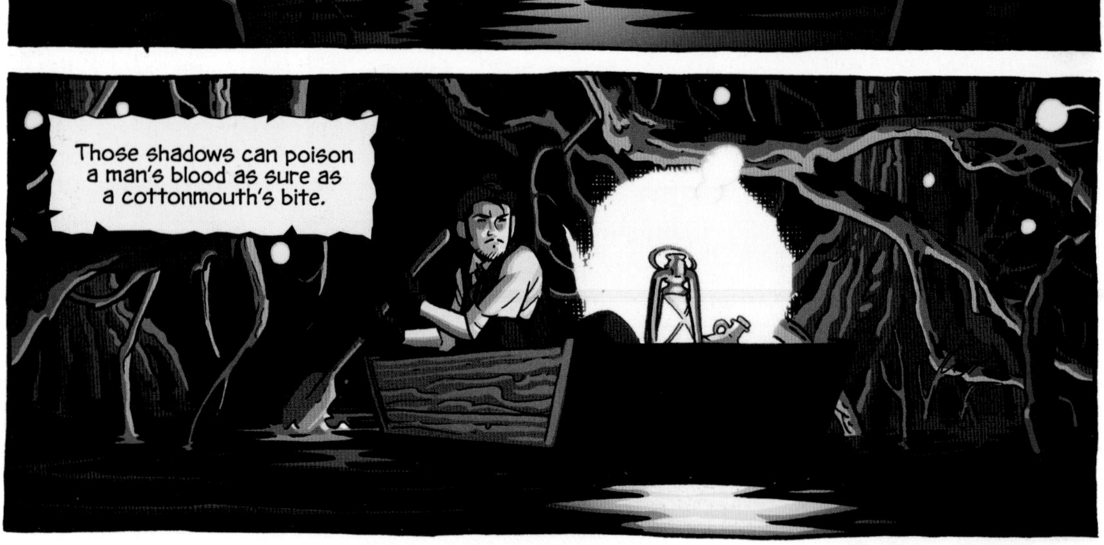
Those shadows can poison a man's blood as sure as a cottonmouth's bite.

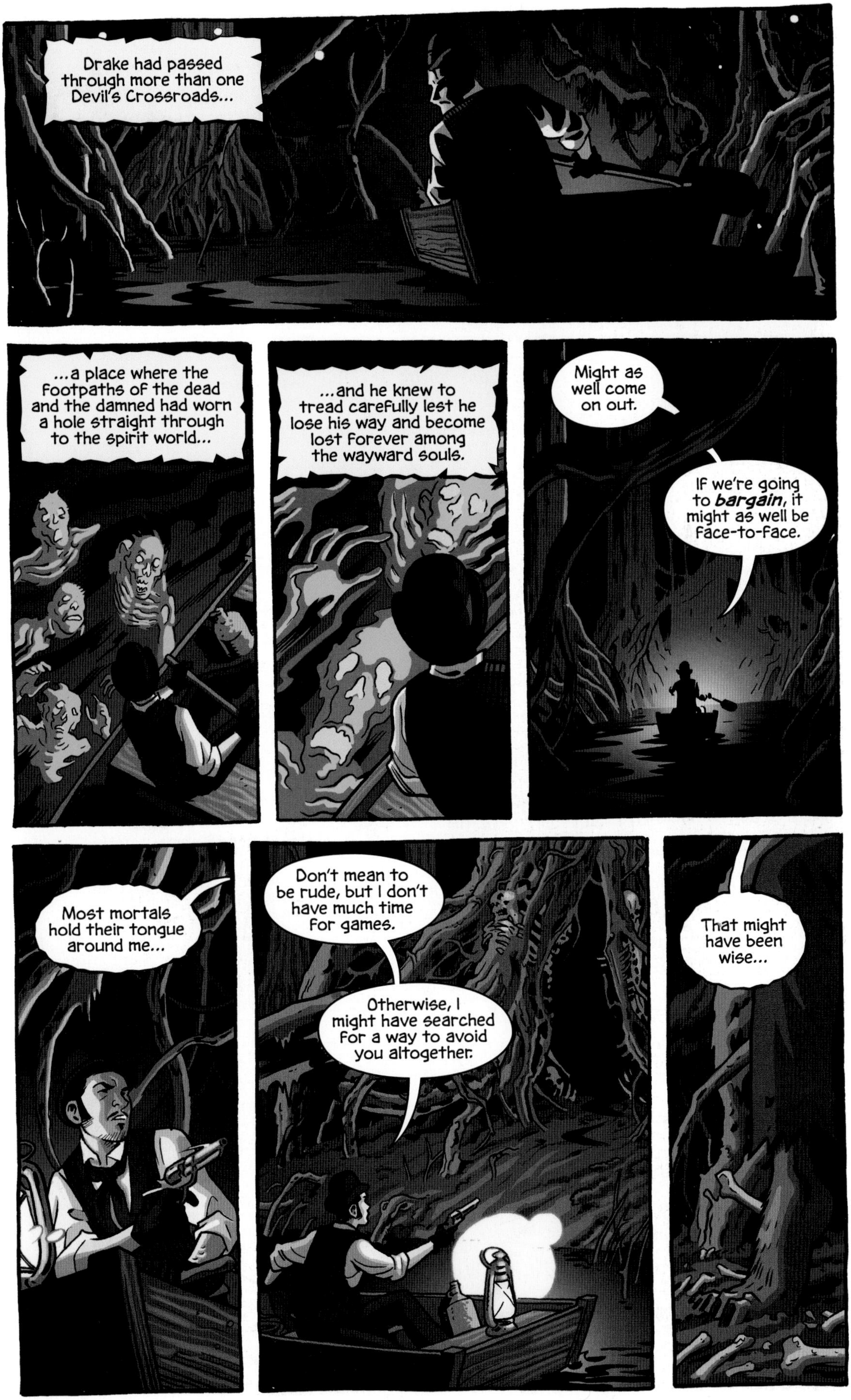

Drake had passed through more than one Devil's Crossroads...
...a place where the footpaths of the dead and the damned had worn a hole straight through to the spirit world...
...and he knew to tread carefully lest he lose his way and become lost forever among the wayward souls.
Might as well come on out.
If we're going to *bargain*, it might as well be face-to-face.
Most mortals hold their tongue around me...
Don't mean to be rude, but I don't have much time for games.
Otherwise, I might have searched for a way to avoid you altogether.
That might have been wise...

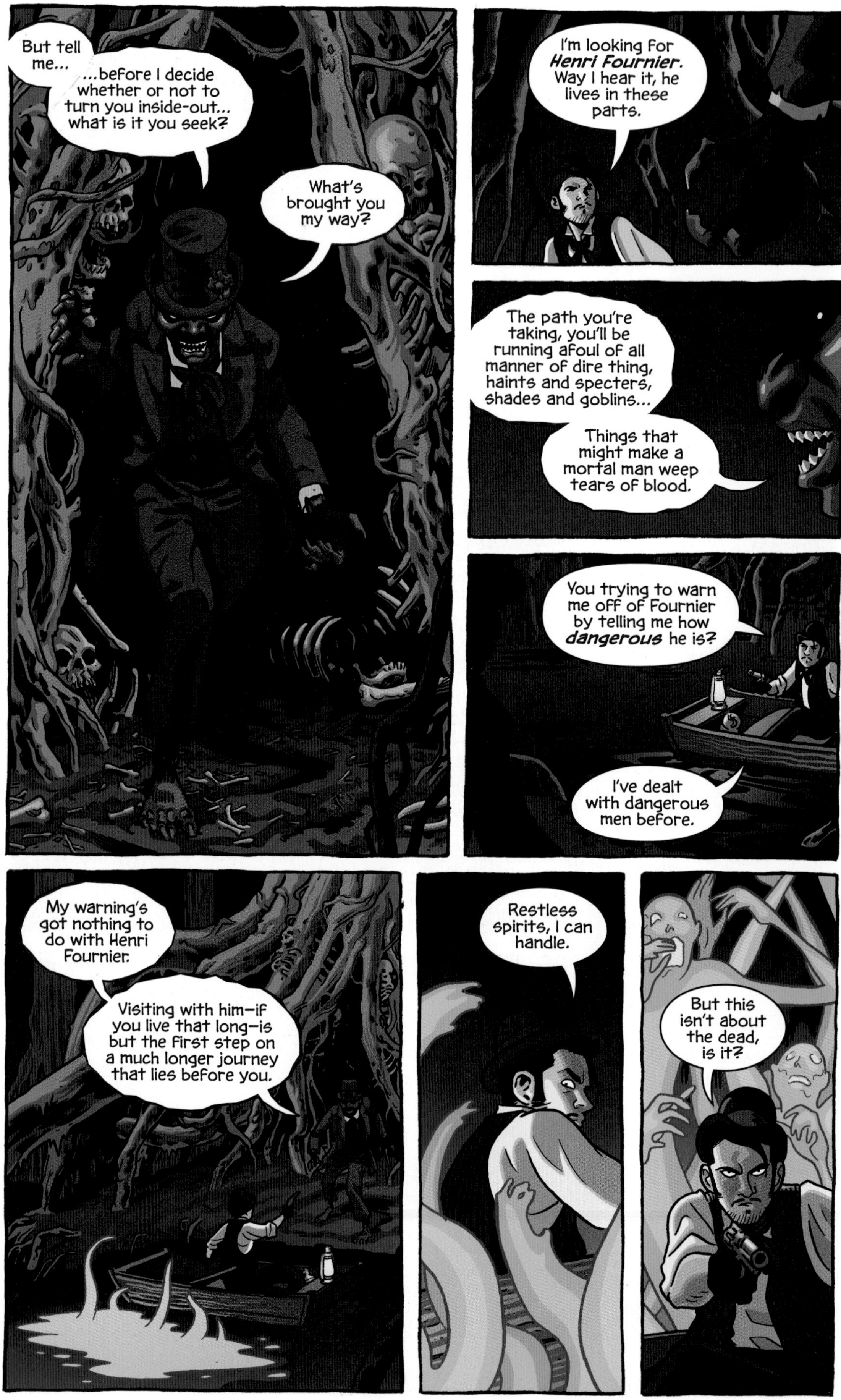
But tell me...
...before I decide whether or not to turn you inside-out... what is it you seek?
What's brought you my way?
I'm looking for **Henri Fournier**. Way I hear it, he lives in these parts.
The path you're taking, you'll be running afoul of all manner of dire thing, haints and specters, shades and goblins...
Things that might make a mortal man weep tears of blood.
You trying to warn me off of Fournier by telling me how *dangerous* he is?
I've dealt with dangerous men before.
My warning's got nothing to do with Henri Fournier.
Visiting with him—if you live that long—is but the first step on a much longer journey that lies before you.
Restless spirits, I can handle.
But this isn't about the dead, is it?

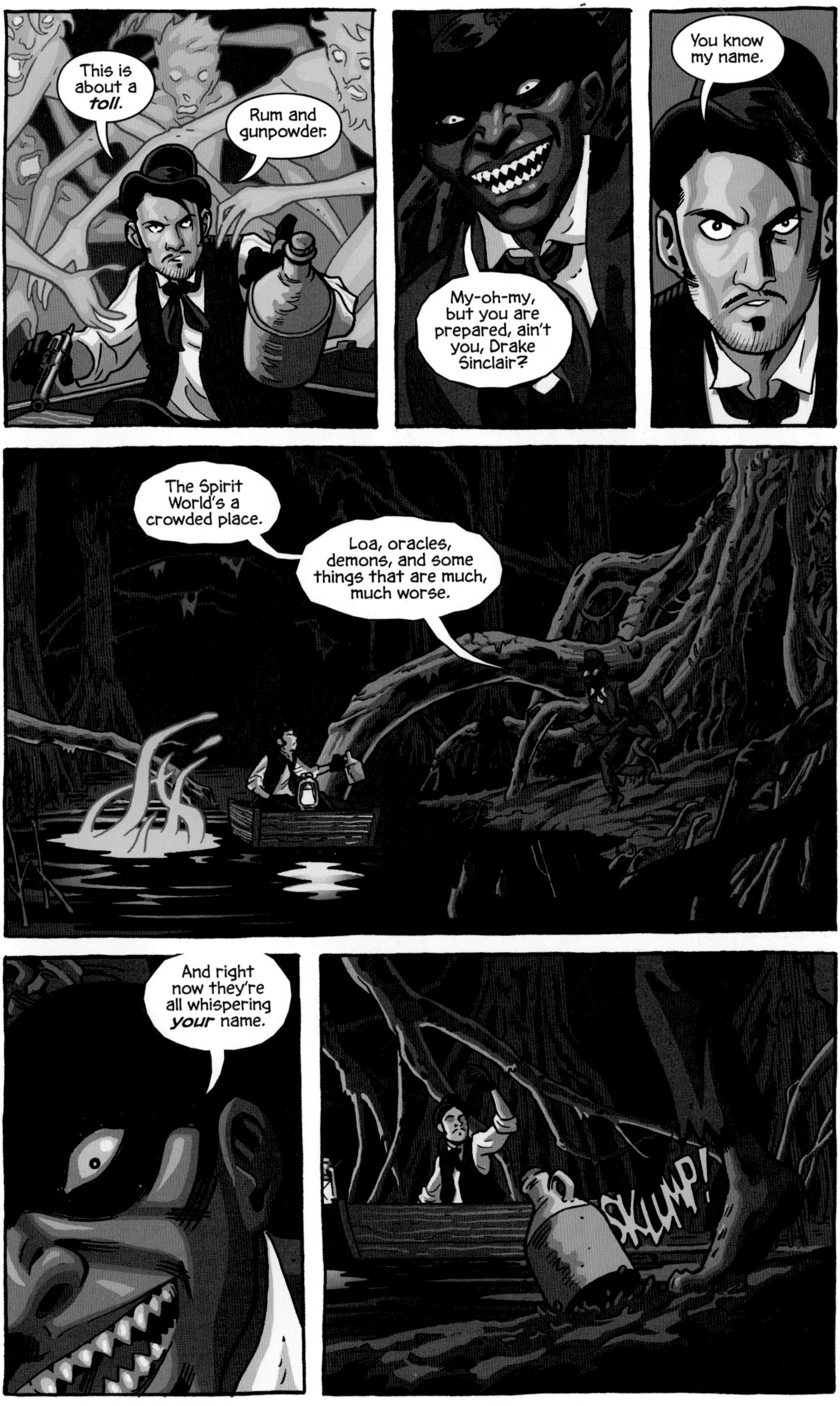
This is about a *toll*.
Rum and gunpowder.
My-oh-my, but you are prepared, ain't you, Drake Sinclair?
You know my name.
The Spirit World's a crowded place.
Loa, oracles, demons, and some things that are much, much worse.
And right now they're all whispering *your* name.
SKLUMP!

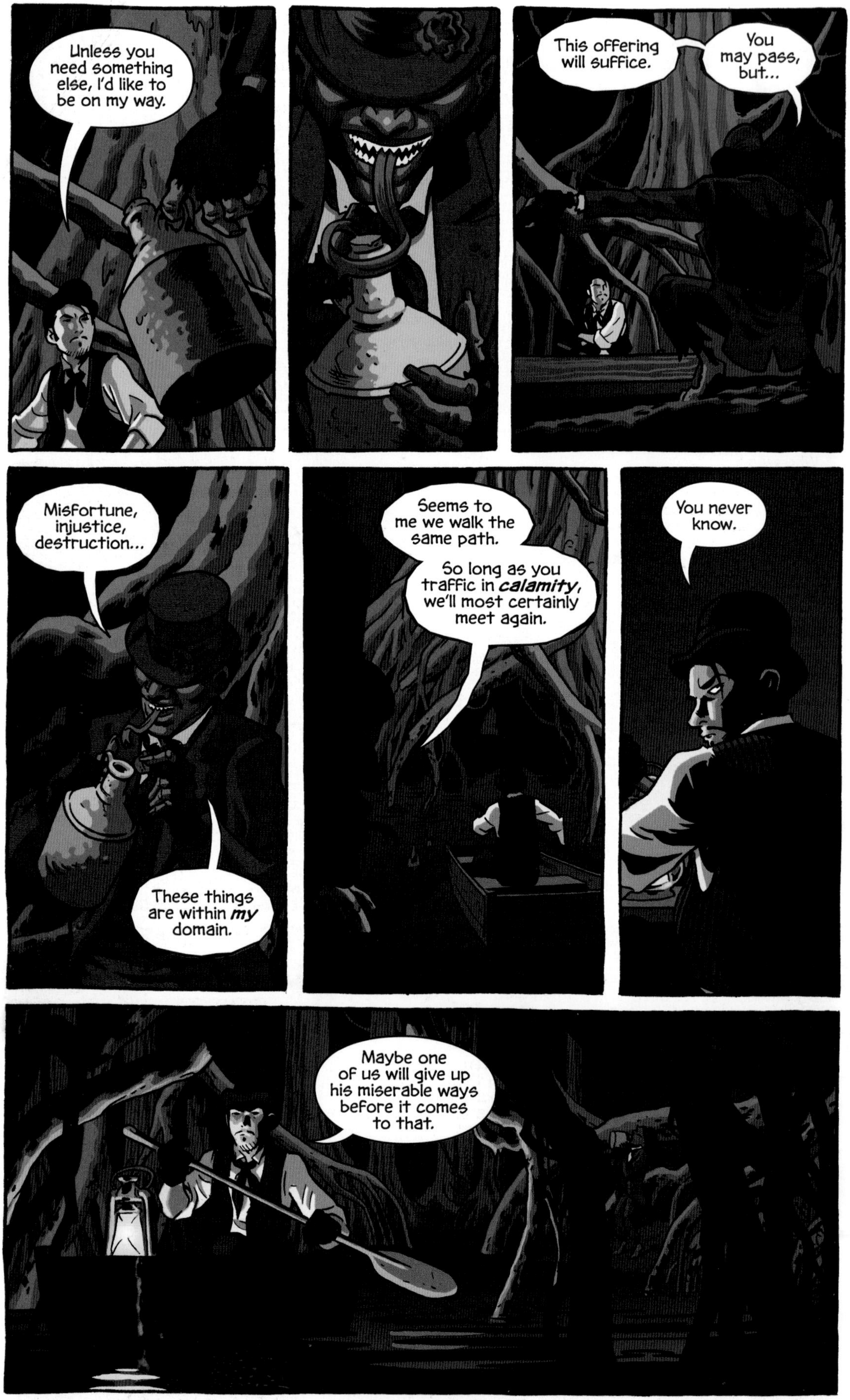
Unless you need something else, I'd like to be on my way.
This offering will suffice.
You may pass, but...
Misfortune, injustice, destruction...
These things are within *my* domain.
Seems to me we walk the same path.
So long as you traffic in *calamity*, we'll most certainly meet again.
You never know.
Maybe one of us will give up his miserable ways before it comes to that.

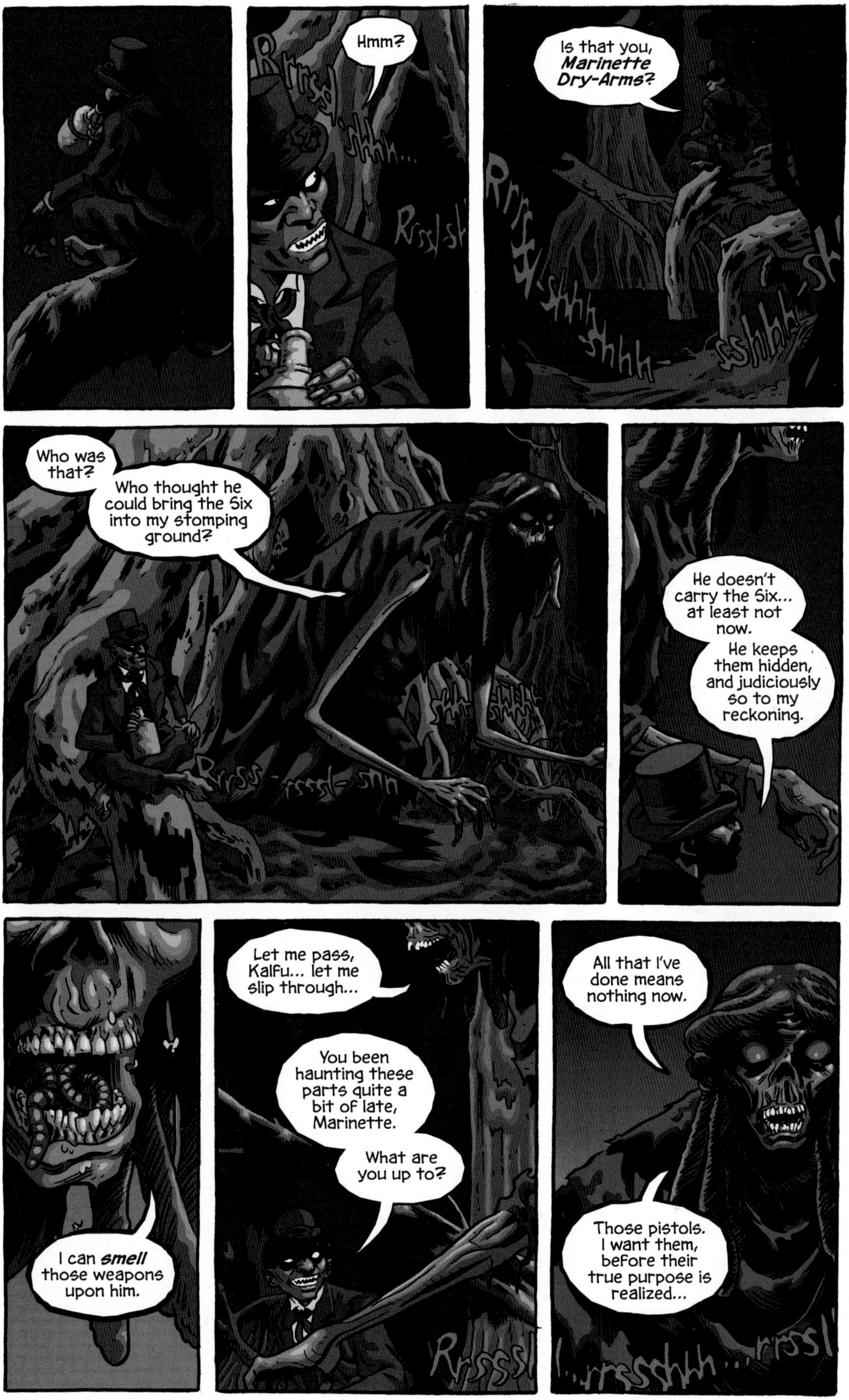
Hmm?
Rrrssl-shhh...
Is that you, *Marinette Dry-Arms?*
Rrrssh-shhh shhh
rsshhh
-sh
Who was that?
Who thought he could bring the Six into my stomping ground?
Rrrss-rrssl-shh
He doesn't carry the Six... at least not now.
He keeps them hidden, and judiciously so to my reckoning.
I can *smell* those weapons upon him.
Let me pass, Kalfu... let me slip through...
You been haunting these parts quite a bit of late, Marinette.
What are you up to?
Rrsssl
All that I've done means nothing now.
Those pistols. I want them, before their true purpose is realized...
...rrsshhh...rrssl

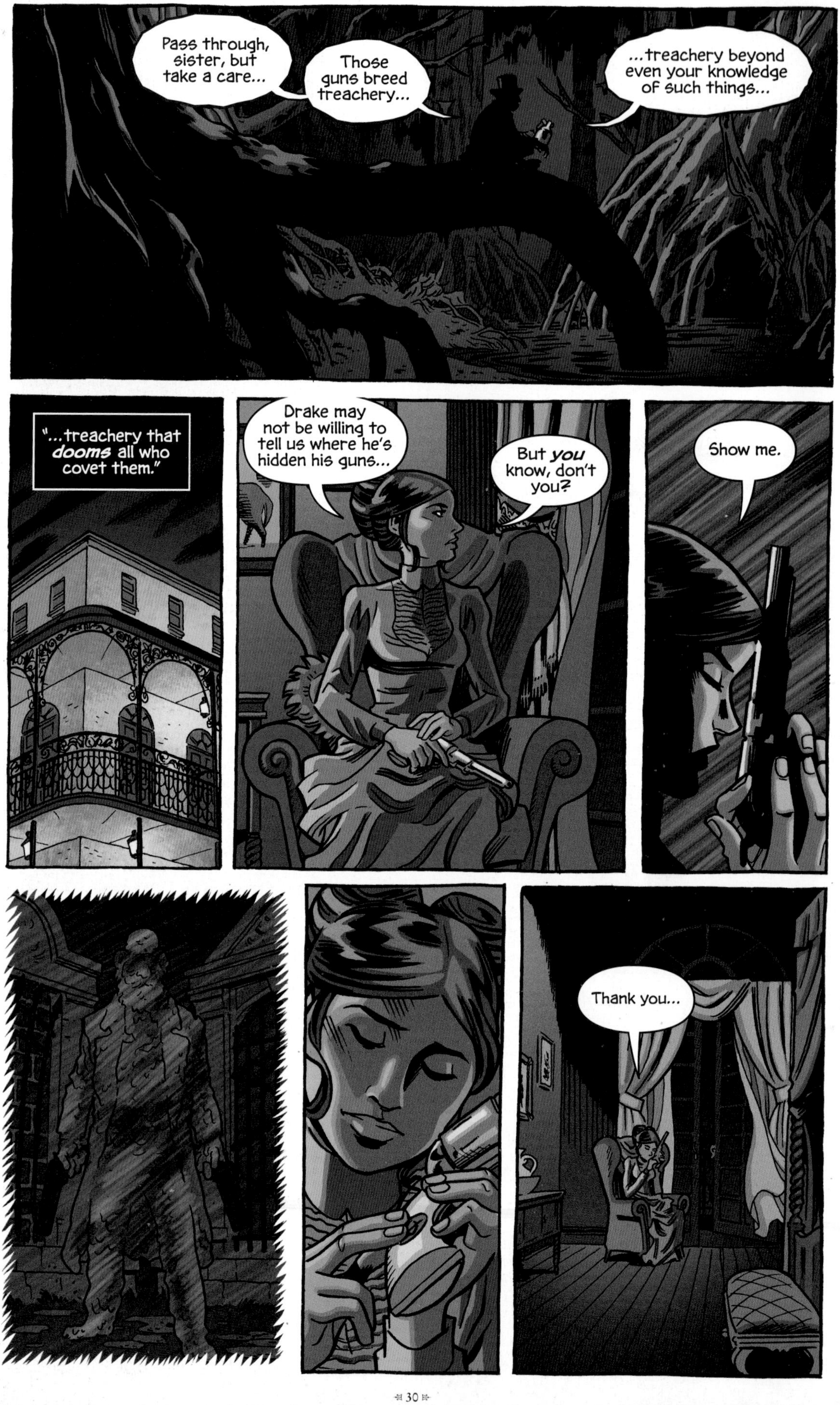

Pass through, sister, but take a care...
Those guns breed treachery...
...treachery beyond even your knowledge of such things...
"...treachery that *dooms* all who covet them."
Drake may not be willing to tell us where he's hidden his guns...
But *you* know, don't you?
Show me.
Thank you...

CHAPTER
TWO

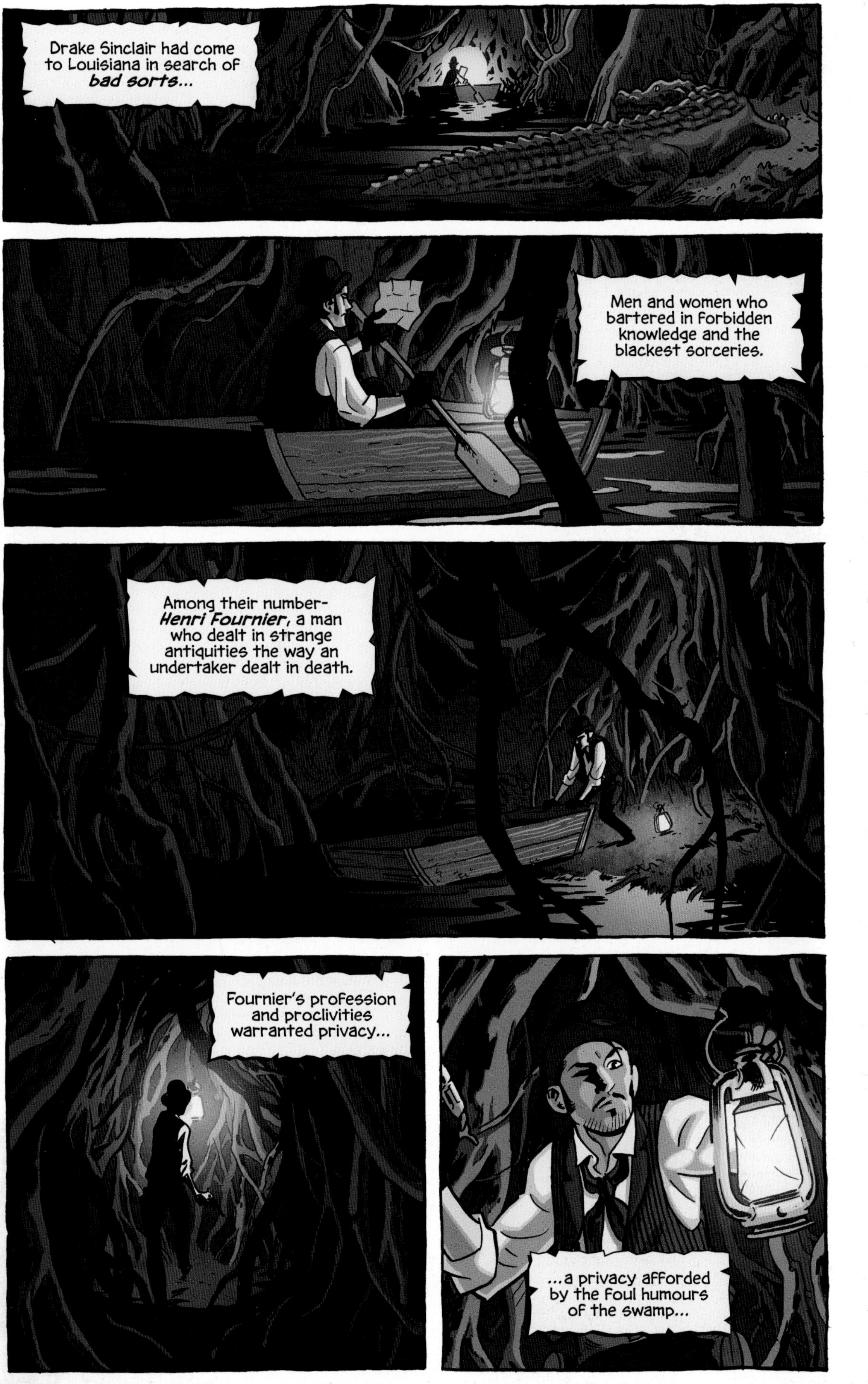

Drake Sinclair had come to Louisiana in search of *bad sorts...*
Men and women who bartered in forbidden knowledge and the blackest sorceries.
Among their number- *Henri Fournier*, a man who dealt in strange antiquities the way an undertaker dealt in death.
Fournier's profession and proclivities warranted privacy...
...a privacy afforded by the foul humours of the swamp...

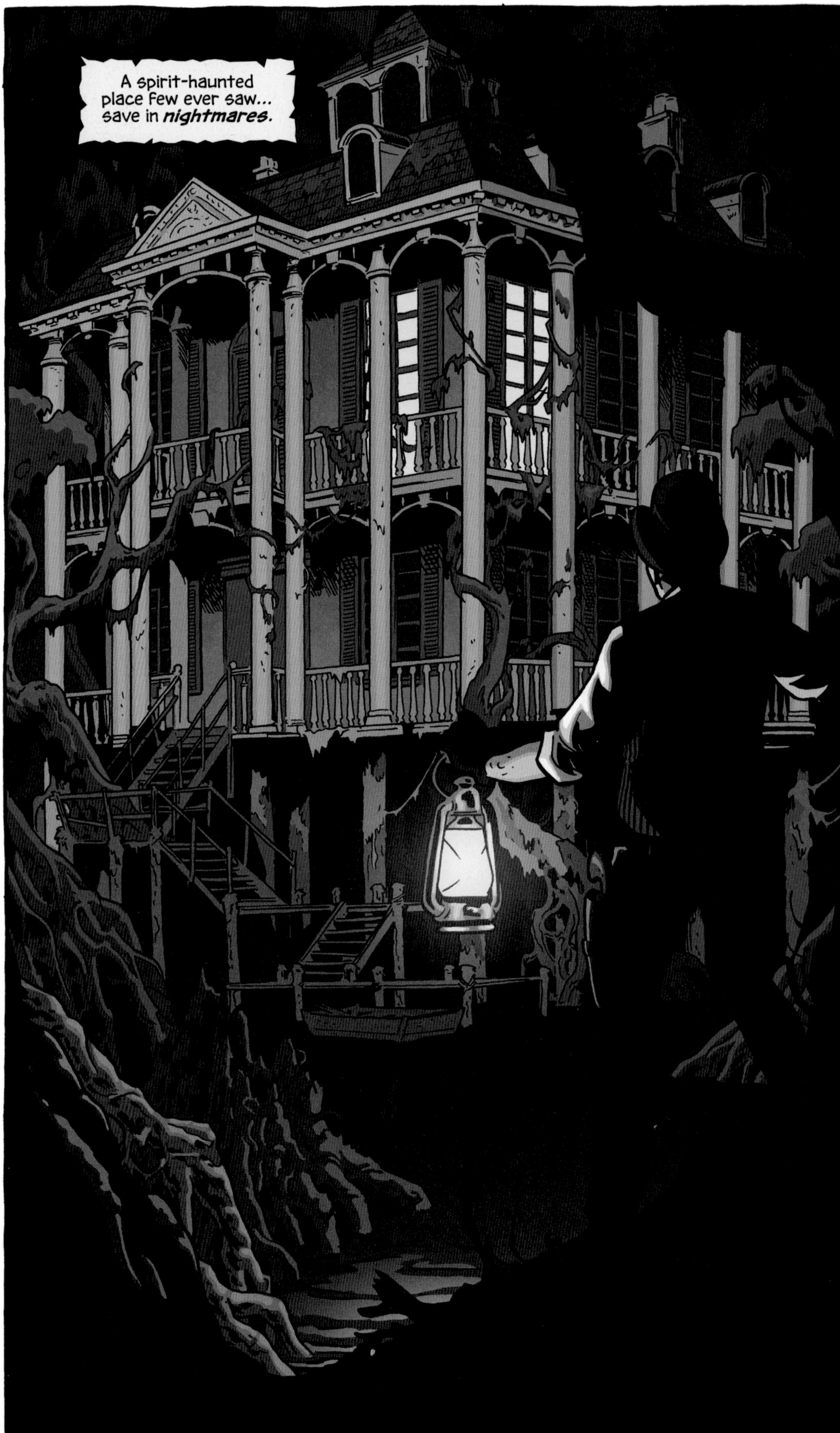
A spirit-haunted place few ever saw... save in *nightmares*.

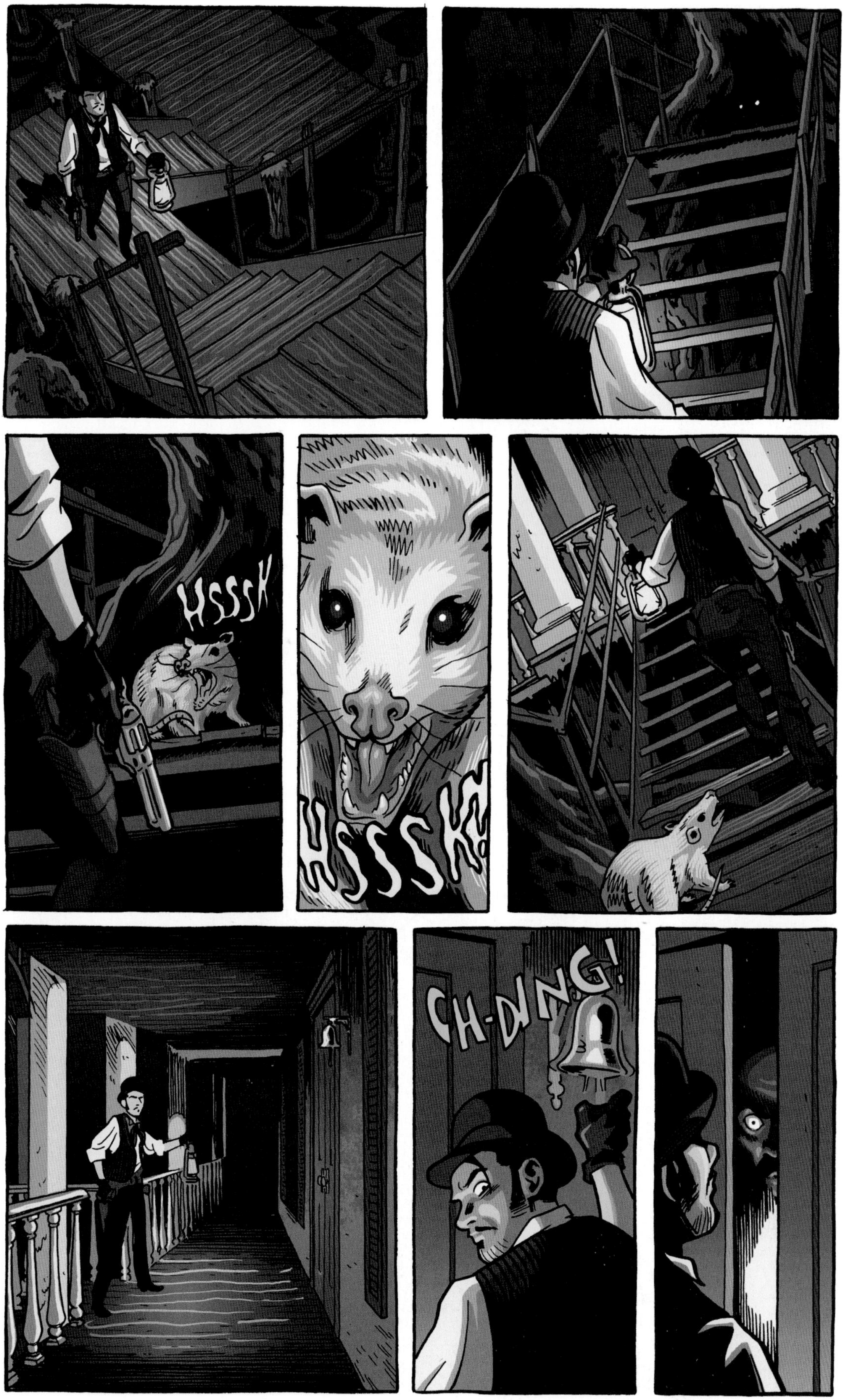
HSSSK
HSSSK!
CH-DING!

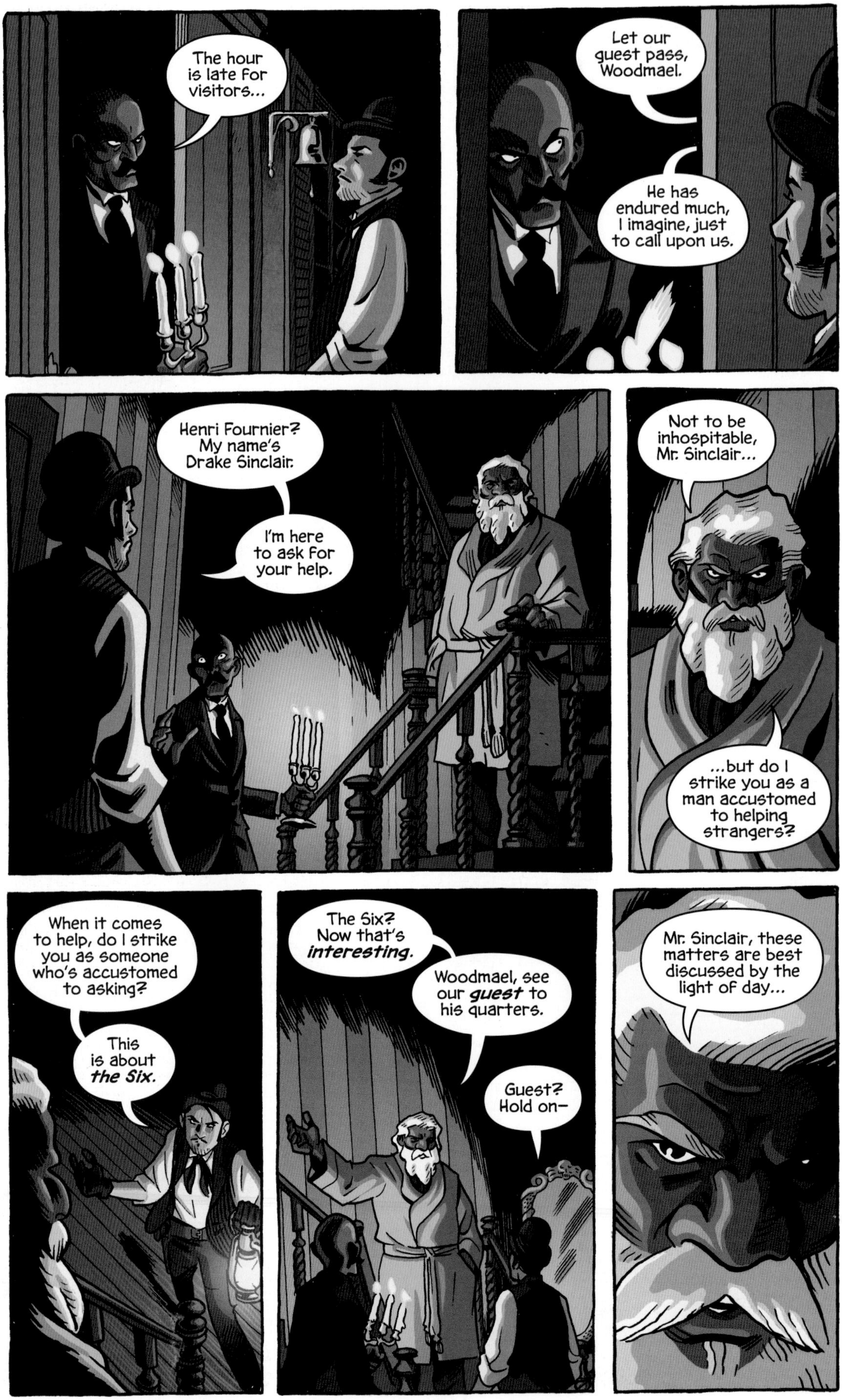
The hour is late for visitors...
Let our guest pass, Woodmael.
He has endured much, I imagine, just to call upon us.
Henri Fournier? My name's Drake Sinclair.
I'm here to ask for your help.
Not to be inhospitable, Mr. Sinclair...
...but do I strike you as a man accustomed to helping strangers?
When it comes to help, do I strike you as someone who's accustomed to asking?
This is about *the Six.*
The Six? Now that's *interesting.*
Woodmael, see our *guest* to his quarters.
Guest? Hold on–
Mr. Sinclair, these matters are best discussed by the light of day...

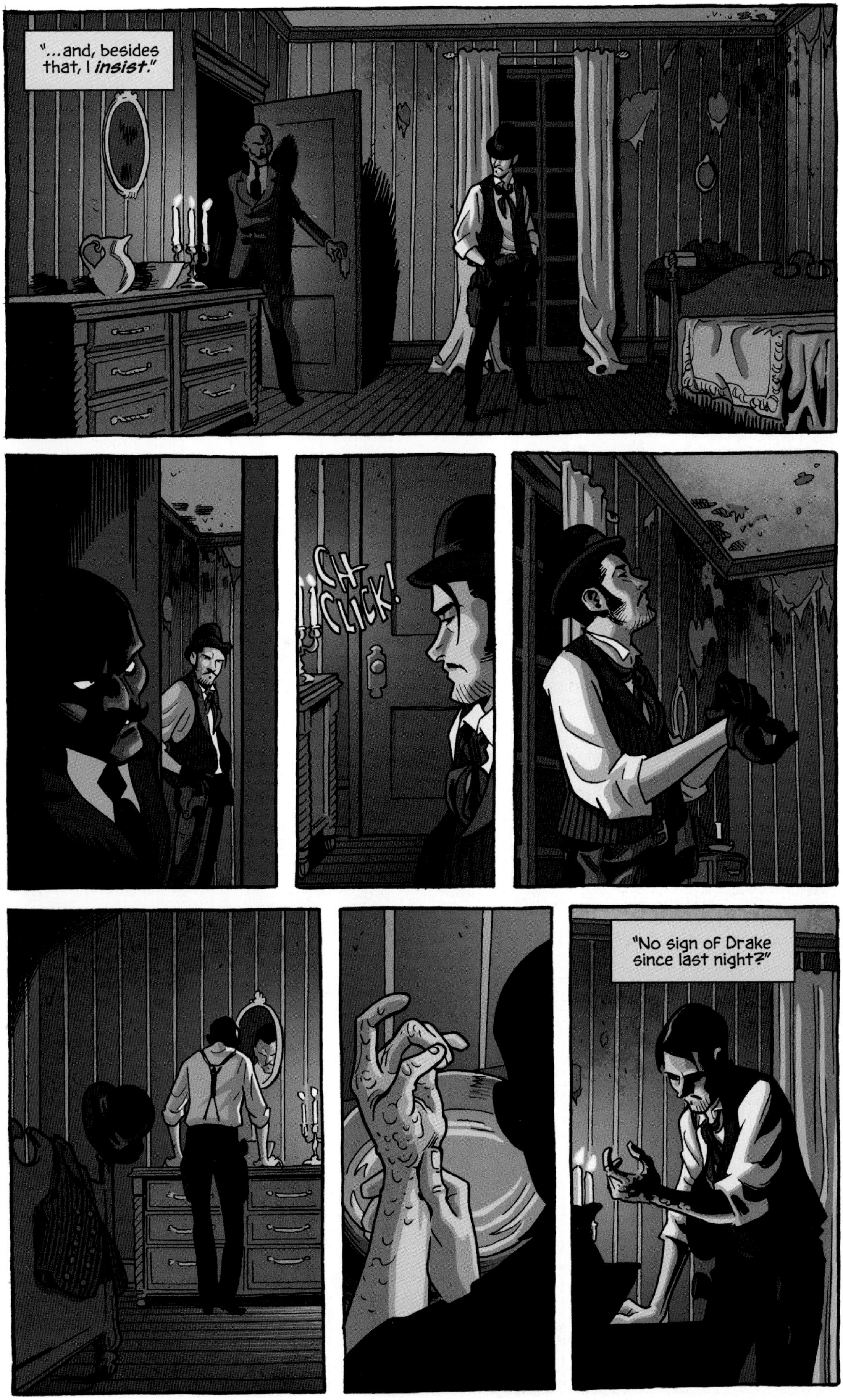
"...and, besides that, I *insist*."
CH CLICK!
"No sign of Drake since last night?"

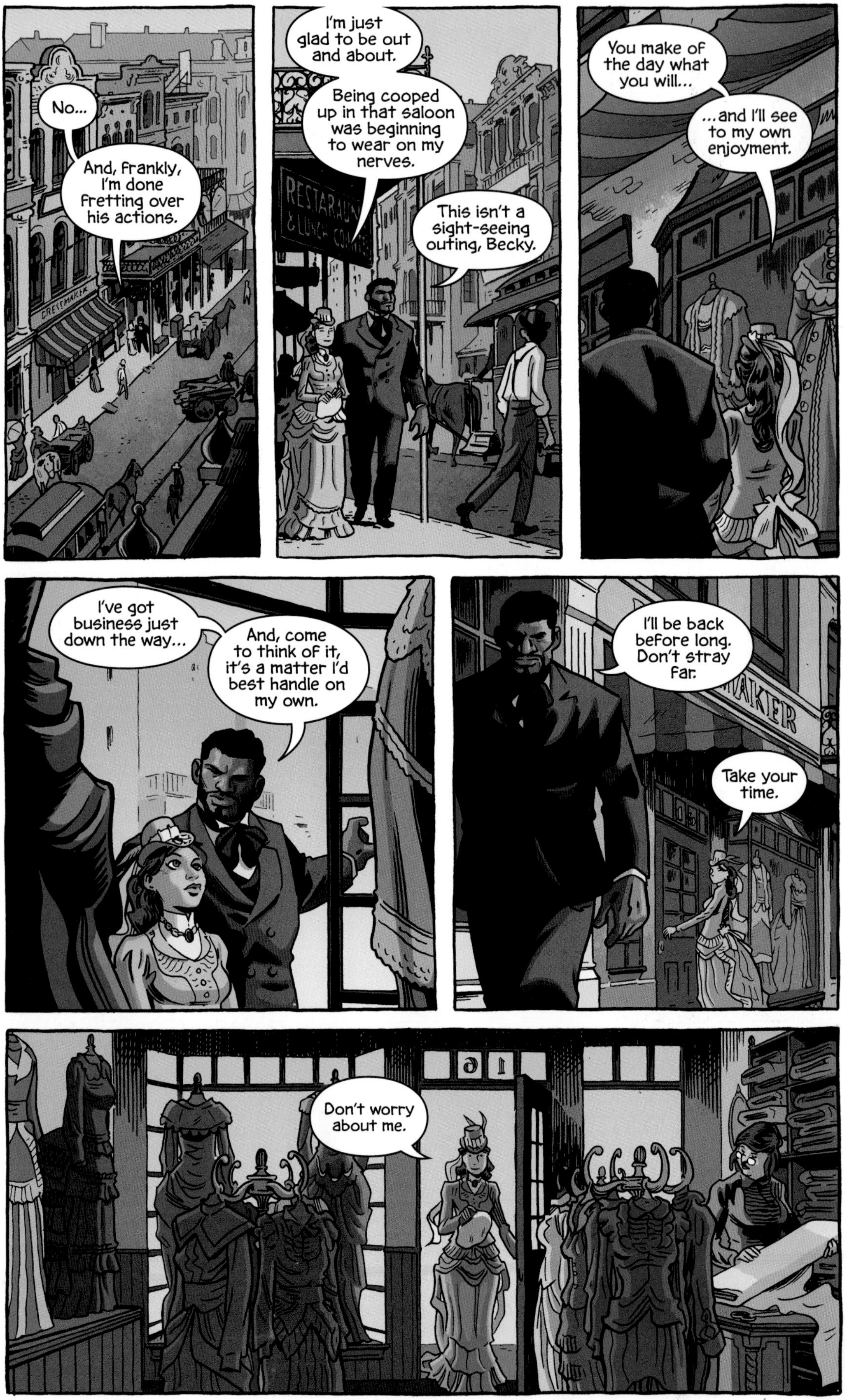
No...
And, frankly, I'm done fretting over his actions.
DRESSMAKER
I'm just glad to be out and about.
Being cooped up in that saloon was beginning to wear on my nerves.
RESTARAUN & LUNCH CO
This isn't a sight-seeing outing, Becky.
You make of the day what you will...
...and I'll see to my own enjoyment.
I've got business just down the way...
And, come to think of it, it's a matter I'd best handle on my own.
I'll be back before long. Don't stray far.
MAKER
Take your time.
Don't worry about me.

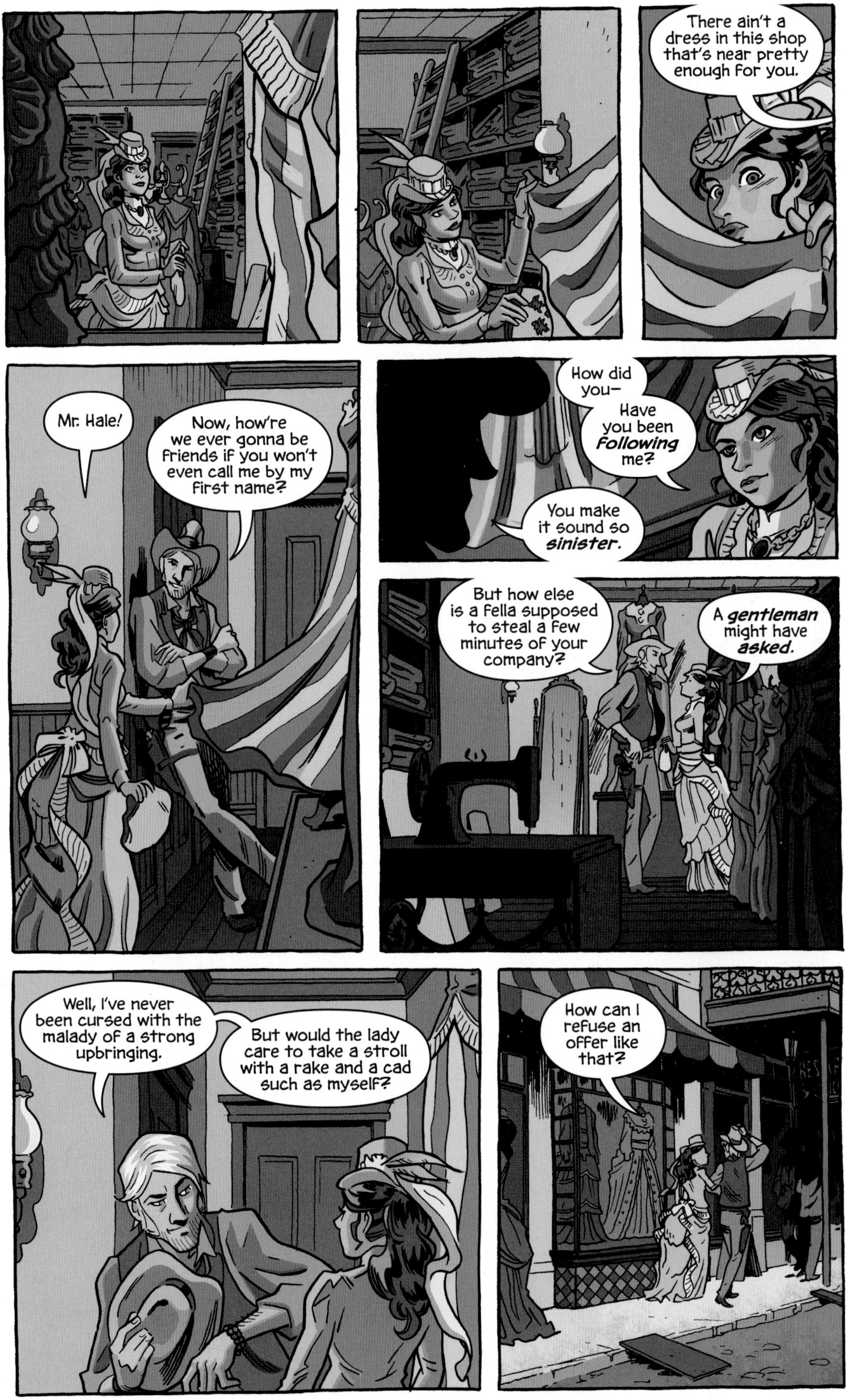
There ain't a dress in this shop that's near pretty enough for you.
Mr. Hale!
Now, how're we ever gonna be friends if you won't even call me by my first name?
How did you—
Have you been *following* me?
You make it sound so *sinister*.
But how else is a fella supposed to steal a few minutes of your company?
A *gentleman* might have *asked*.
Well, I've never been cursed with the malady of a strong upbringing.
But would the lady care to take a stroll with a rake and a cad such as myself?
How can I refuse an offer like that?

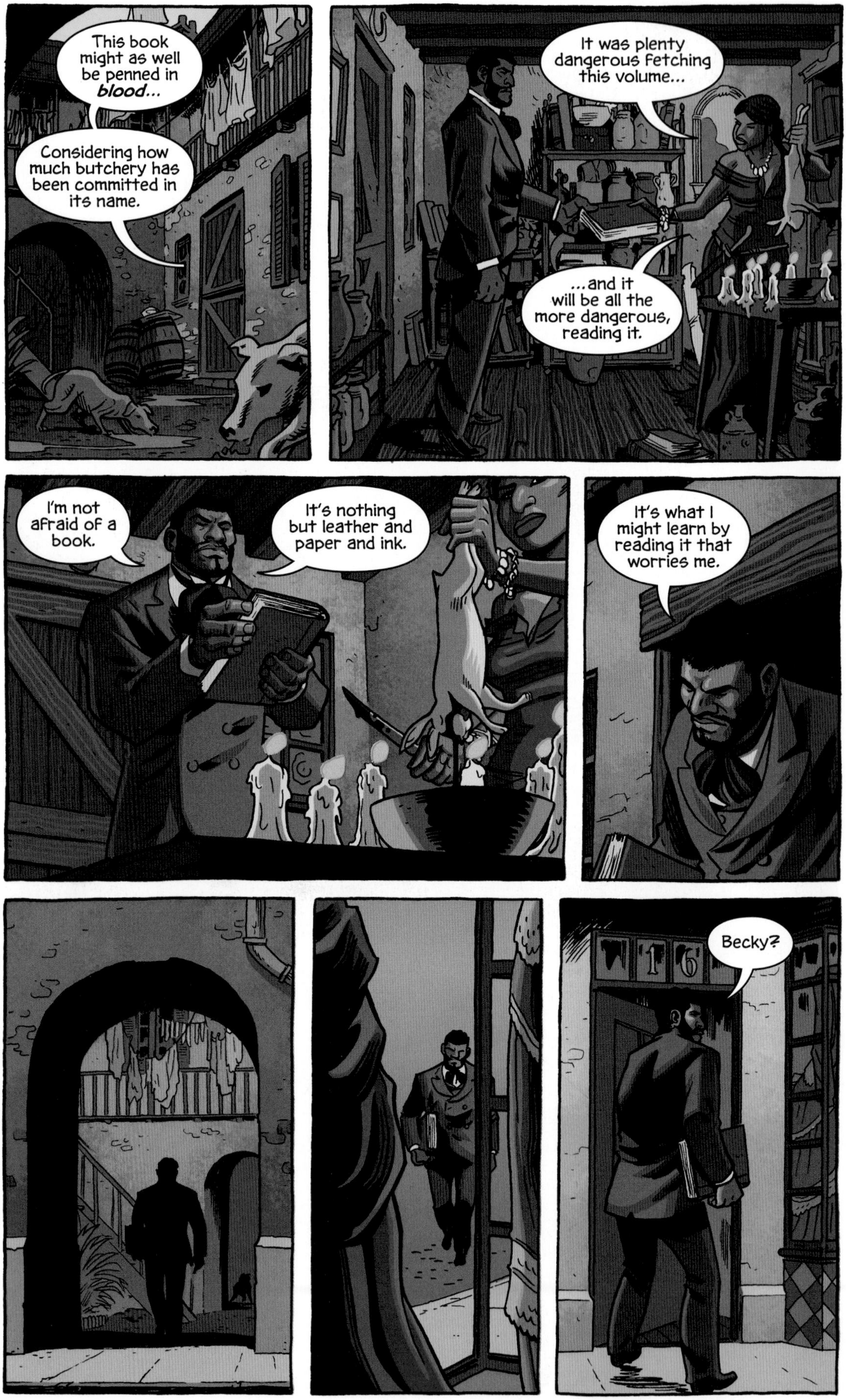
This book might as well be penned in *blood*...
Considering how much butchery has been committed in its name.
It was plenty dangerous fetching this volume...
...and it will be all the more dangerous, reading it.
I'm not afraid of a book.
It's nothing but leather and paper and ink.
It's what I might learn by reading it that worries me.
16
Becky?

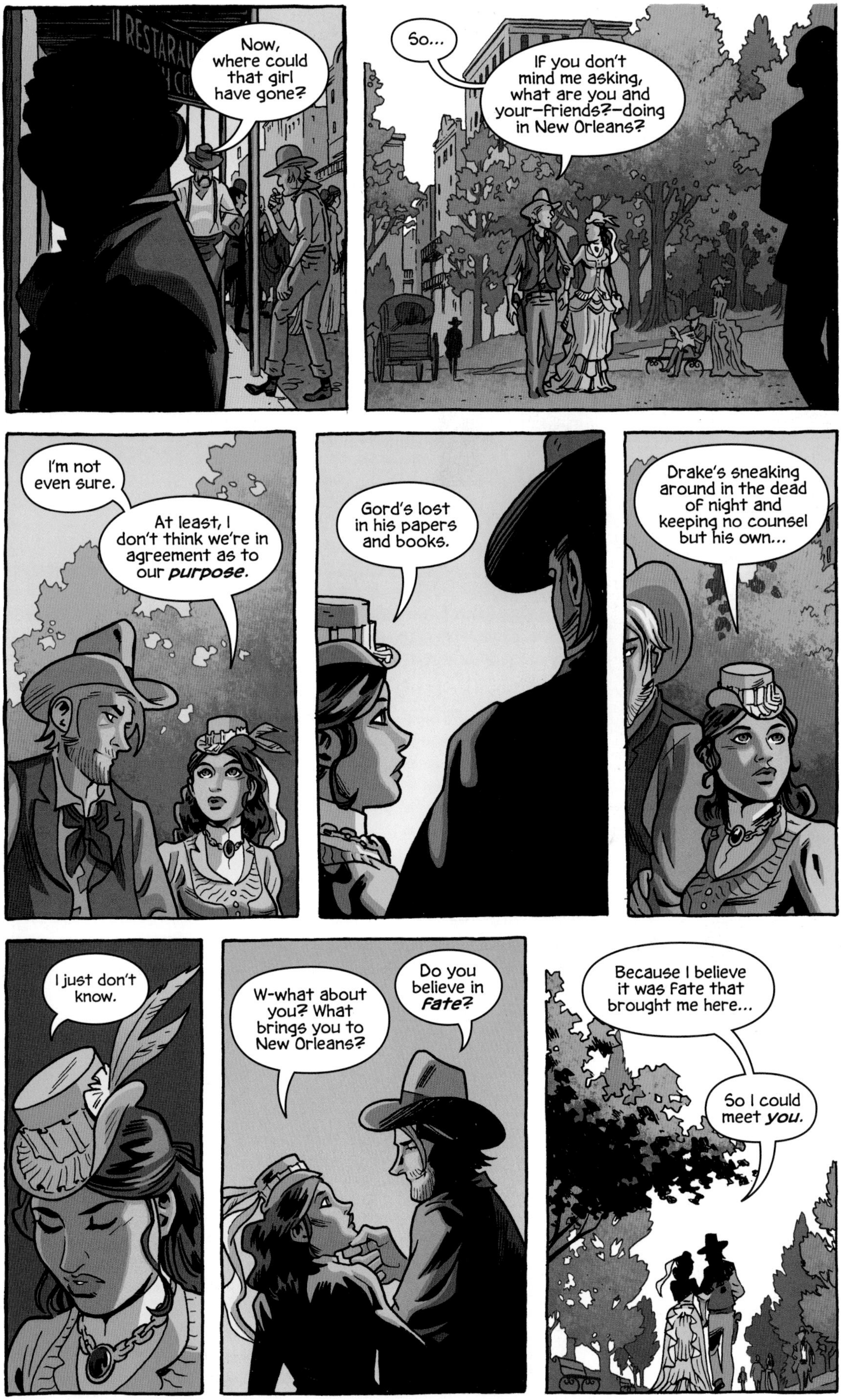
RESTARAU
Now, where could that girl have gone?
So...
If you don't mind me asking, what are you and your—friends?—doing in New Orleans?
I'm not even sure.
At least, I don't think we're in agreement as to our *purpose*.
Gord's lost in his papers and books.
Drake's sneaking around in the dead of night and keeping no counsel but his own...
I just don't know.
W-what about you? What brings you to New Orleans?
Do you believe in *fate?*
Because I believe it was fate that brought me here...
So I could meet *you.*

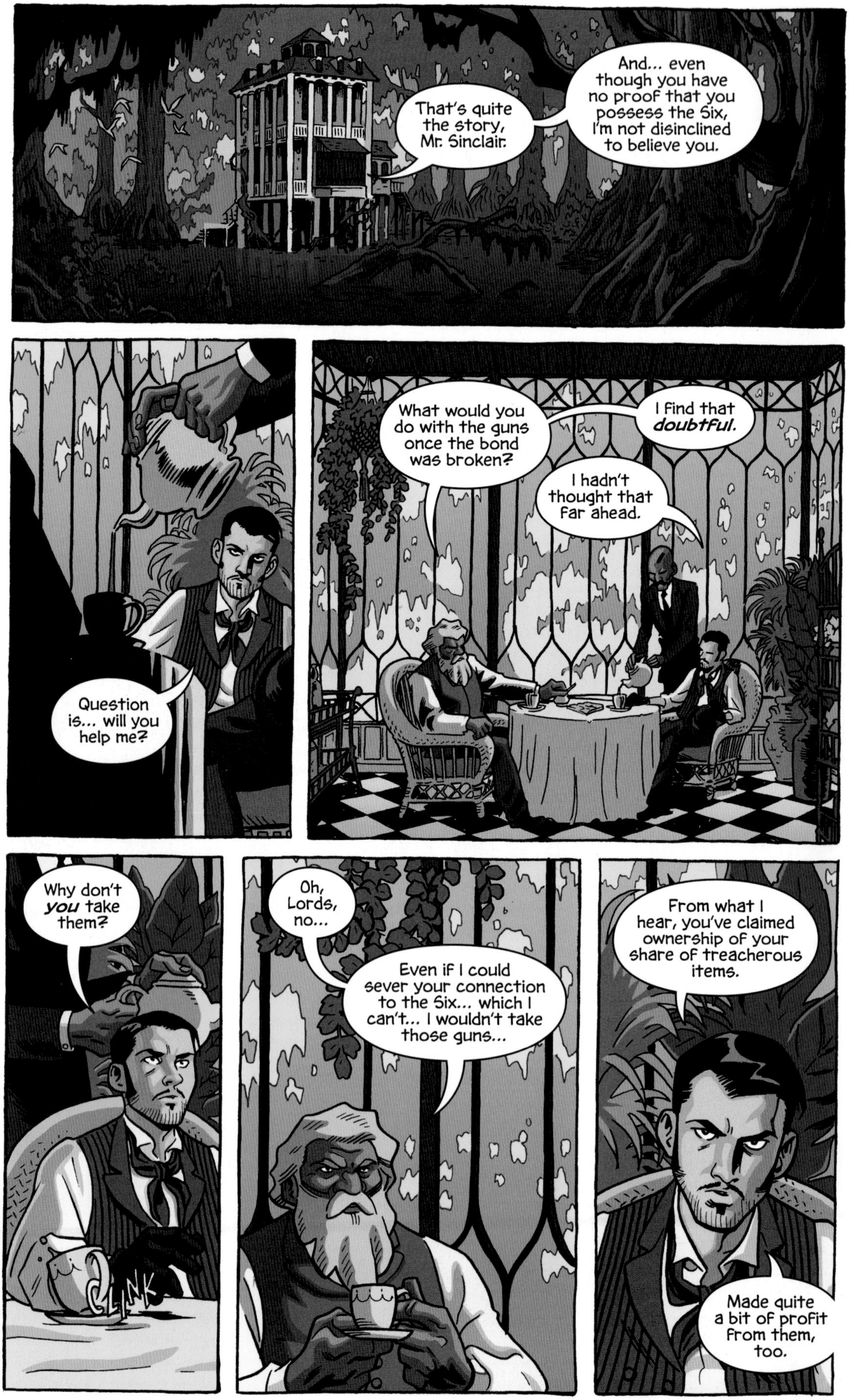

That's quite the story, Mr. Sinclair.
And... even though you have no proof that you possess the Six, I'm not disinclined to believe you.
Question is... will you help me?
What would you do with the guns once the bond was broken?
I find that *doubtful.*
I hadn't thought that far ahead.
Why don't *you* take them?
CLINK
Oh, Lords, no...
Even if I could sever your connection to the Six... which I can't... I wouldn't take those guns...
From what I hear, you've claimed ownership of your share of treacherous items.
Made quite a bit of profit from them, too.

Did you come here hoping to *sell* those guns, Mr. Sinclair?

The Six can't be traded for anything quite so common as money... not by me... and most certainly not by you.

The people—the forces— who would want the guns... they can't be bargained with.

They'll kill you and take the guns from your corpse.

Only a *dead man's hand* can trade those weapons.

But, as I said, I've no desire for the Six.

Nor does your death serve me in any way that matters.

There was a man... in the swamp.

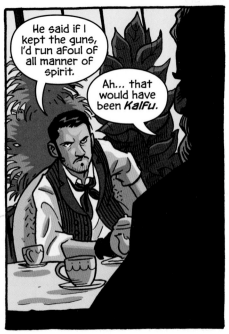

He said if I kept the guns, I'd run afoul of all manner of spirit.

Ah... that would have been *Kalfu*.

"A powerful *Loa*...

"A gatekeeper of sorts... granting or forbidding passage into our world to those things that might wish to cross over."

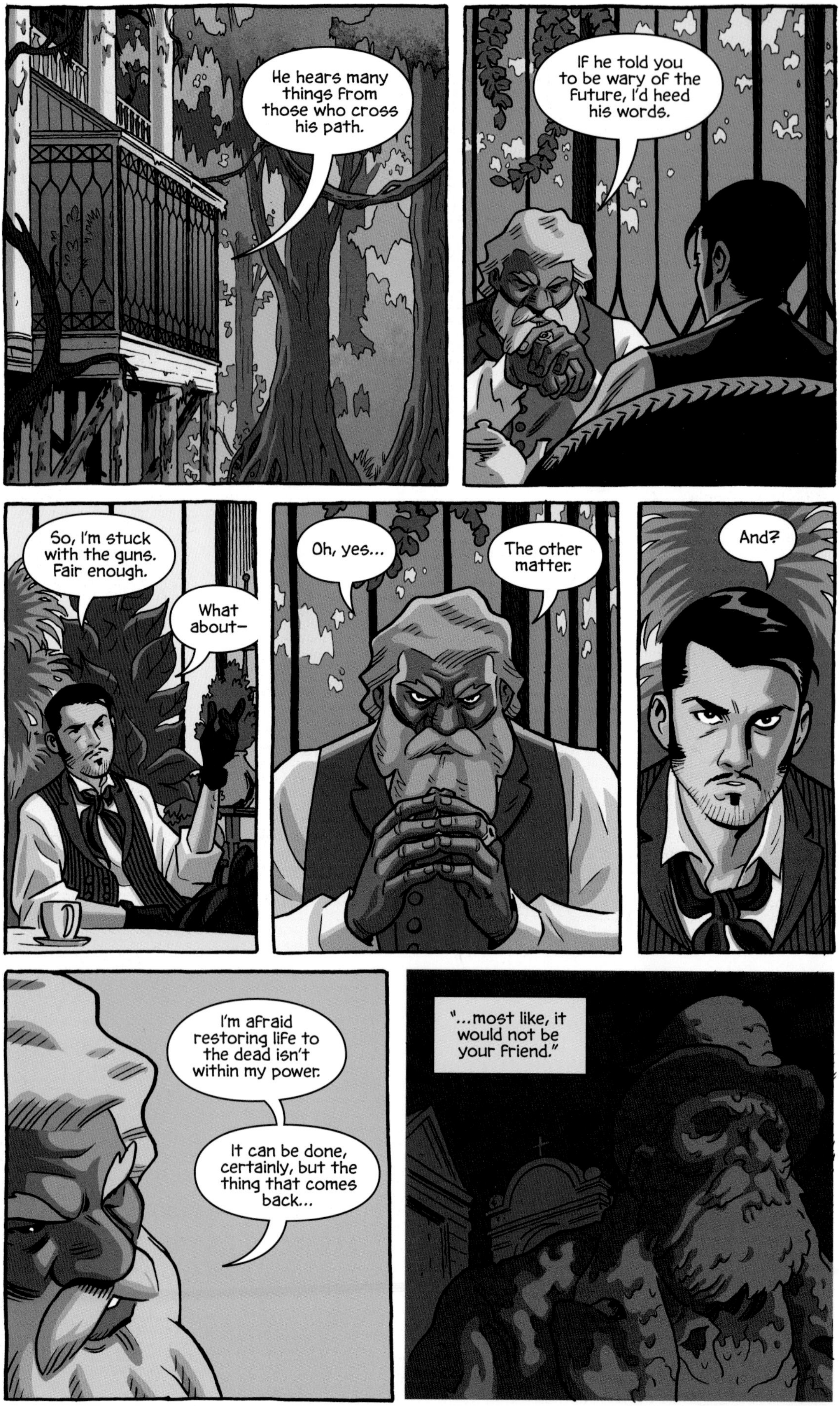
He hears many things from those who cross his path.
If he told you to be wary of the future, I'd heed his words.
So, I'm stuck with the guns. Fair enough.
What about–
Oh, yes...
The other matter.
And?
I'm afraid restoring life to the dead isn't within my power.
It can be done, certainly, but the thing that comes back...
"...most like, it would not be your friend."

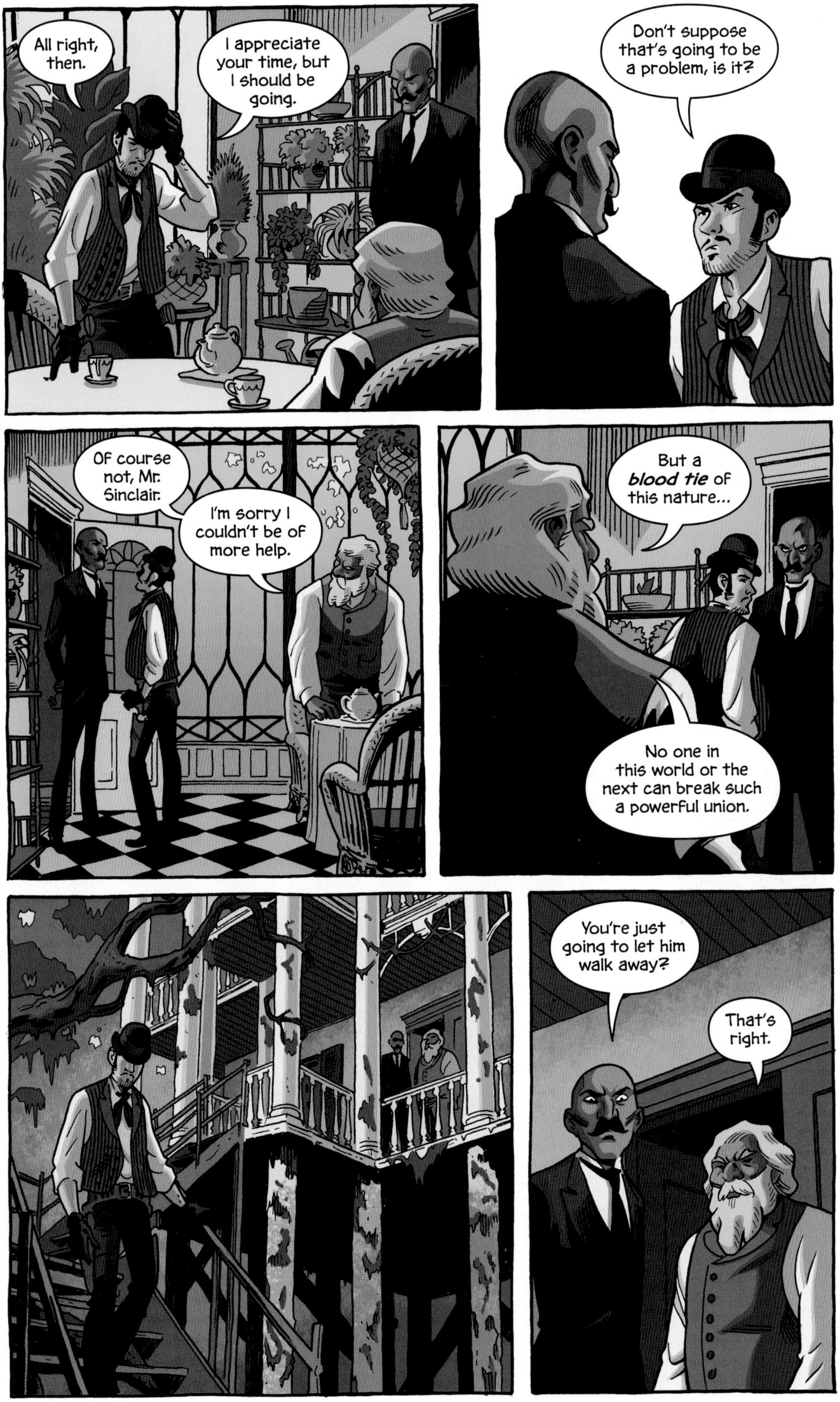
All right, then.
I appreciate your time, but I should be going.
Don't suppose that's going to be a problem, is it?
Of course not, Mr. Sinclair.
I'm sorry I couldn't be of more help.
But a *blood tie* of this nature...
No one in this world or the next can break such a powerful union.
You're just going to let him walk away?
That's right.

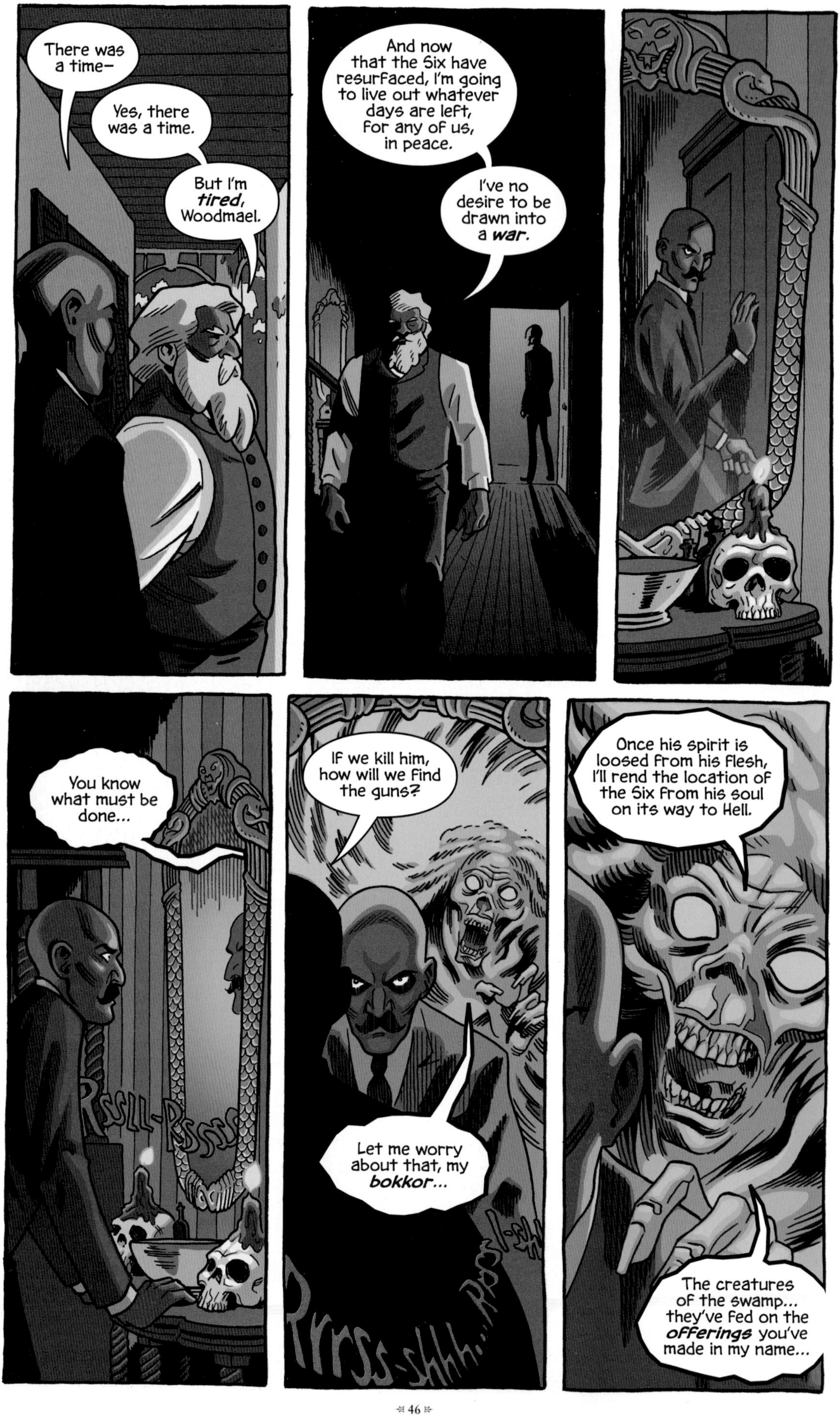
There was a time—
Yes, there was a time.
But I'm *tired*, Woodmael.
And now that the Six have resurfaced, I'm going to live out whatever days are left, for any of us, in peace.
I've no desire to be drawn into a *war*.
You know what must be done...
If we kill him, how will we find the guns?
Let me worry about that, my *bokkor*...
Once his spirit is loosed from his flesh, I'll rend the location of the Six from his soul on its way to Hell.
The creatures of the swamp... they've fed on the *offerings* you've made in my name...

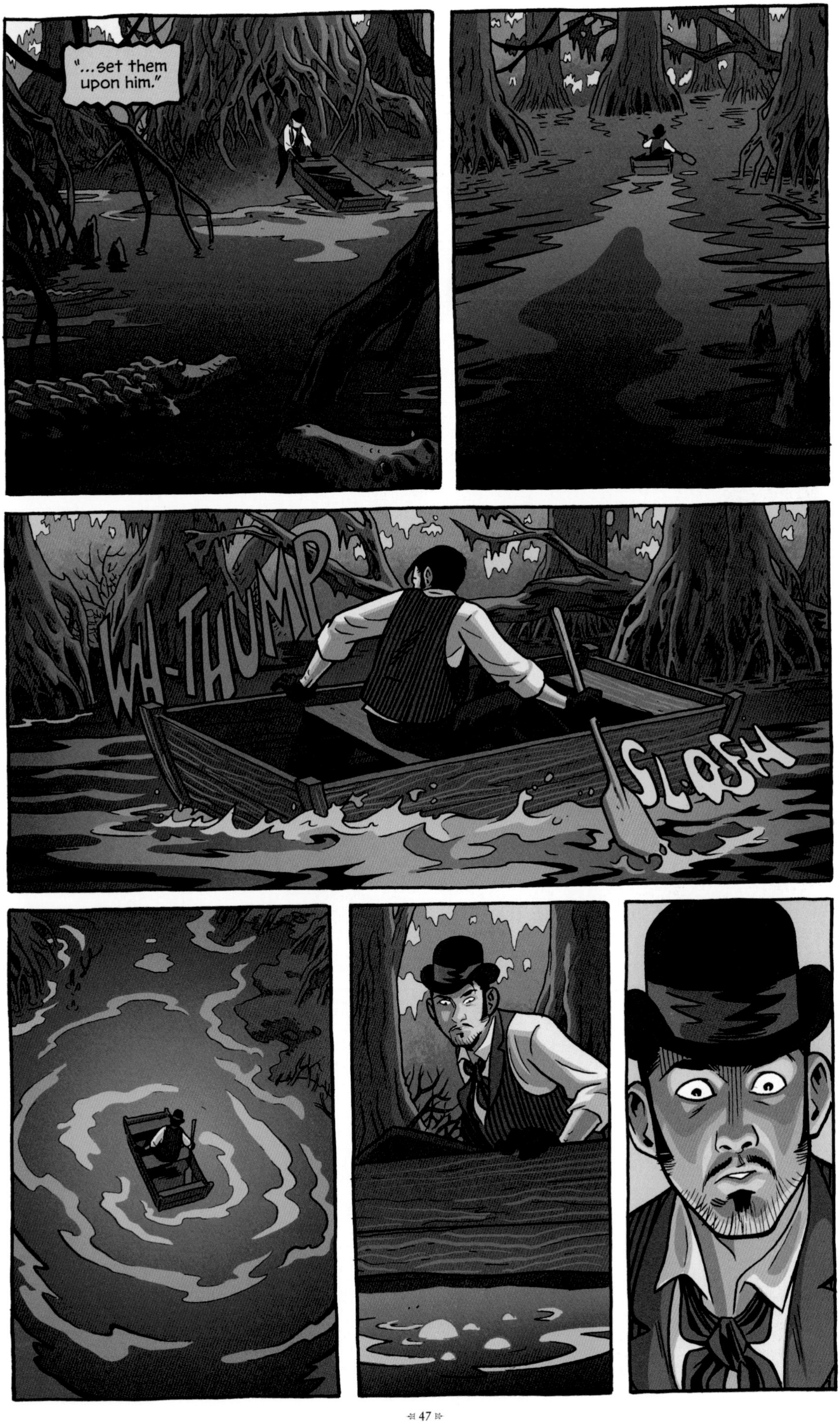
"...set them upon him."
WA-THUMP
SLOSH

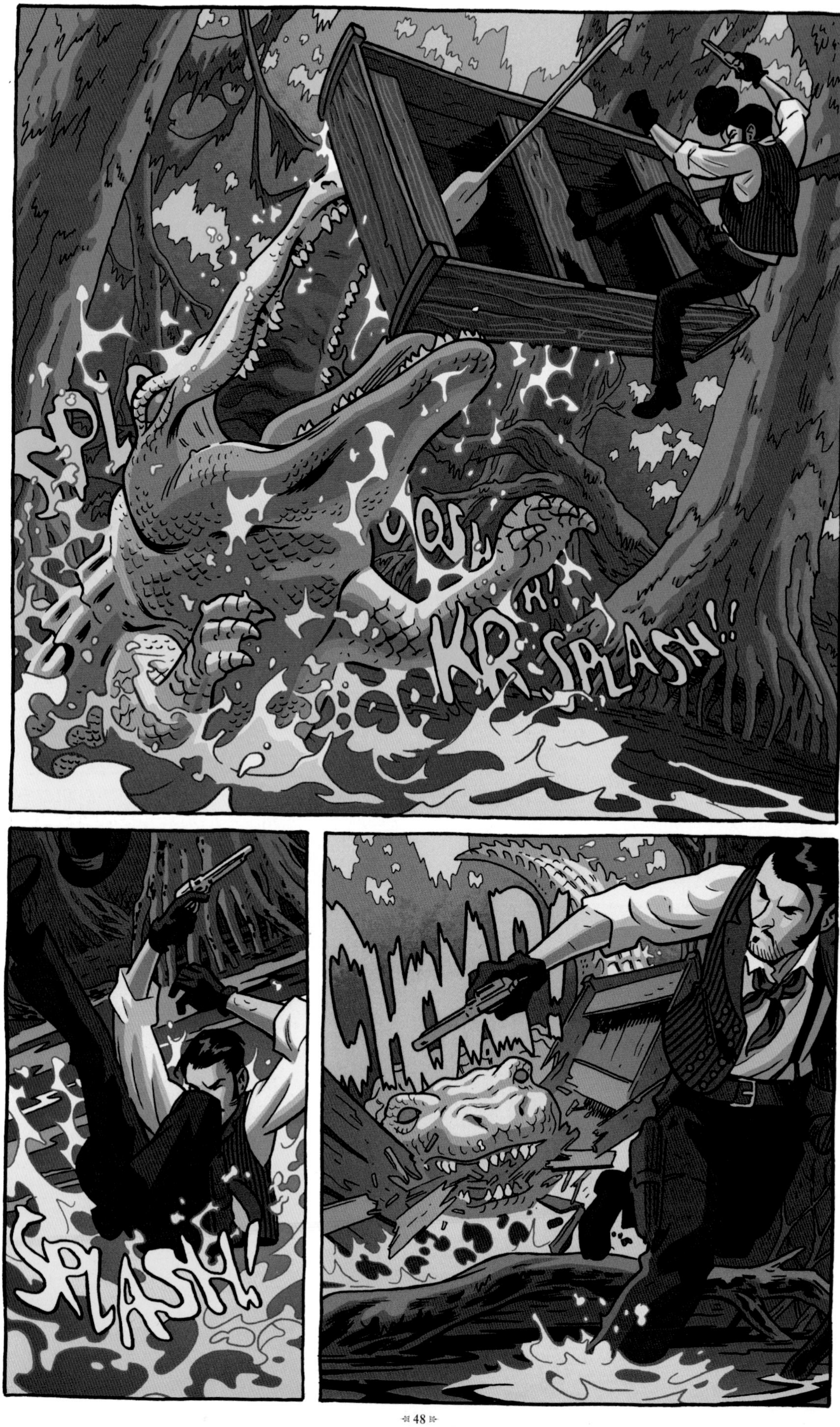
KRSPLASH!!
SPLASH!

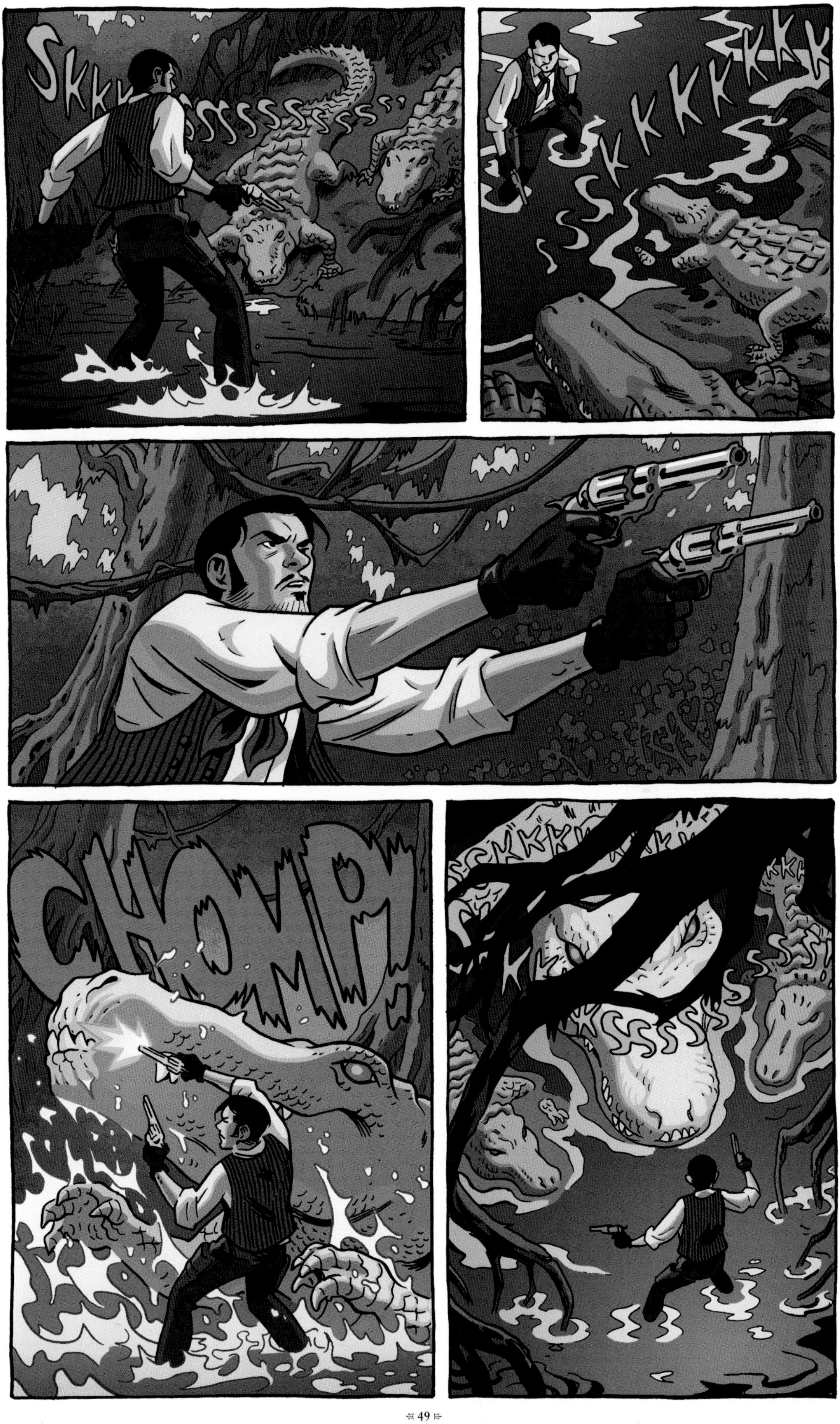
CHOMP!

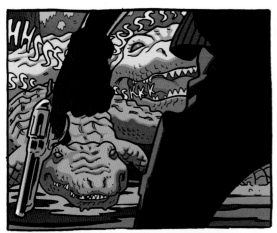

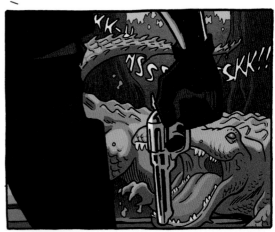

BLAM! BLAM!

CRK CRK CRK BLAM

WHUMP! OOF!

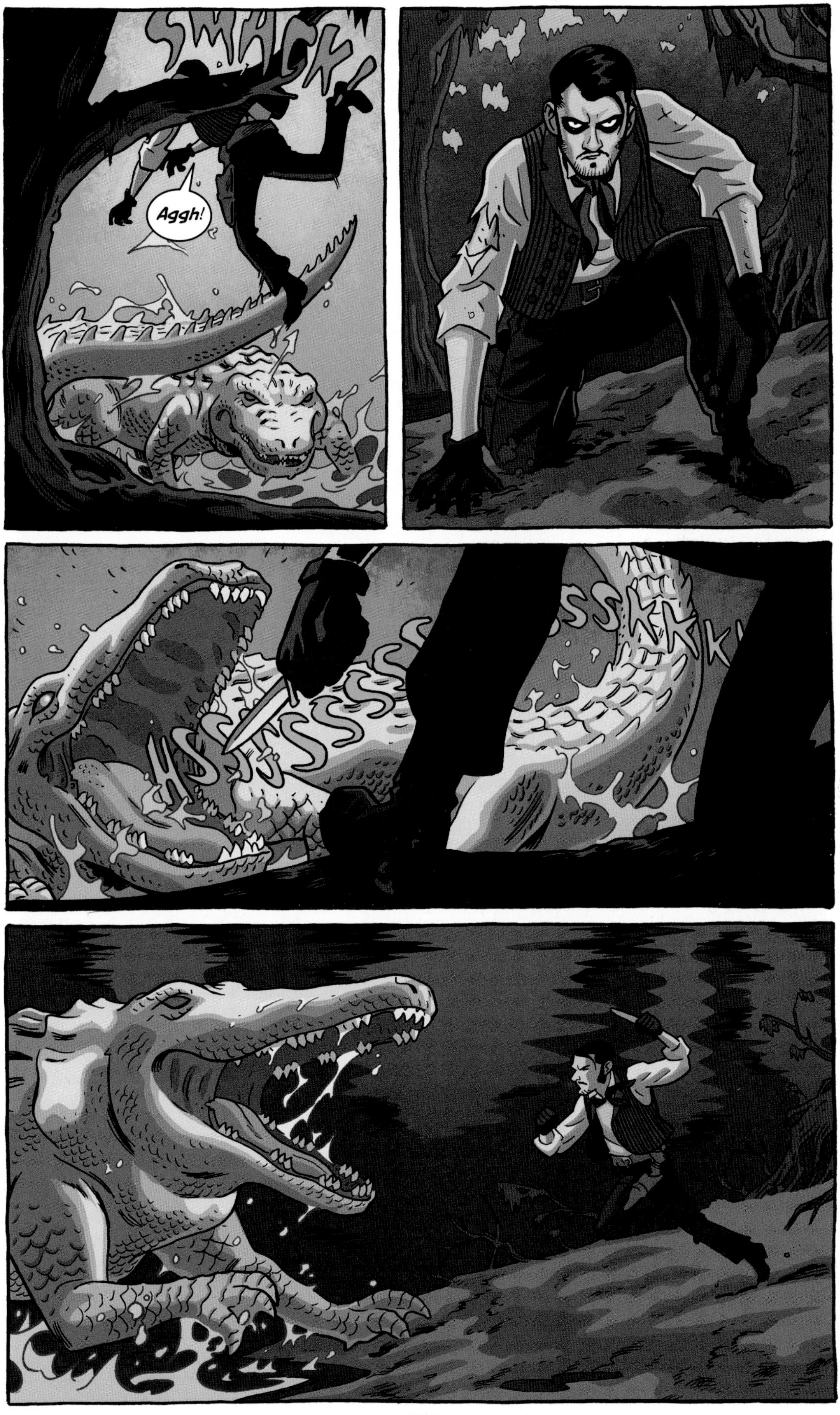
SMACK!
Aggh!
HSSSSSSSSSKKK!

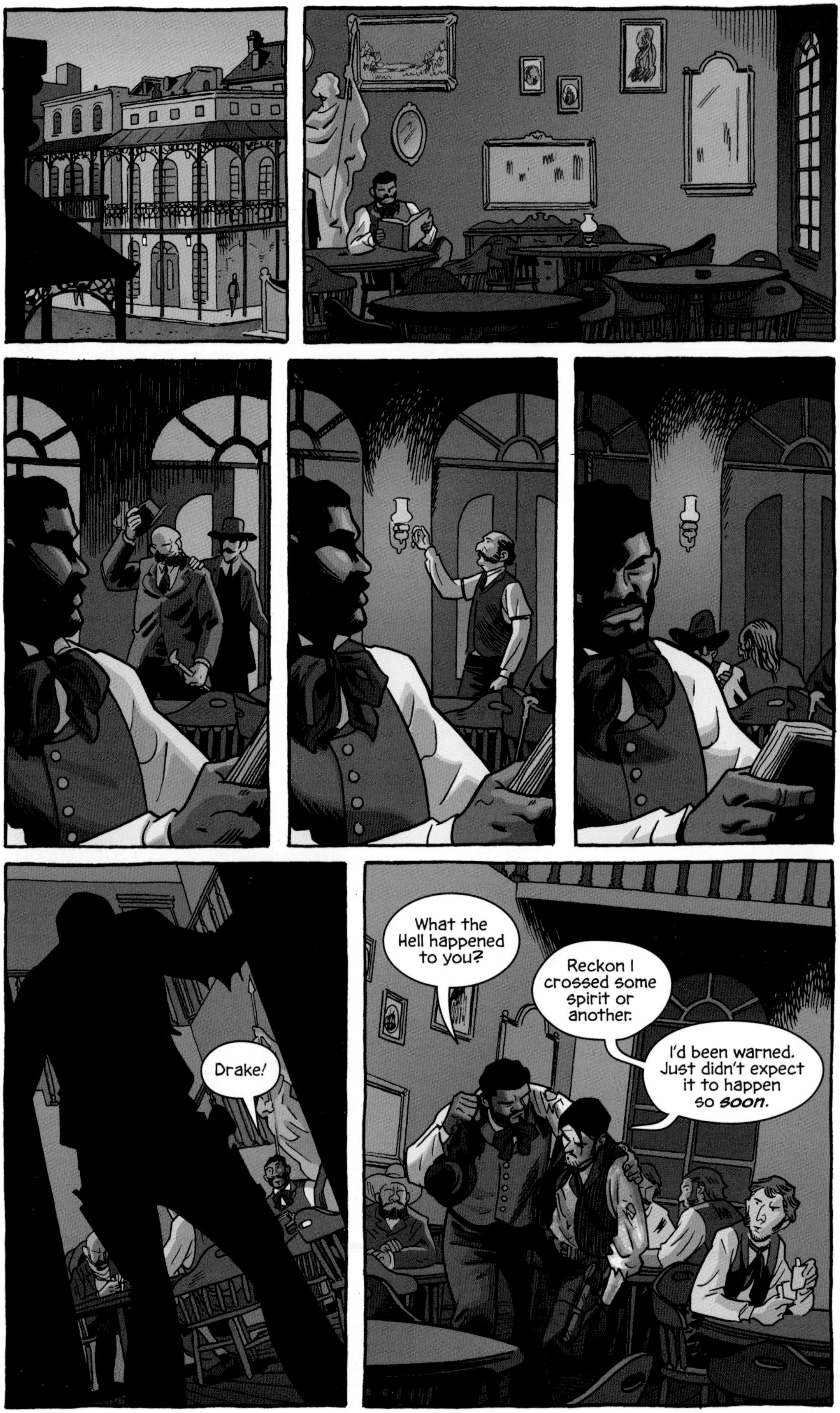
Drake!
What the Hell happened to you?
Reckon I crossed some spirit or another.
I'd been warned. Just didn't expect it to happen so soon.

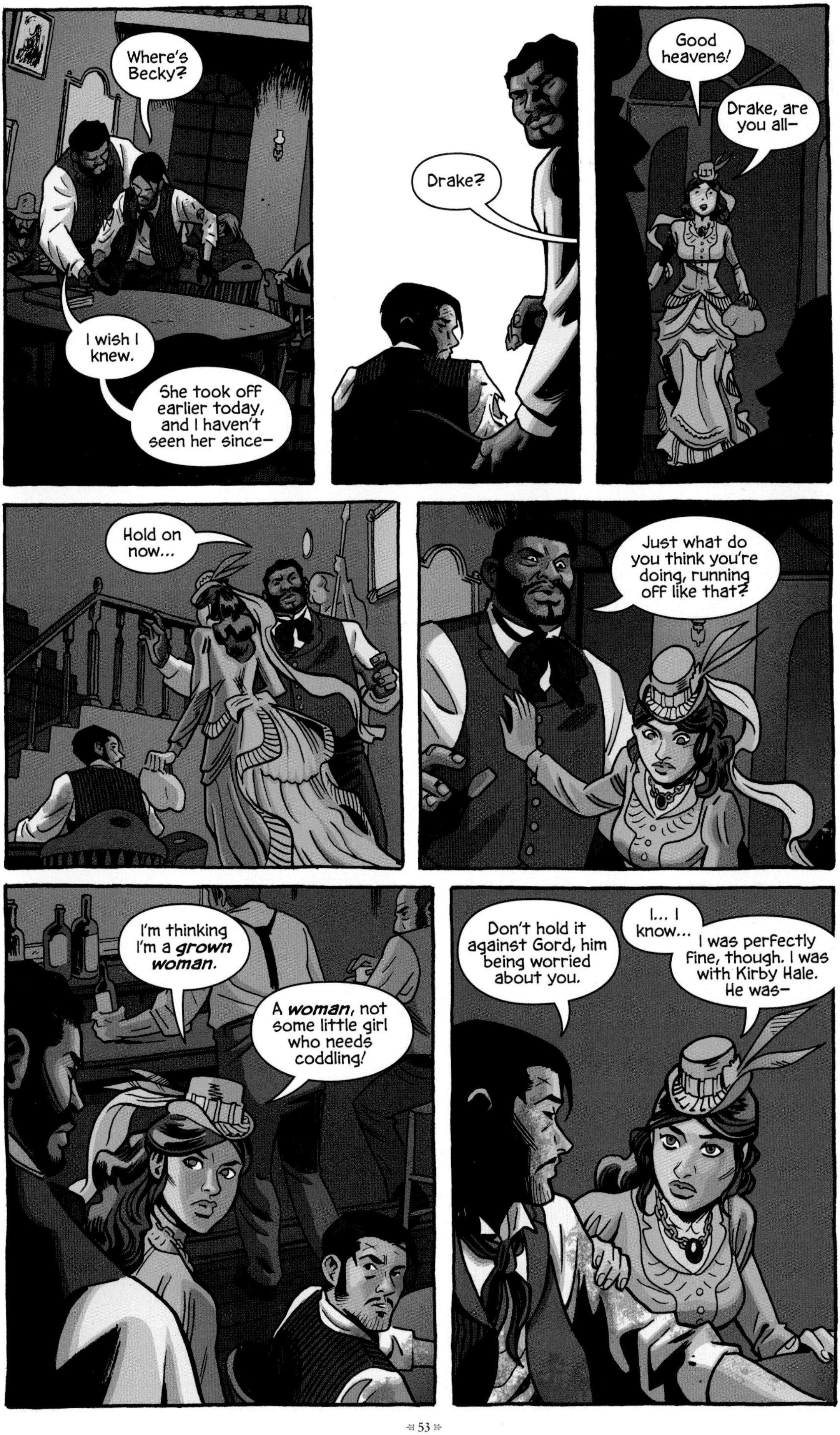
Where's Becky?
I wish I knew.
She took off earlier today, and I haven't seen her since–
Drake?
Good heavens!
Drake, are you all–
Hold on now...
Just what do you think you're doing, running off like that?
I'm thinking I'm a ***grown woman***.
A ***woman***, not some little girl who needs coddling!
Don't hold it against Gord, him being worried about you.
I... I know...
I was perfectly fine, though. I was with Kirby Hale. He was–

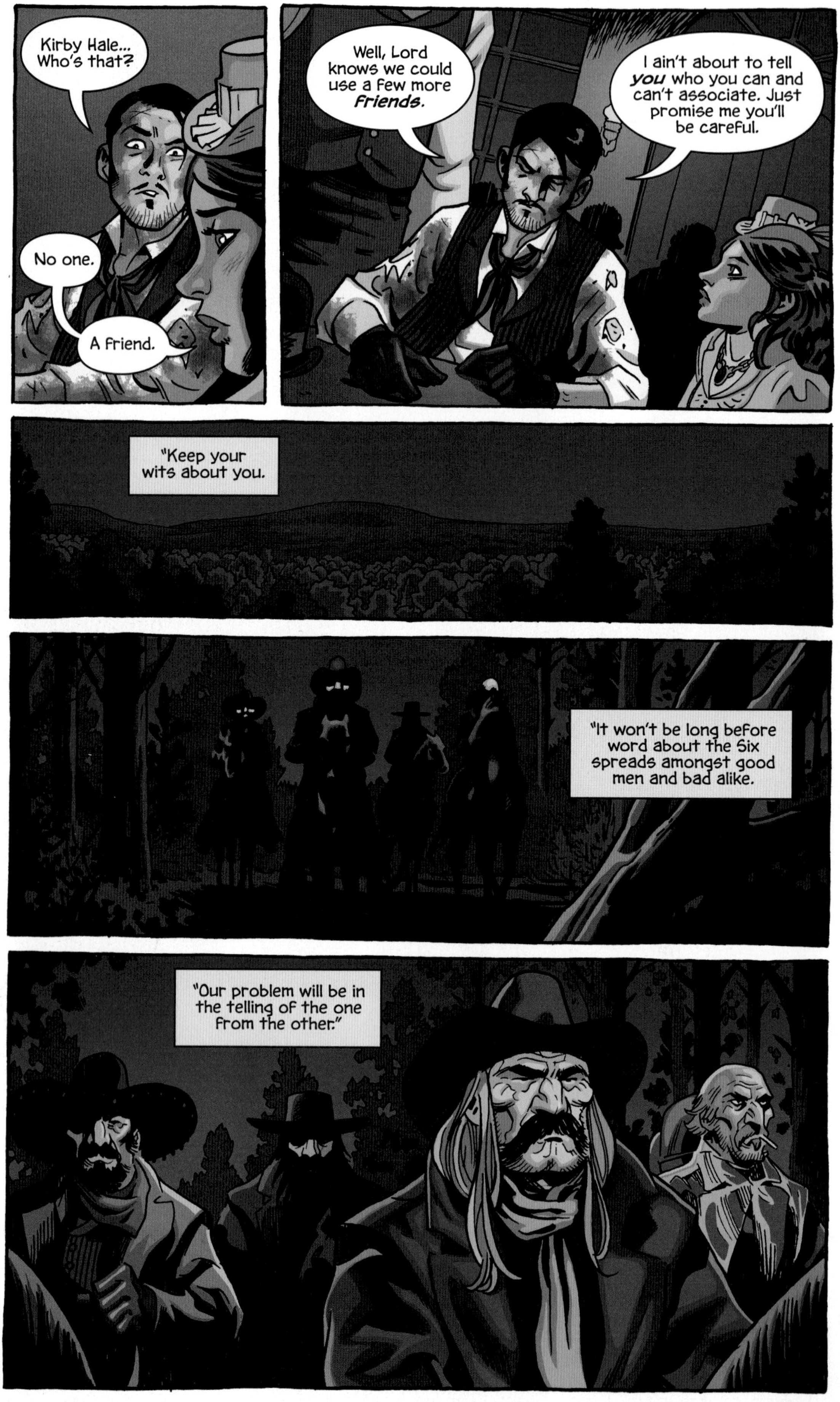
Kirby Hale... Who's that?
No one.
A friend.
Well, Lord knows we could use a few more *friends.*
I ain't about to tell *you* who you can and can't associate. Just promise me you'll be careful.
"Keep your wits about you.
"It won't be long before word about the Six spreads amongst good men and bad alike.
"Our problem will be in the telling of the one from the other."

CHAPTER THREE

...explain it to me again.

After what happened at the Maw, I couldn't stop thinking about those guns...

About what they mean in the grand scheme of things, about what they have to do with that vault that you and me were so dead set on opening...

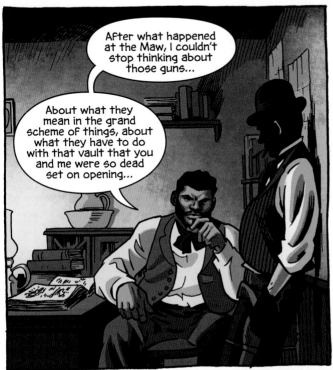

This book was written by *Albrecht Krieg,* a German madman and prophet who lived more than two hundred years ago.

He claimed that the end of days would be brought about by *six weapons*...

Are you suggesting he was talking about the pistols?

The guns aren't—

I know.

But Becky said that the guns had assumed many different forms over the centuries, didn't she?

It stands to reason, then, that the vault's assumed different forms, too.

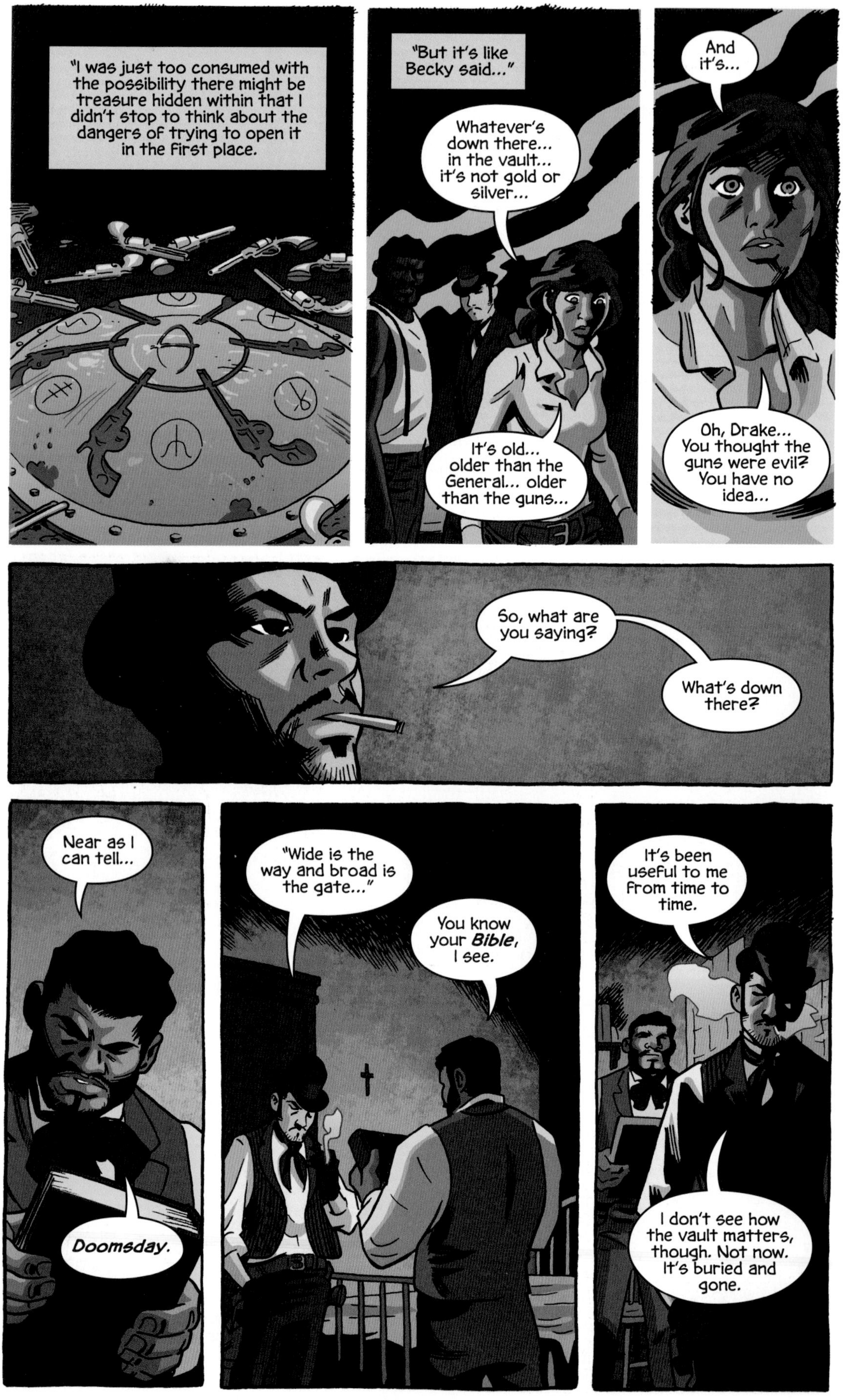
"I was just too consumed with the possibility there might be treasure hidden within that I didn't stop to think about the dangers of trying to open it in the first place.
"But it's like Becky said..."
Whatever's down there... in the vault... it's not gold or silver...
It's old... older than the General... older than the guns...
And it's...
Oh, Drake... You thought the guns were evil? You have no idea...
So, what are you saying?
What's down there?
Near as I can tell...
Doomsday.
"Wide is the way and broad is the gate..."
You know your Bible, I see.
It's been useful to me from time to time.
I don't see how the vault matters, though. Not now. It's buried and gone.

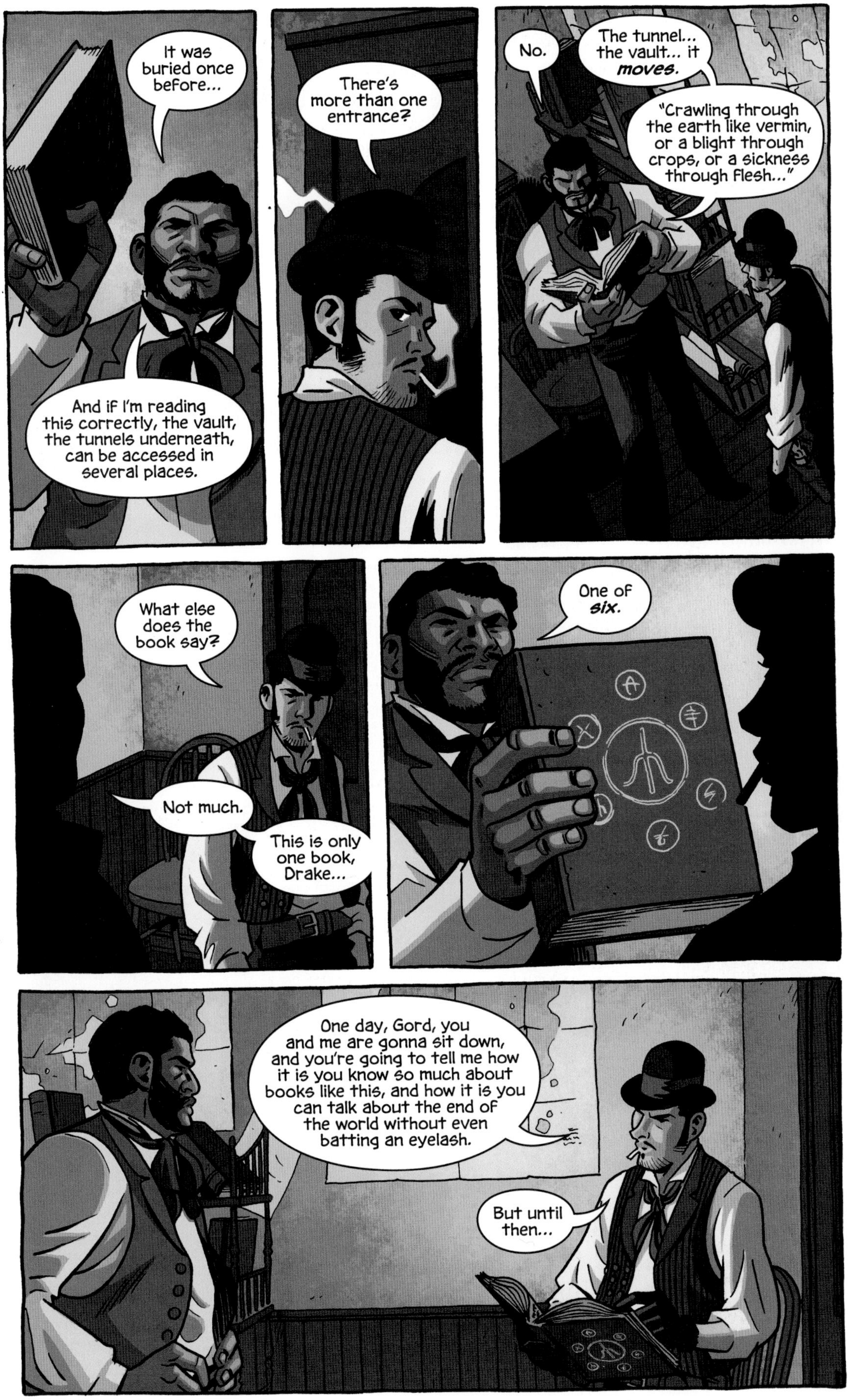

It was buried once before...
And if I'm reading this correctly, the vault, the tunnels underneath, can be accessed in several places.
There's more than one entrance?
No.
The tunnel... the vault... it *moves.*
"Crawling through the earth like vermin, or a blight through crops, or a sickness through flesh..."
What else does the book say?
Not much.
This is only one book, Drake...
One of *six.*
One day, Gord, you and me are gonna sit down, and you're going to tell me how it is you know so much about books like this, and how it is you can talk about the end of the world without even batting an eyelash.
But until then...

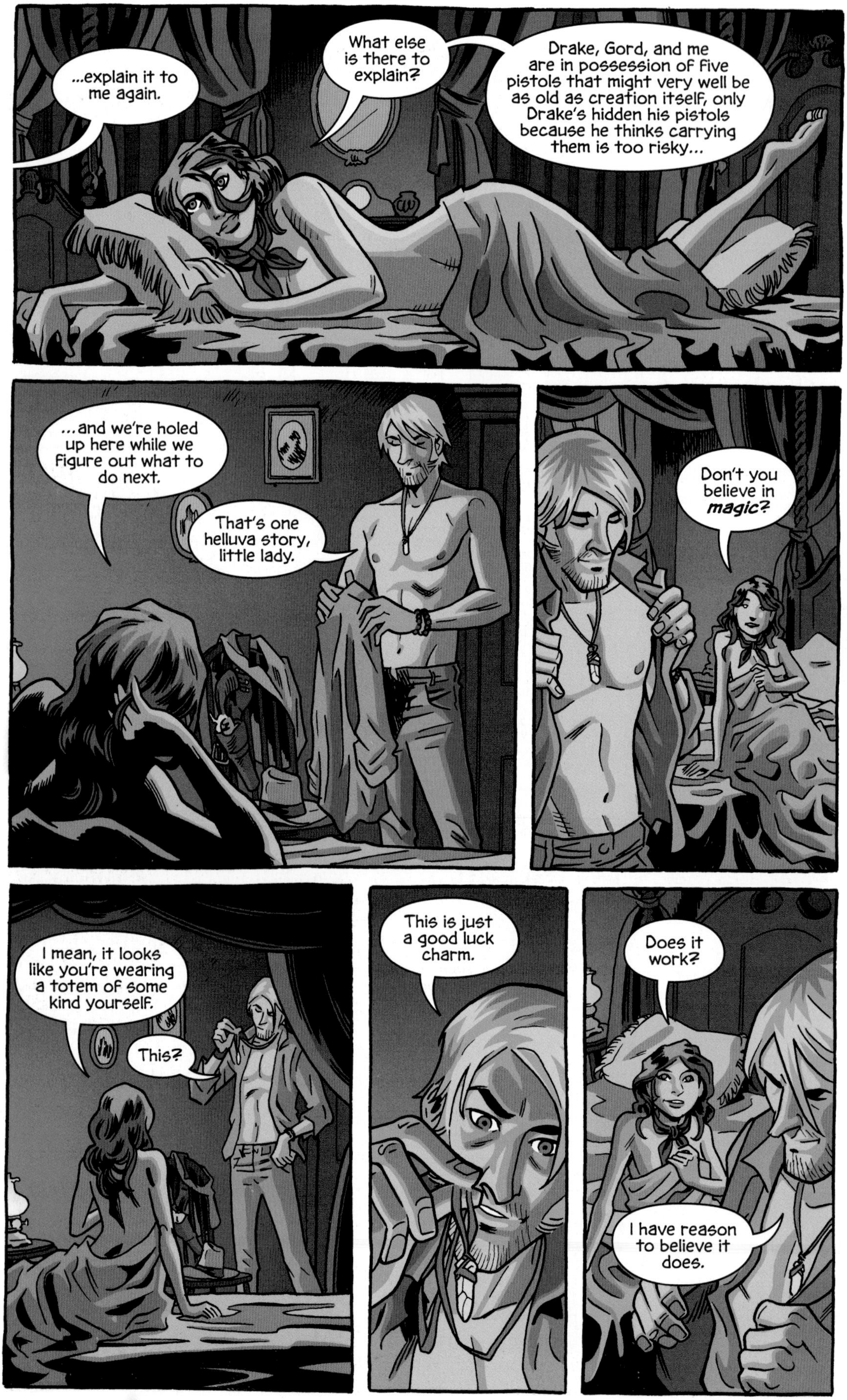
...explain it to me again.
What else is there to explain?
Drake, Gord, and me are in possession of five pistols that might very well be as old as creation itself, only Drake's hidden his pistols because he thinks carrying them is too risky...
...and we're holed up here while we figure out what to do next.
That's one helluva story, little lady.
Don't you believe in *magic*?
I mean, it looks like you're wearing a totem of some kind yourself.
This?
This is just a good luck charm.
Does it work?
I have reason to believe it does.

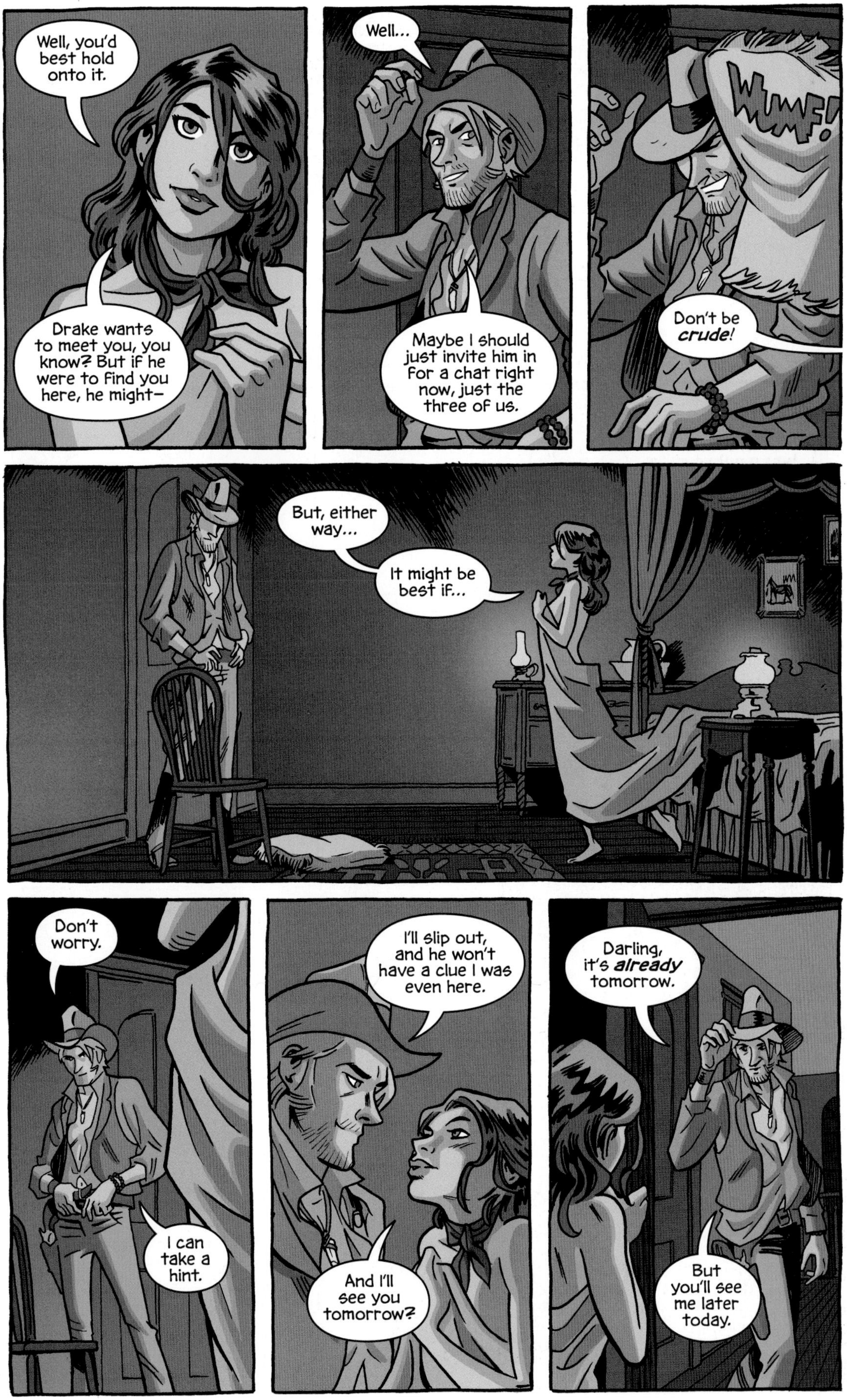
Well, you'd best hold onto it.
Drake wants to meet you, you know? But if he were to find you here, he might–
Well...
Maybe I should just invite him in for a chat right now, just the three of us.
WUMF!
Don't be *crude*!
But, either way...
It might be best if...
Don't worry.
I can take a hint.
I'll slip out, and he won't have a clue I was even here.
And I'll see you tomorrow?
Darling, it's *already* tomorrow.
But you'll see me later today.

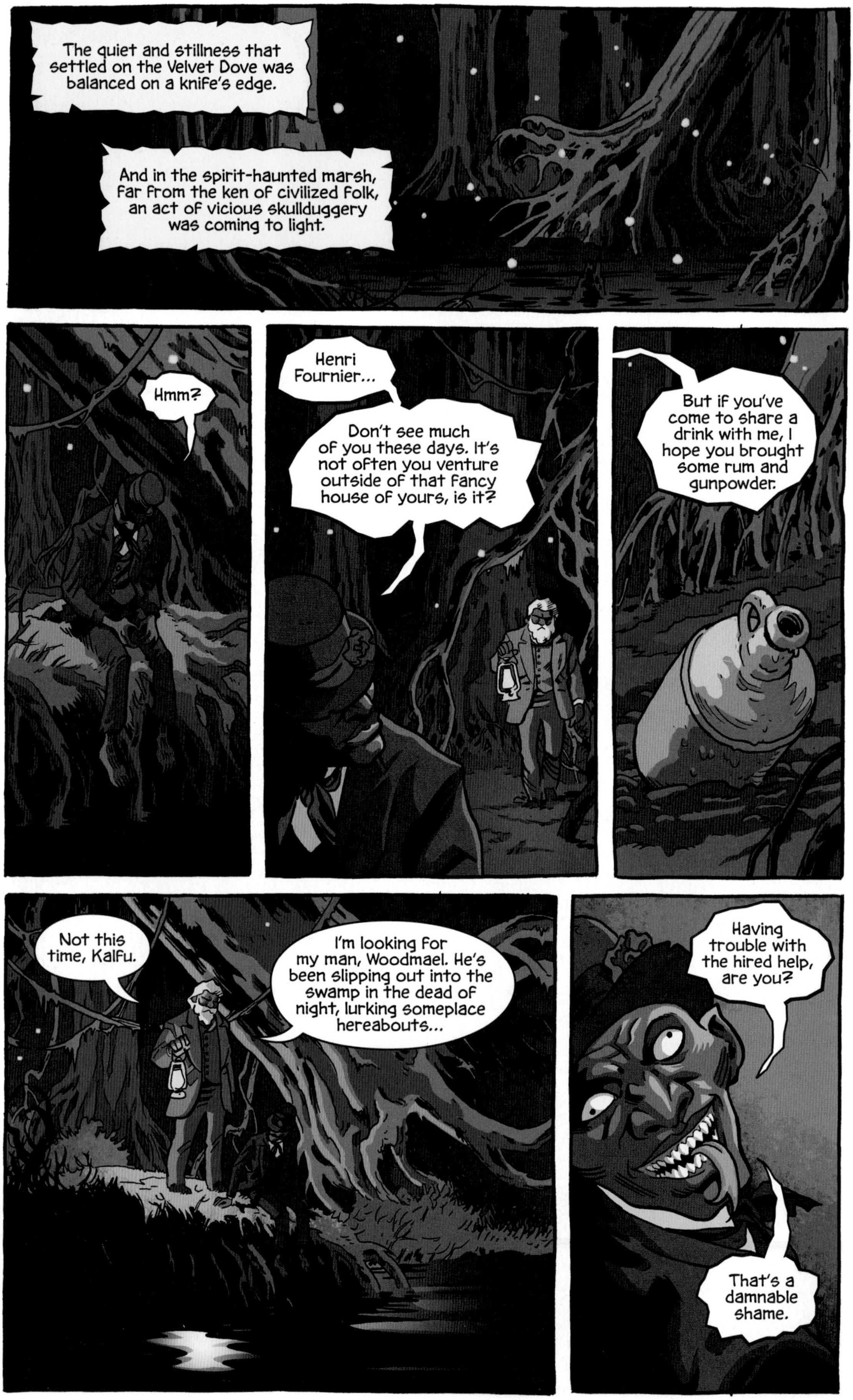
The quiet and stillness that settled on the Velvet Dove was balanced on a knife's edge.
And in the spirit-haunted marsh, far from the ken of civilized folk, an act of vicious skullduggery was coming to light.
Hmm?
Henri Fournier...
Don't see much of you these days. It's not often you venture outside of that fancy house of yours, is it?
But if you've come to share a drink with me, I hope you brought some rum and gunpowder.
Not this time, Kalfu.
I'm looking for my man, Woodmael. He's been slipping out into the swamp in the dead of night, lurking someplace hereabouts...
Having trouble with the hired help, are you?
That's a damnable shame.

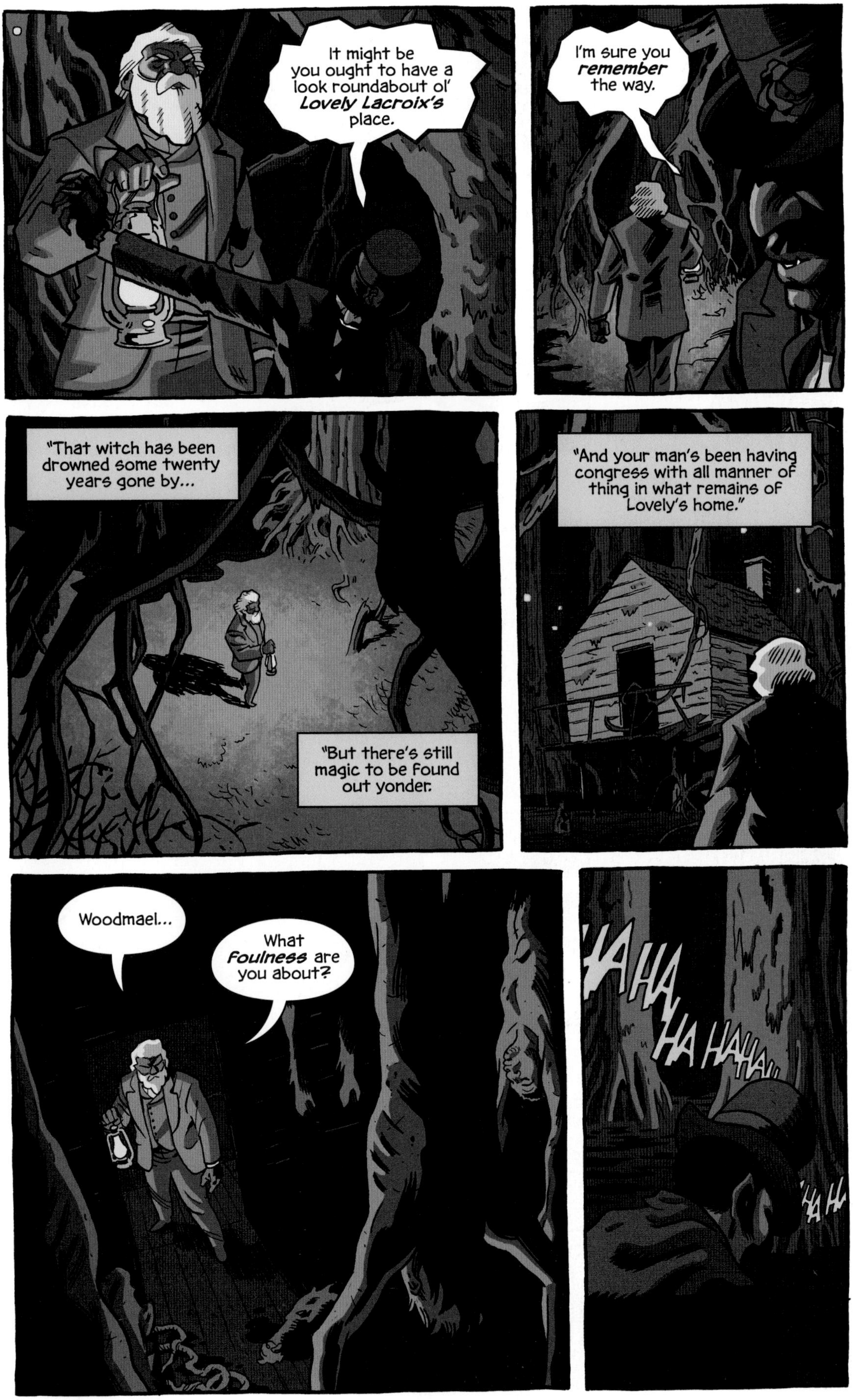
It might be you ought to have a look roundabout ol' *Lovely Lacroix's* place.
I'm sure you *remember* the way.
"That witch has been drowned some twenty years gone by...
"But there's still magic to be found out yonder.
"And your man's been having congress with all manner of thing in what remains of Lovely's home."
Woodmael...
What *foulness* are you about?
HA HA HA HA HAHA
HA HA

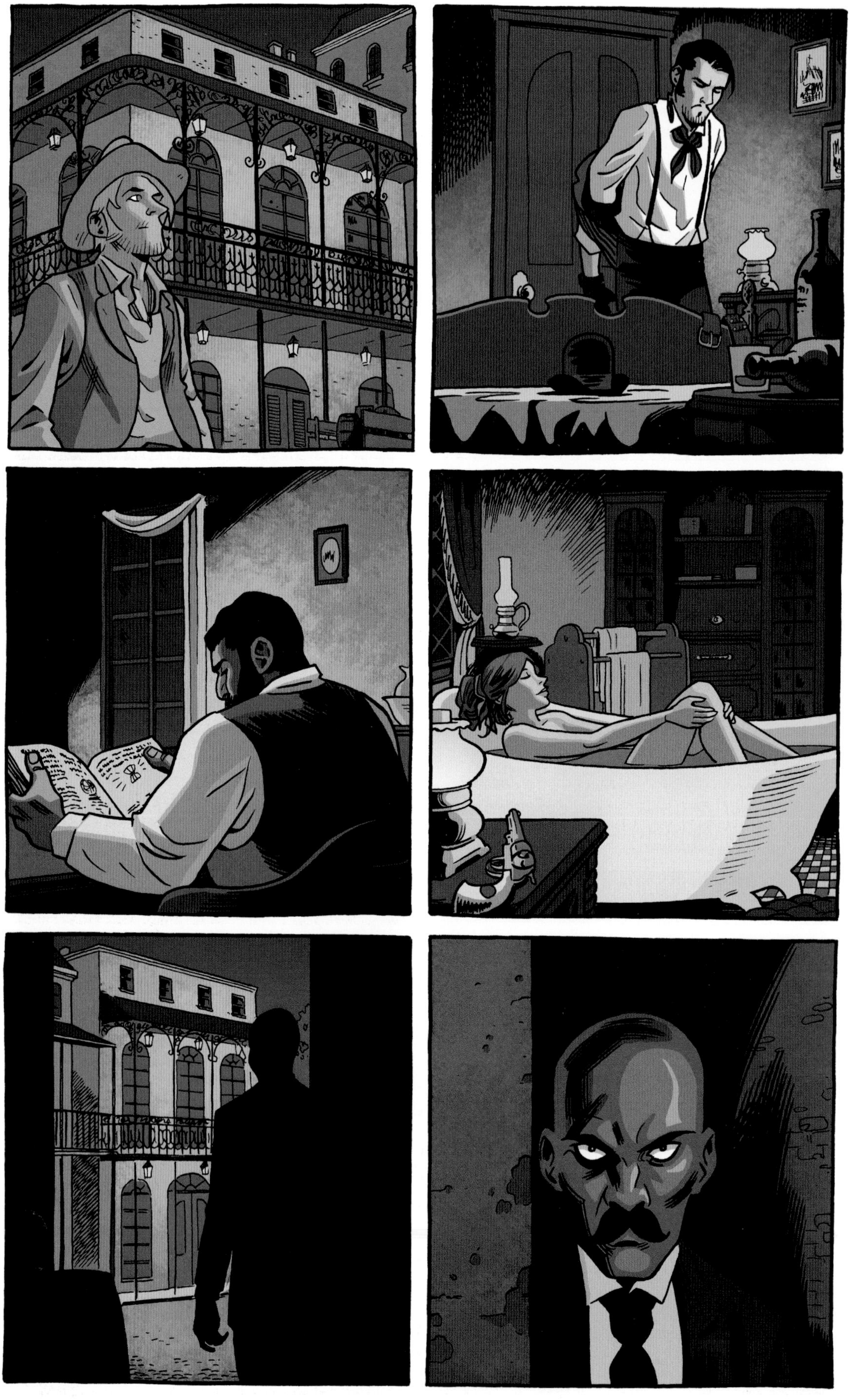

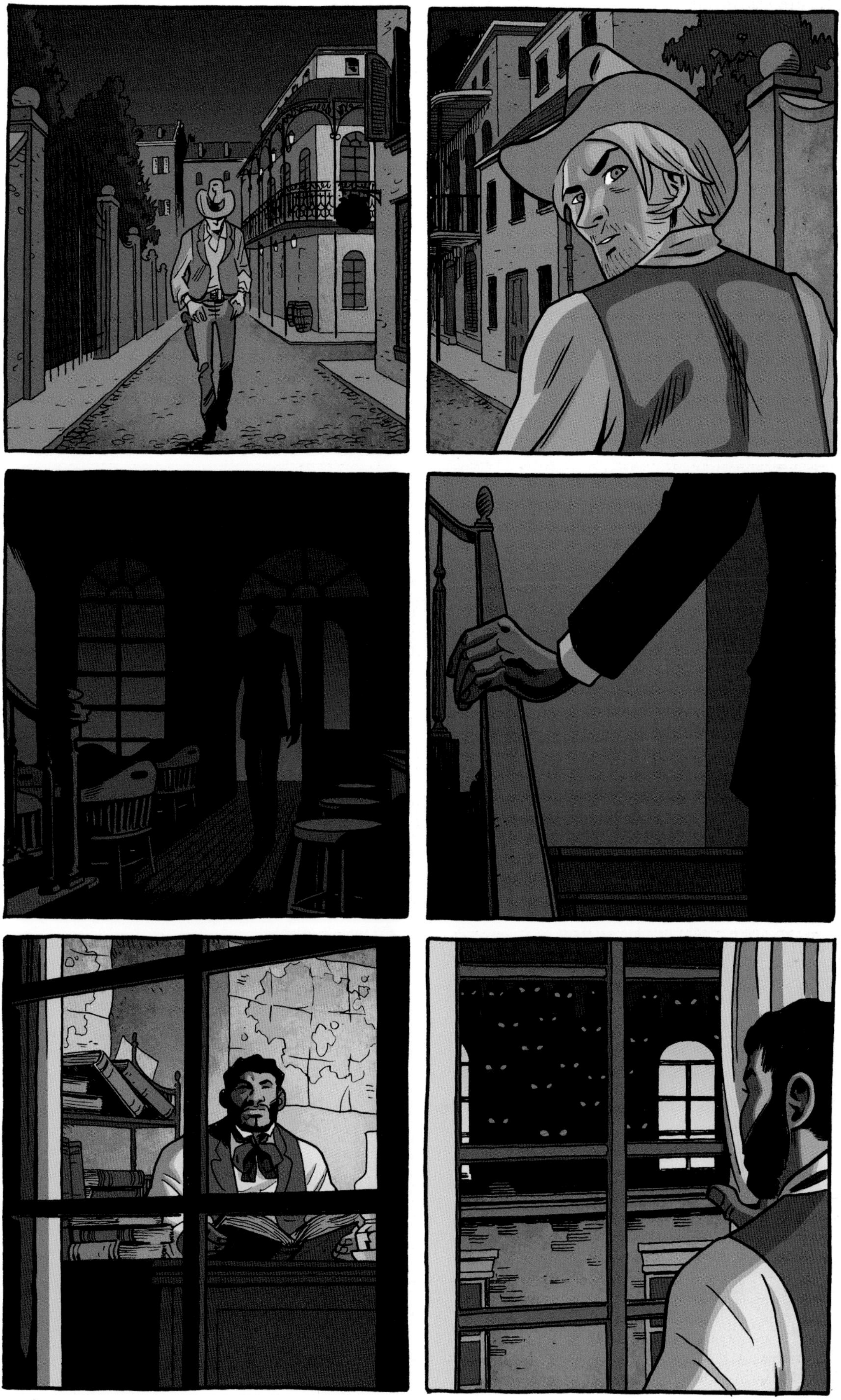

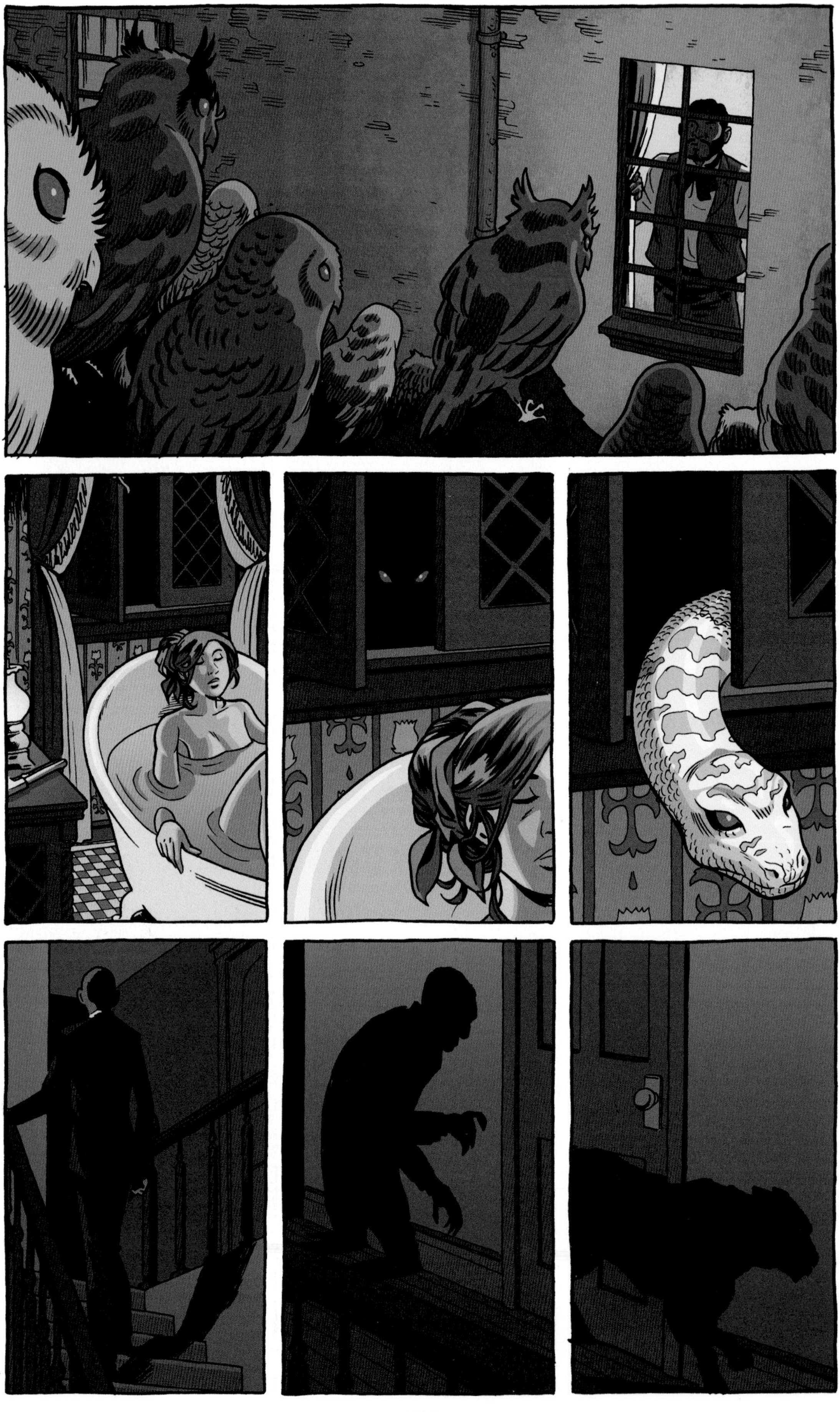

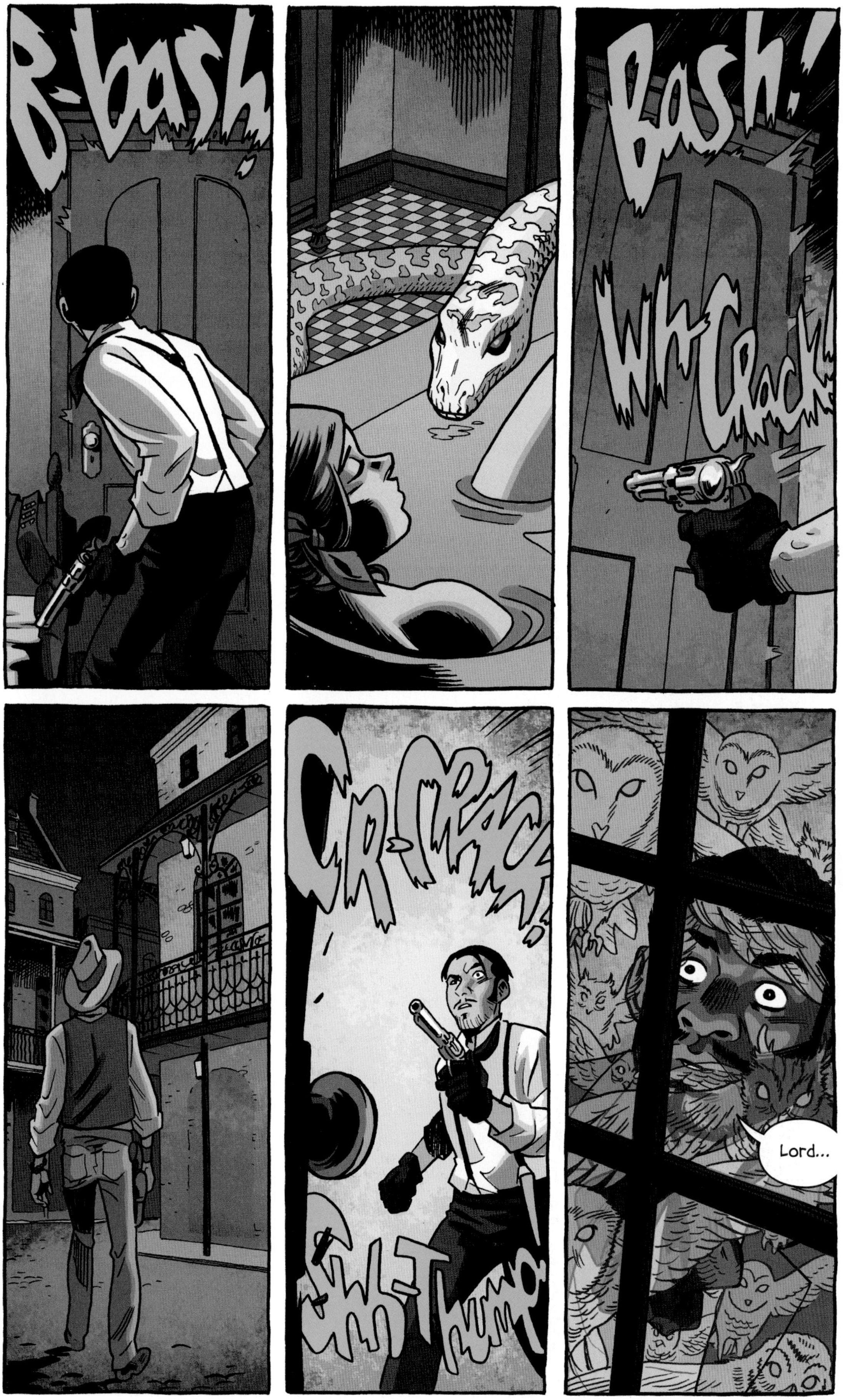
B-bash
Bash!
Wh Crack!
Cr-Crack!
Shh-Thump
Lord...

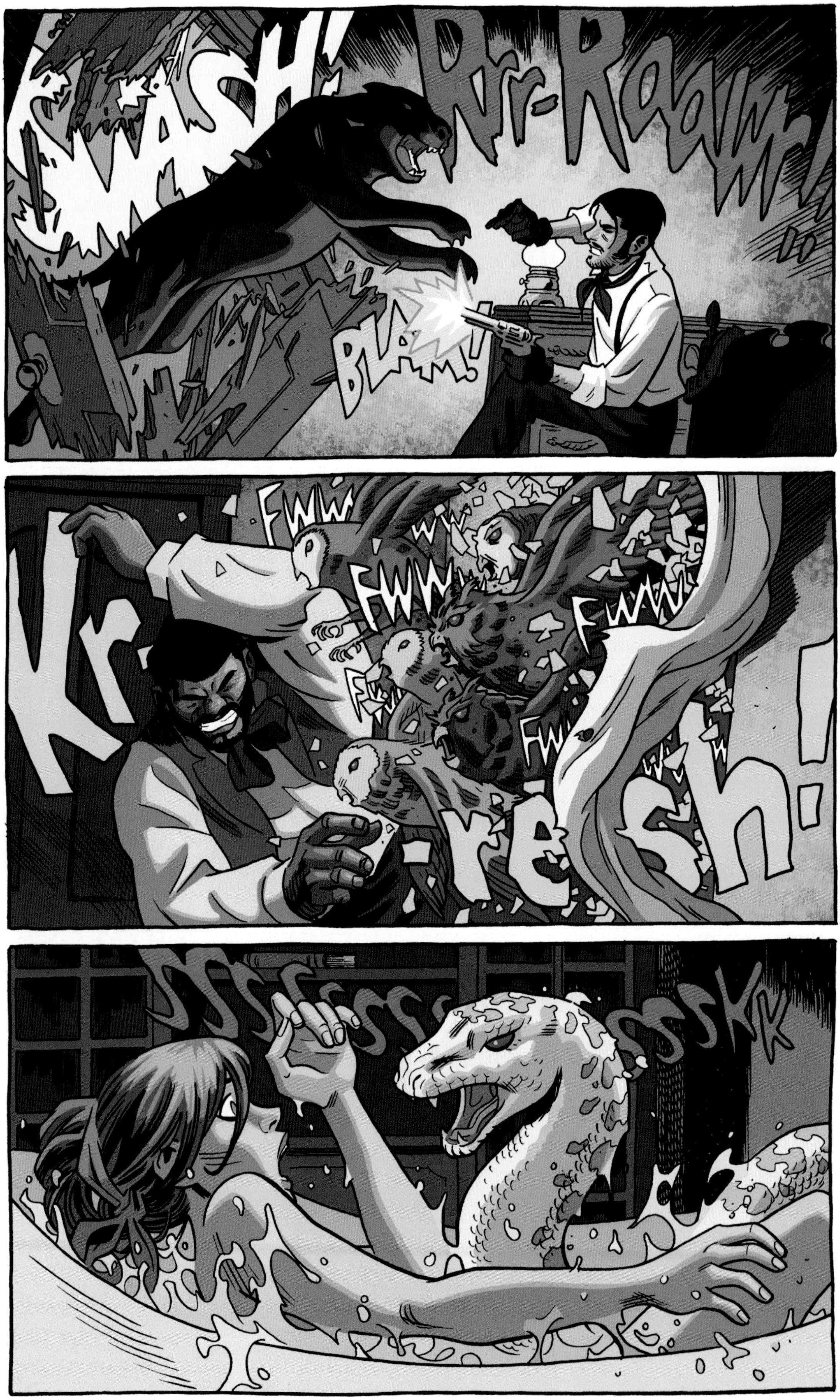
BLAM!
FWW
FWW
FWW
Kresh!

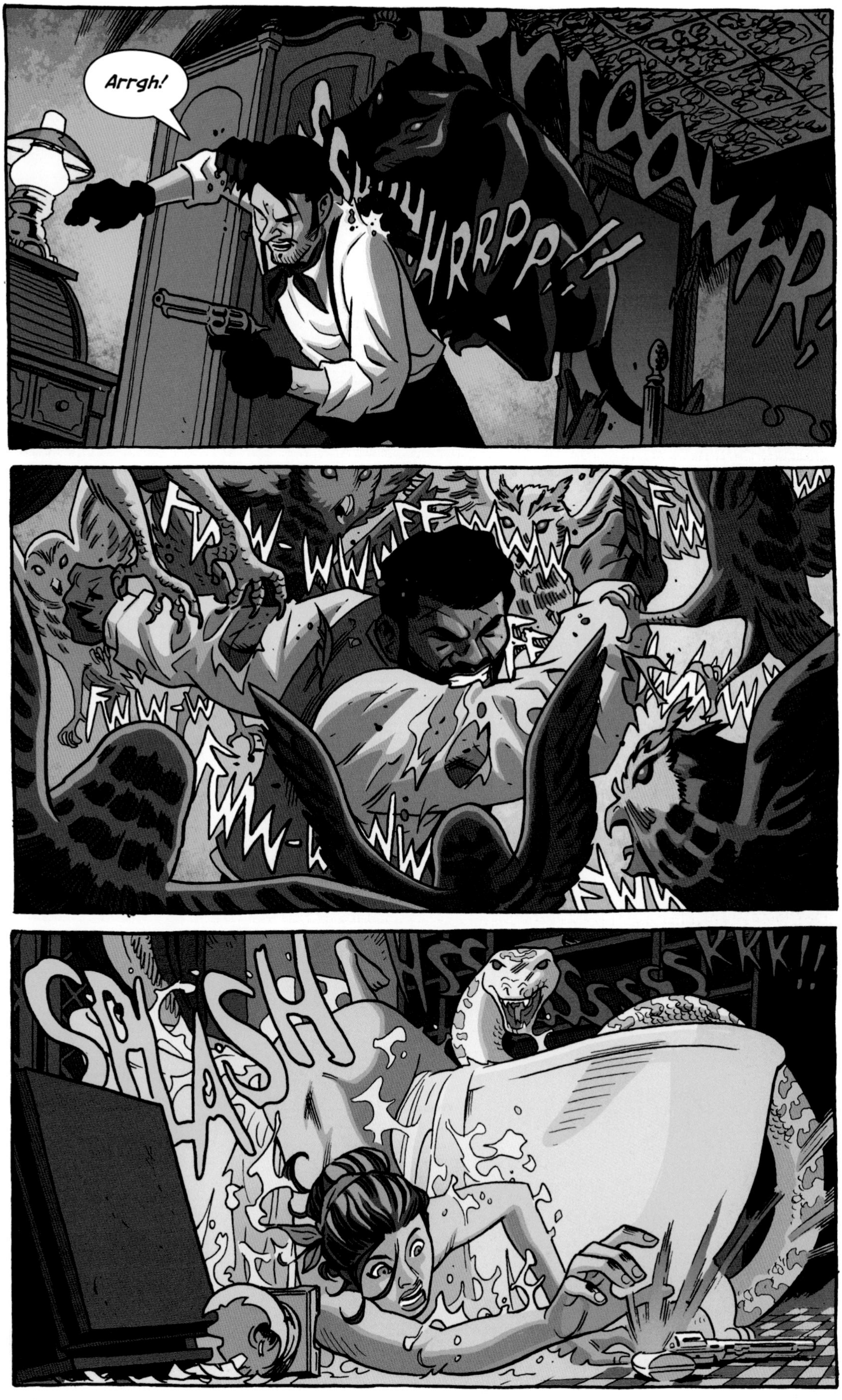
Arrgh!

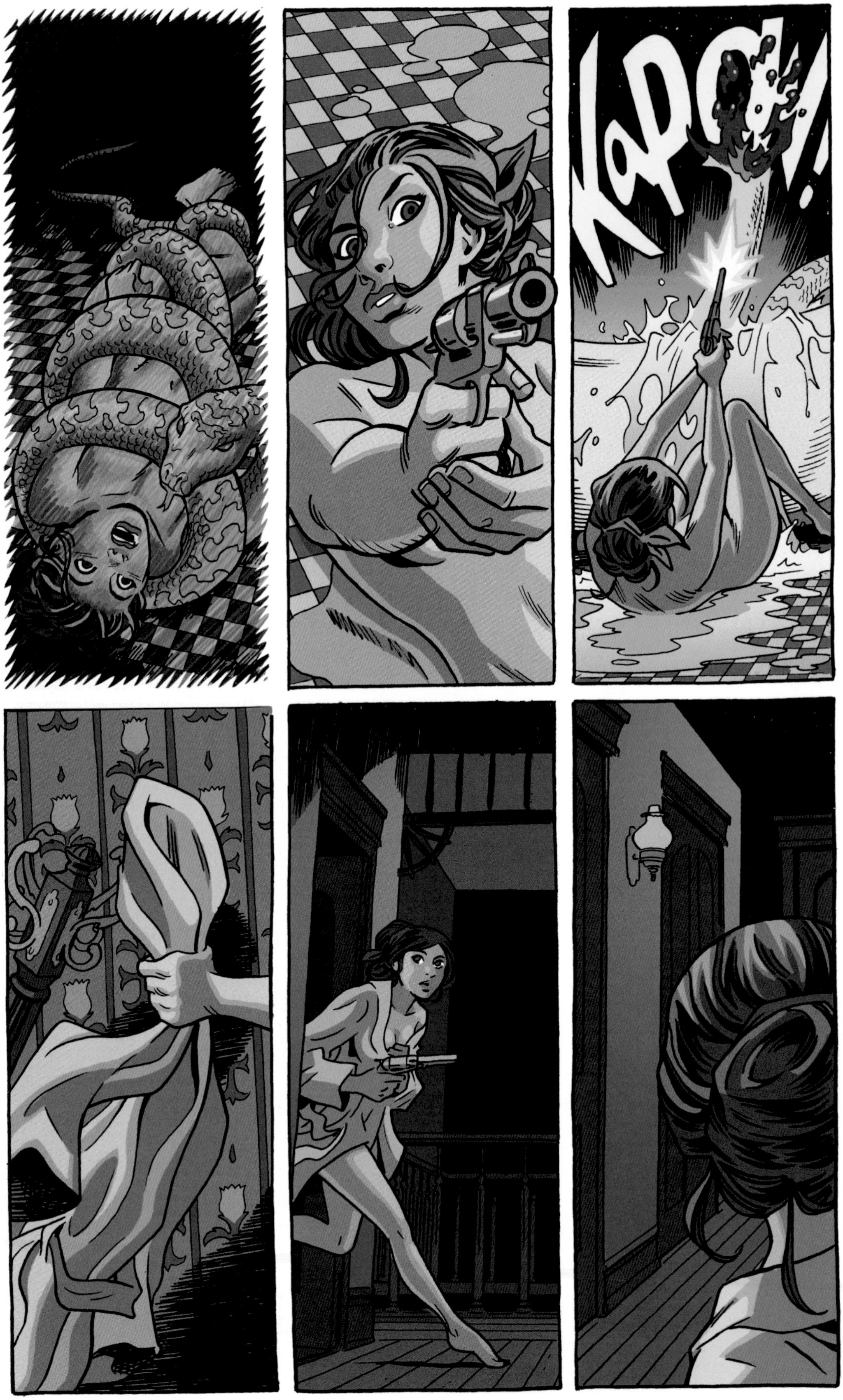
KAPOW!

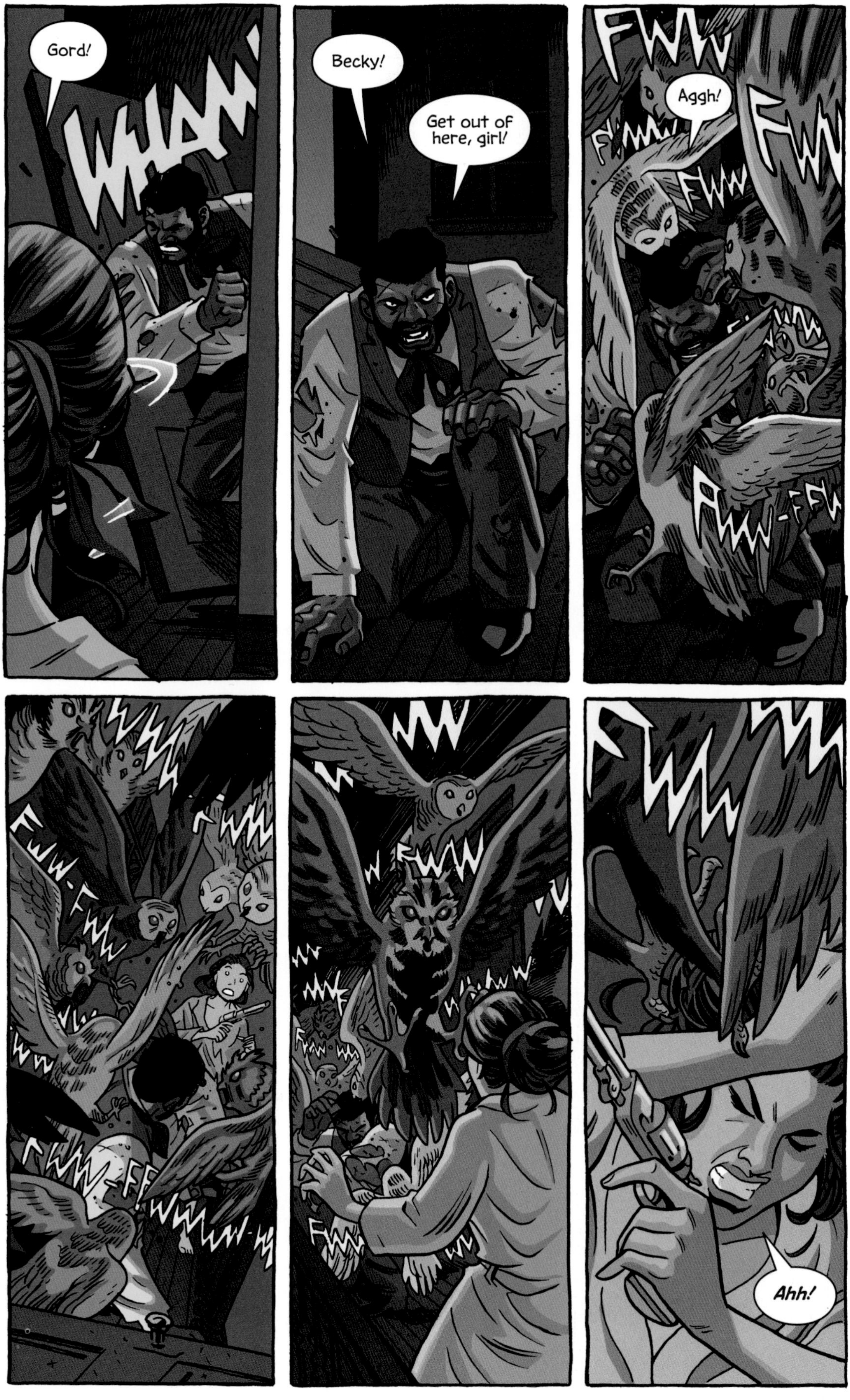
Gord!
WHAM
Becky!
Get out of here, girl!
FWW
Aggh!
FWW
FWW
FWW
AWW-FFW
FWW-FWW
FWW-FF
FWW
FWW
FWW
Ahh!

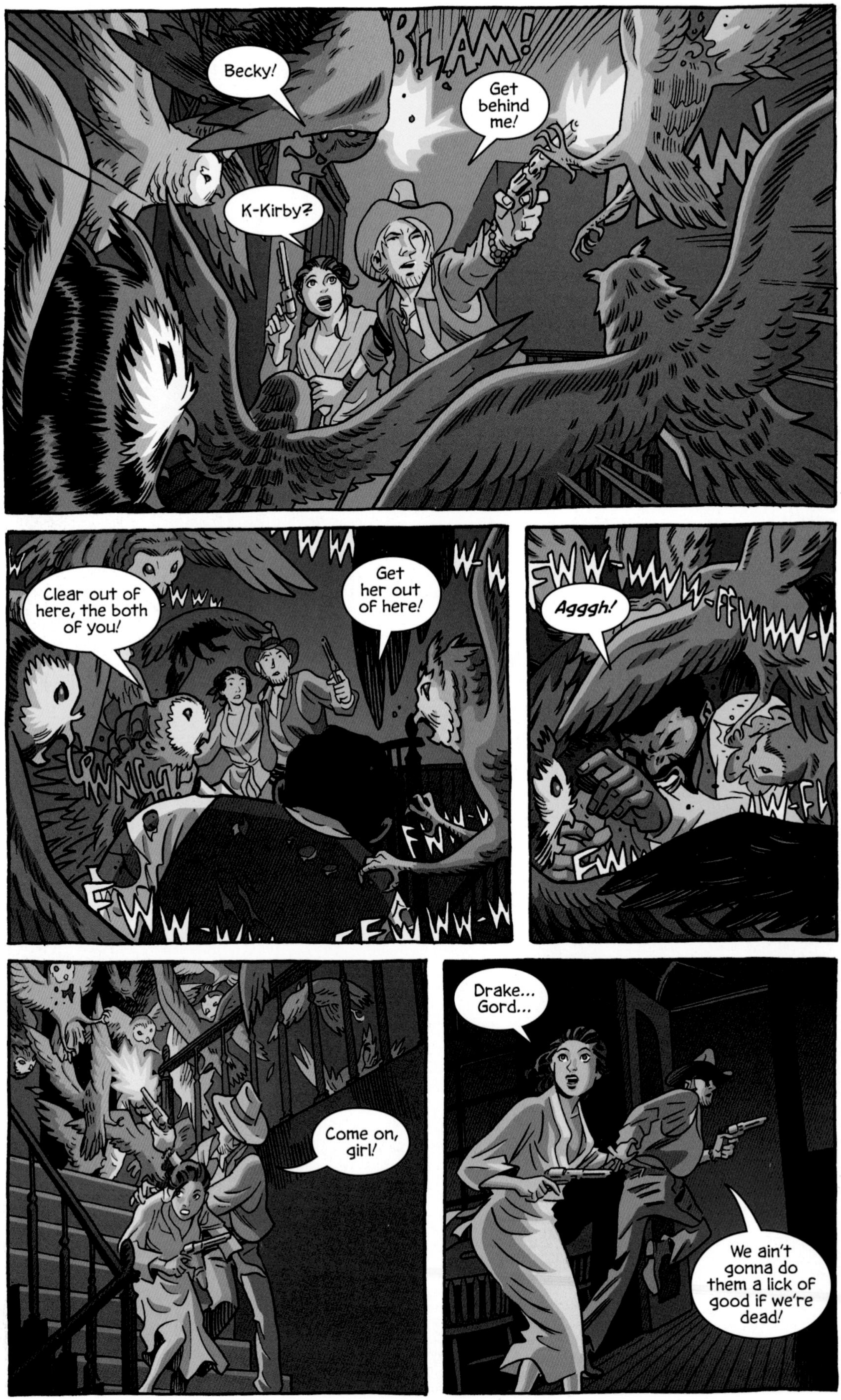
BLAM!
Becky!
Get behind me!
K-Kirby?
Clear out of here, the both of you!
Get her out of here!
Agggh!
Come on, girl!
Drake... Gord...
We ain't gonna do them a lick of good if we're dead!

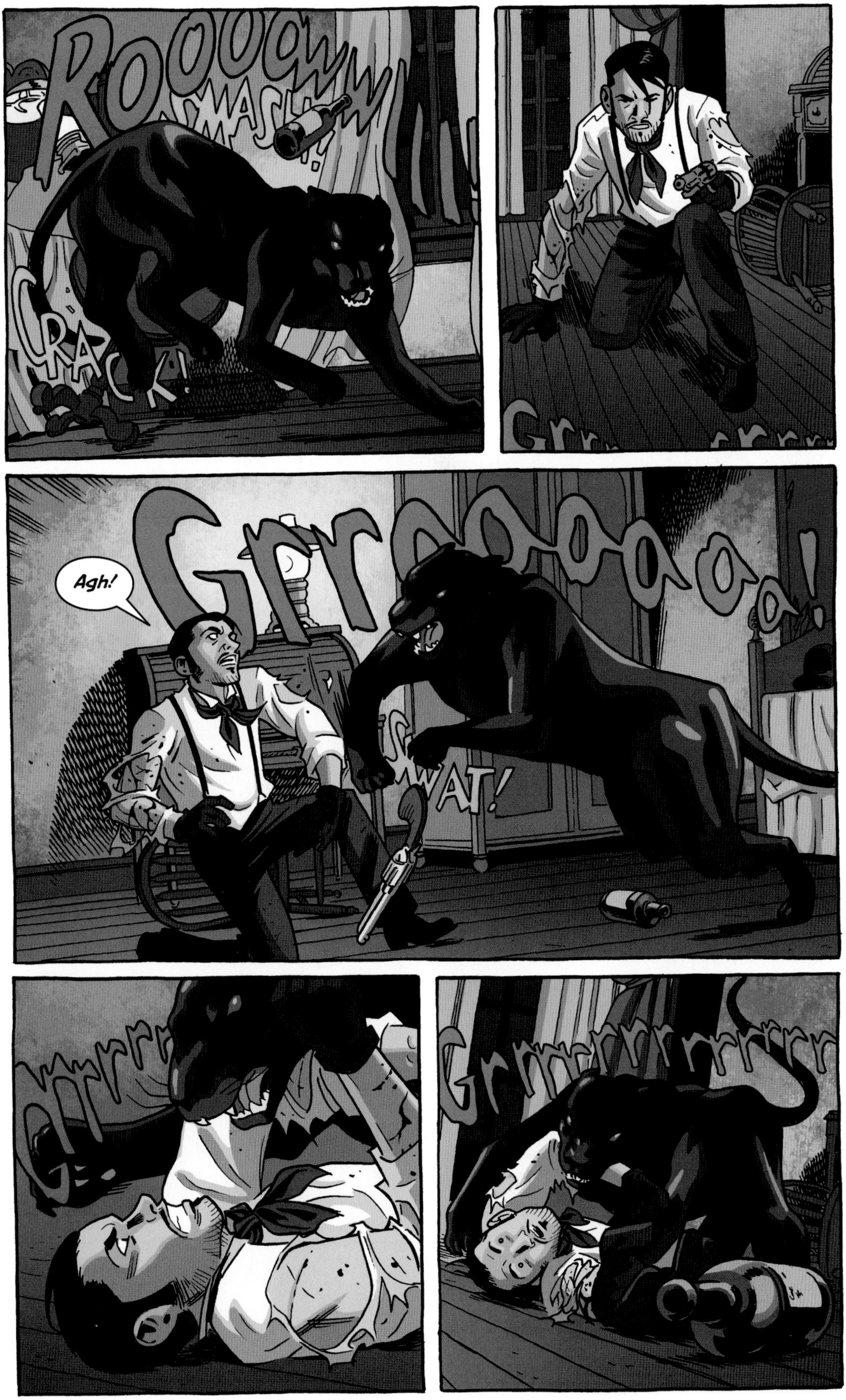
SMASH!!
CRACK!
Agh!
SWAT!
Grrrrrrrrrrrr

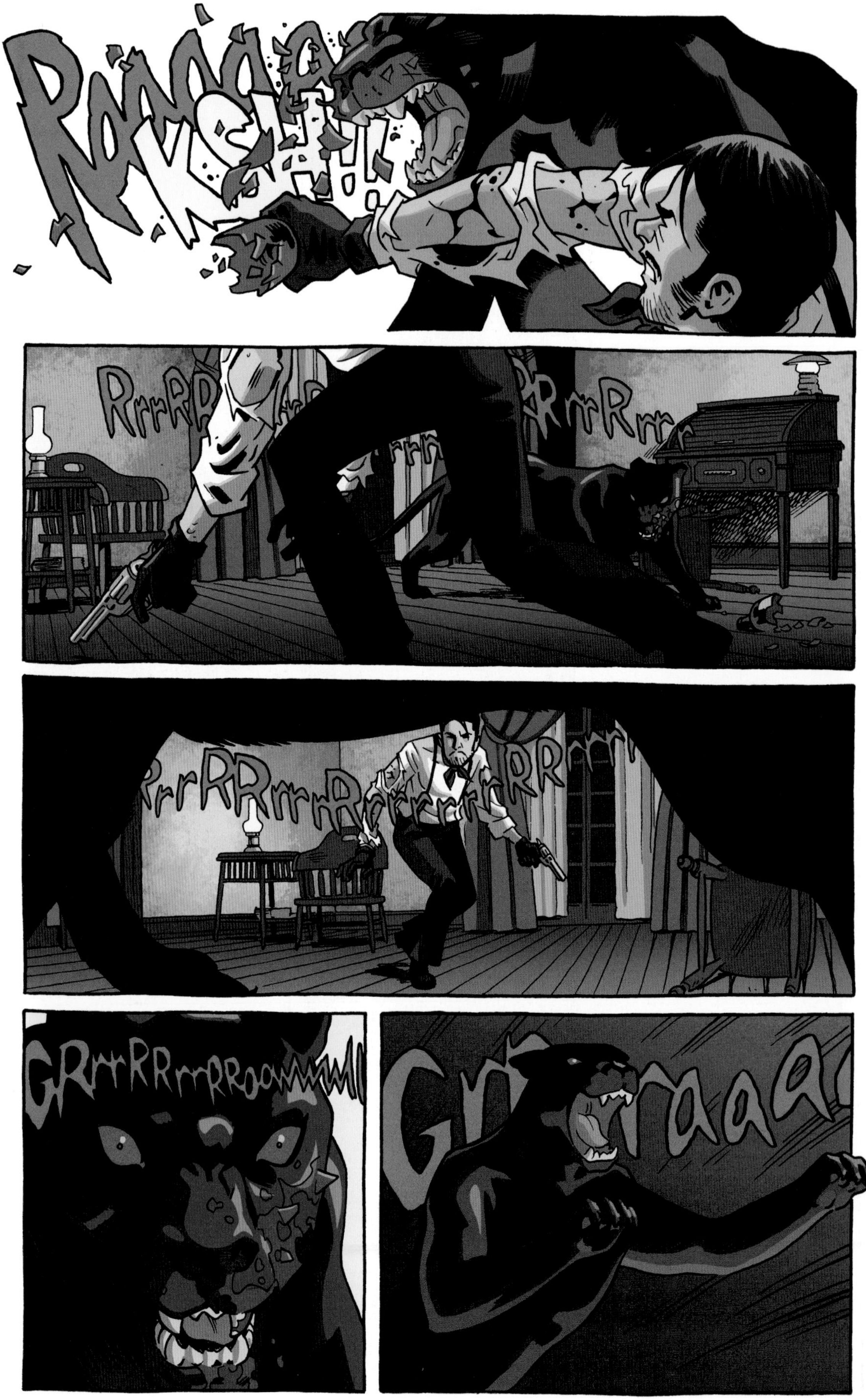
GRrrRRrrRROOWWWL

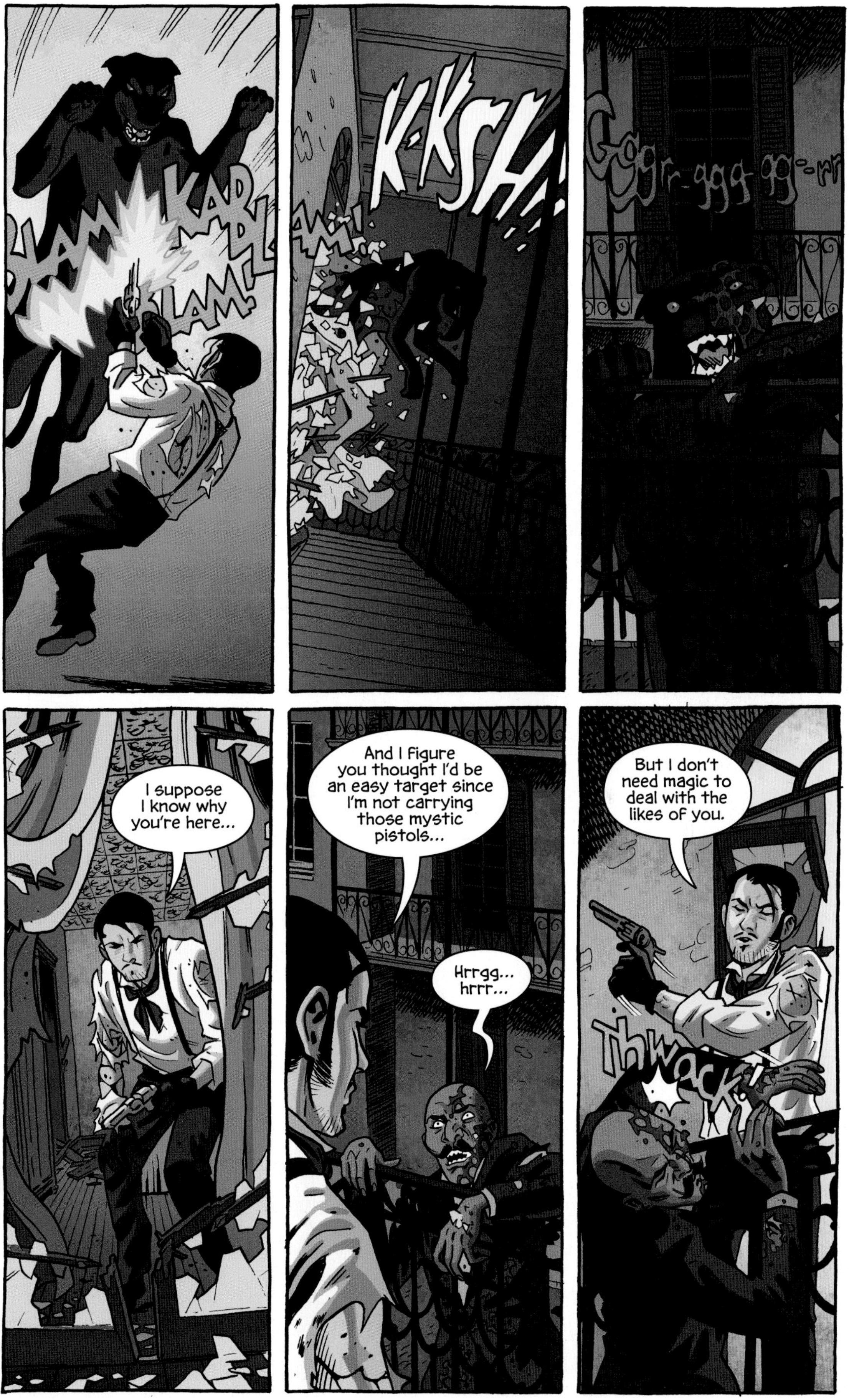
BLAM KABLAM BLAM!
BLAM!
K-KSH!
Gggrr-ggg-gg-rrr
I suppose I know why you're here...
And I figure you thought I'd be an easy target since I'm not carrying those mystic pistols...
Hrrgg... hrrr...
But I don't need magic to deal with the likes of you.
THWACK!

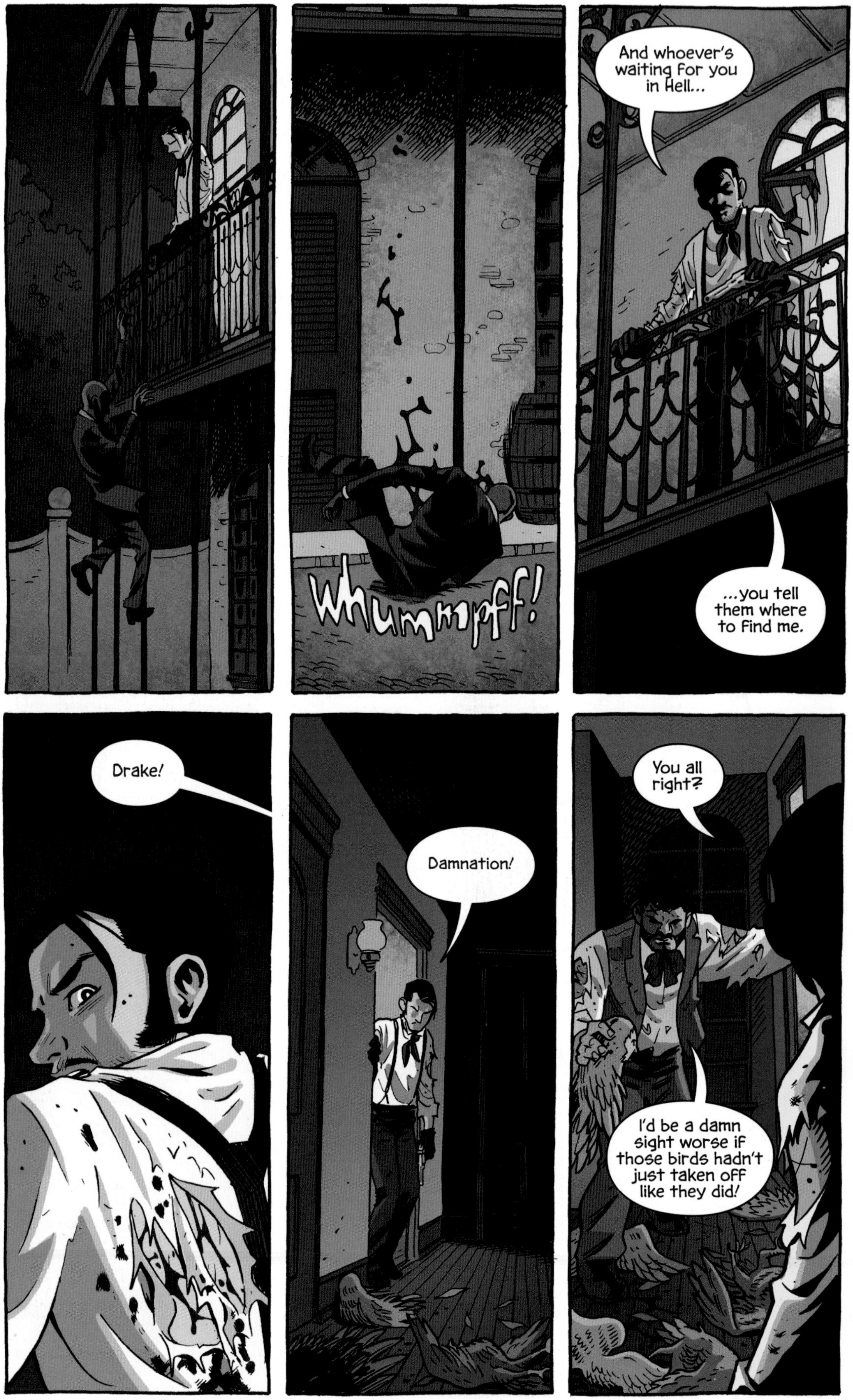
Whummpff!
And whoever's waiting for you in Hell...
...you tell them where to find me.
Drake!
Damnation!
You all right?
I'd be a damn sight worse if those birds hadn't just taken off like they did!

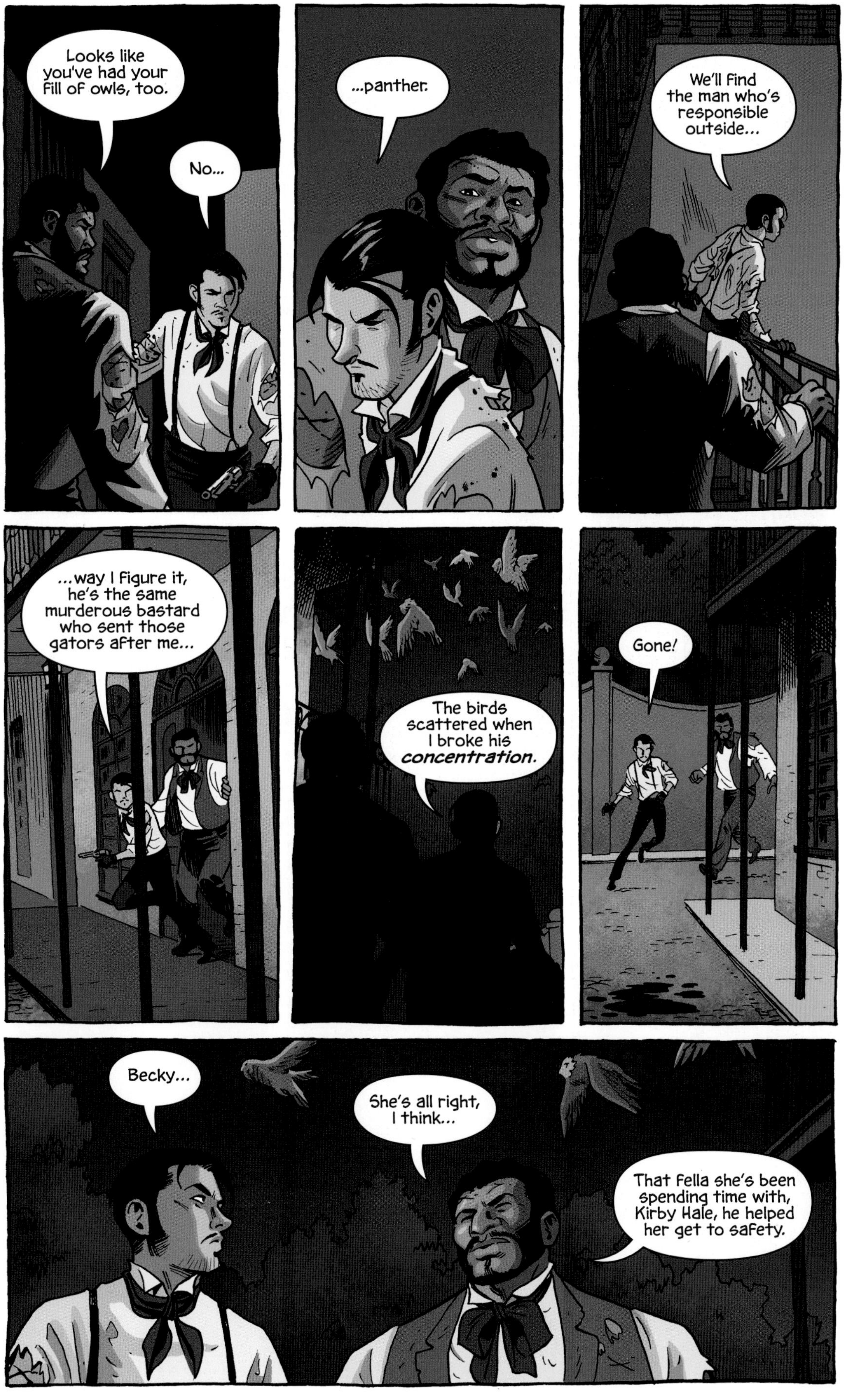
Looks like you've had your fill of owls, too.
No...
...panther.
We'll find the man who's responsible outside...
...way I figure it, he's the same murderous bastard who sent those gators after me...
The birds scattered when I broke his *concentration*.
Gone!
Becky...
She's all right, I think...
That fella she's been spending time with, Kirby Hale, he helped her get to safety.

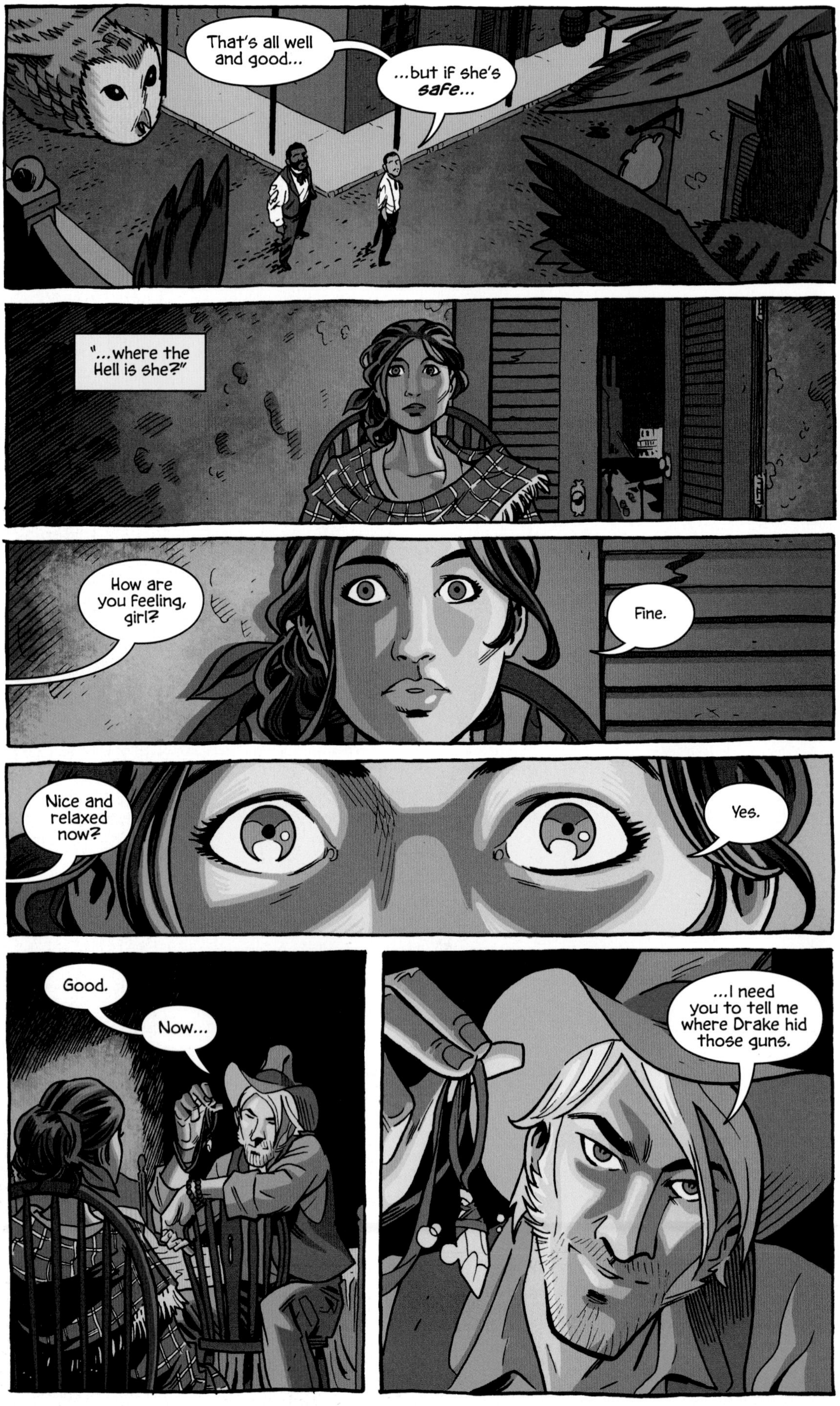

That's all well and good...
...but if she's *safe*...
"...where the Hell is she?"
How are you feeling, girl?
Fine.
Nice and relaxed now?
Yes.
Good.
Now...
...I need you to tell me where Drake hid those guns.

CHAPTER FOUR

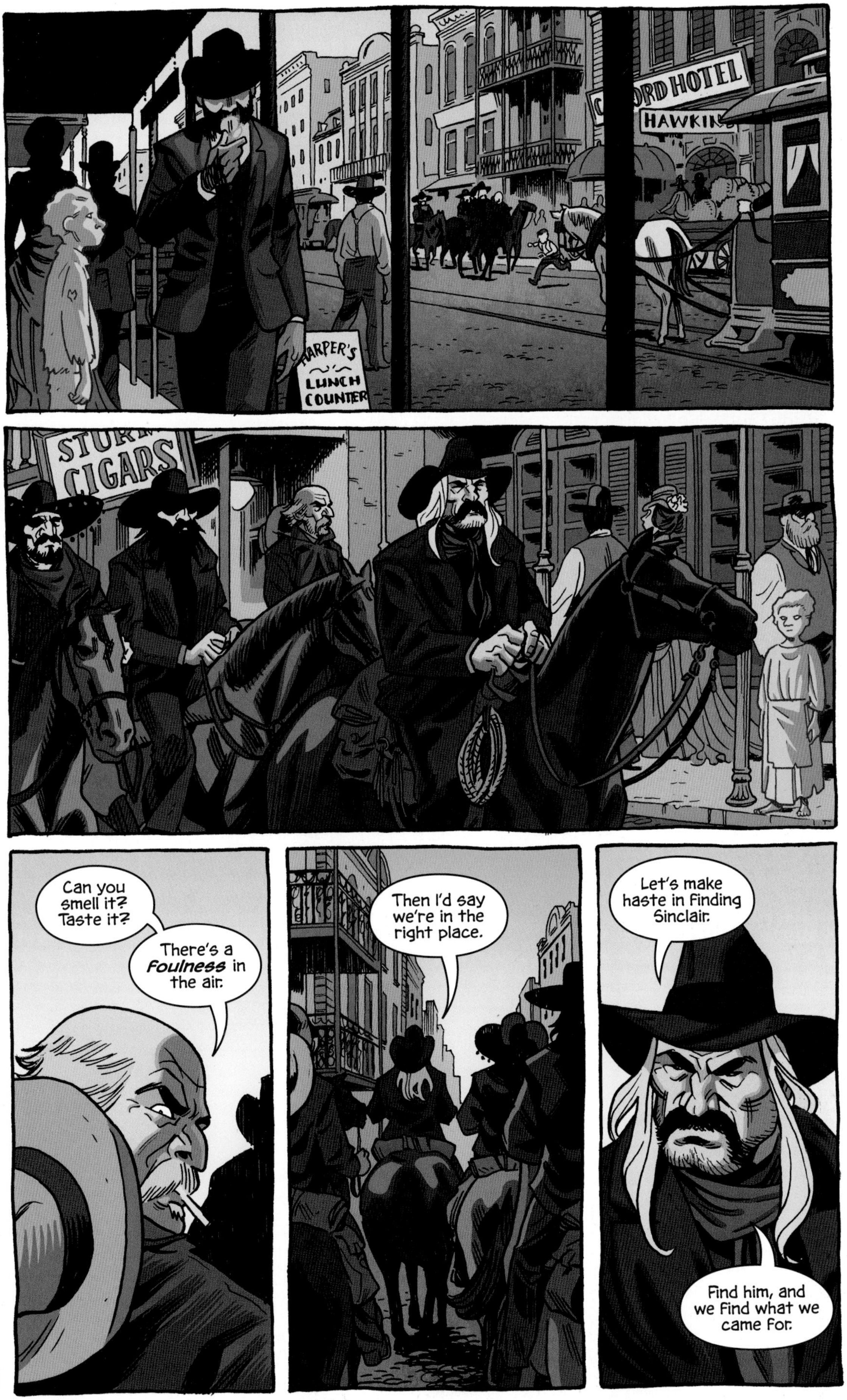

ORD HOTEL
HAWKIN
HARPER'S
LUNCH
COUNTER
CIGARS
Can you smell it? Taste it?
There's a *foulness* in the air.
Then I'd say we're in the right place.
Let's make haste in finding Sinclair.
Find him, and we find what we came for.

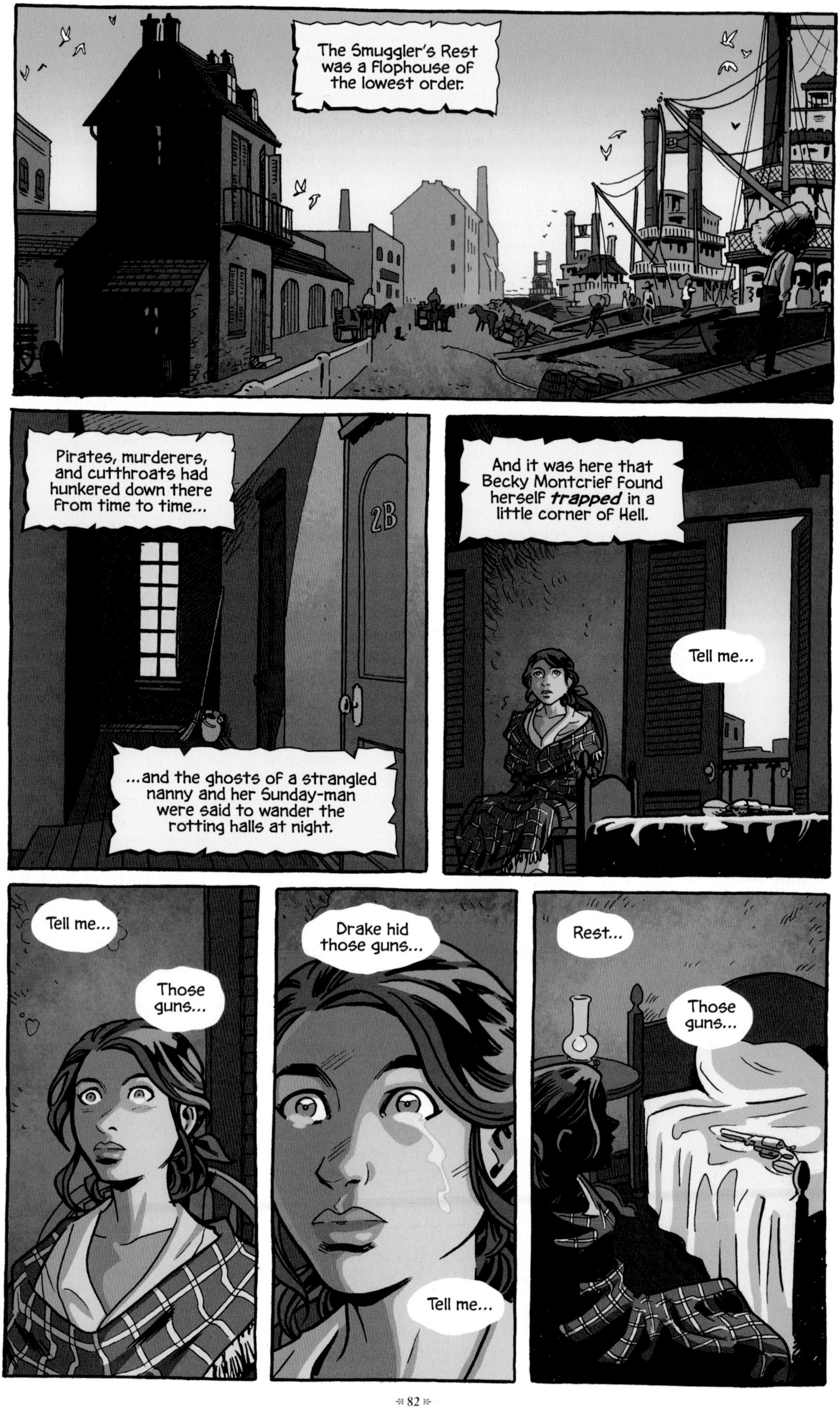
The Smuggler's Rest was a flophouse of the lowest order.
Pirates, murderers, and cutthroats had hunkered down there from time to time...
2B
...and the ghosts of a strangled nanny and her Sunday-man were said to wander the rotting halls at night.
And it was here that Becky Montcrief found herself *trapped* in a little corner of Hell.
Tell me...
Tell me...
Those guns...
Drake hid those guns...
Tell me...
Rest...
Those guns...

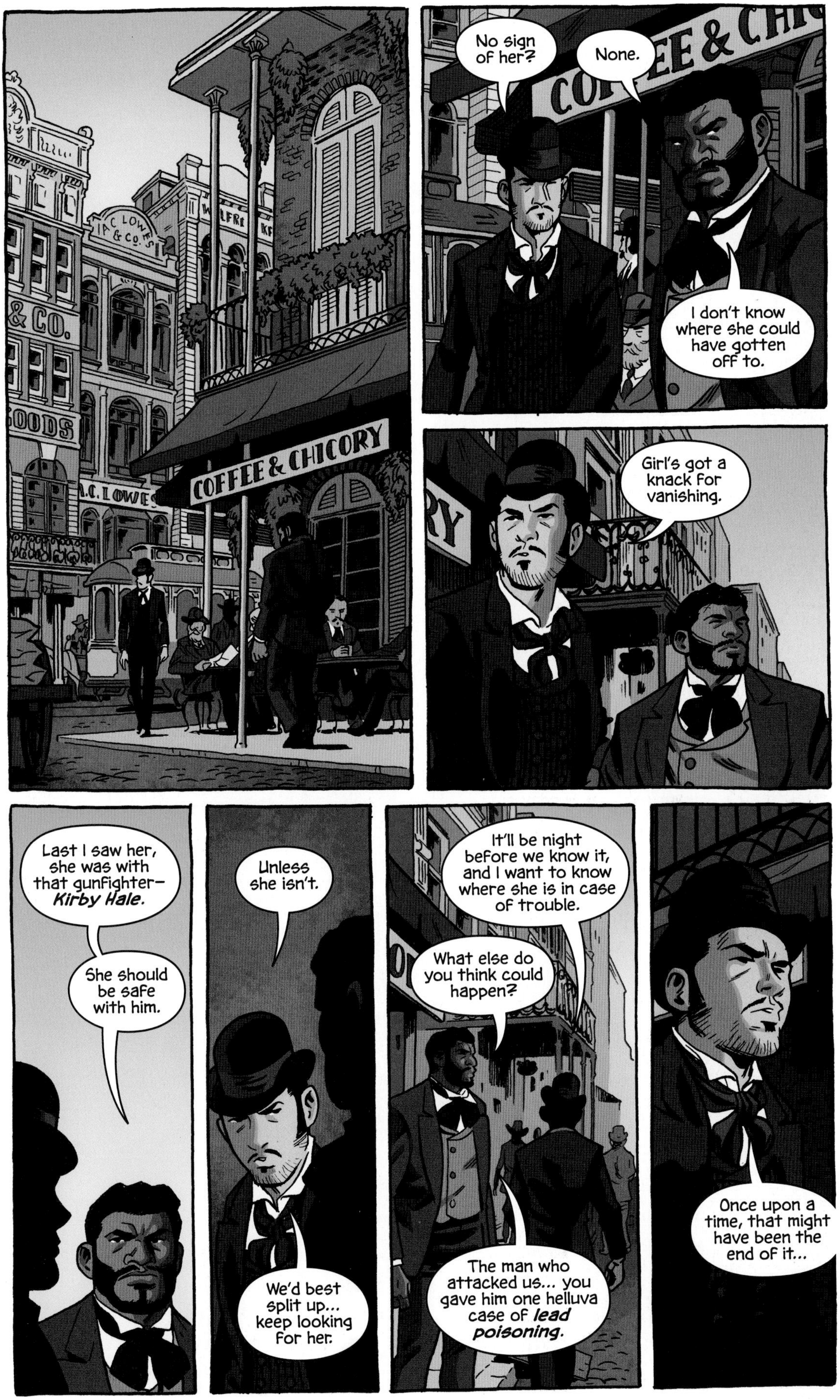
COFFEE & CHICORY
A.C. LOWES
No sign of her?
None.
I don't know where she could have gotten off to.
Girl's got a knack for vanishing.
Last I saw her, she was with that gunfighter— *Kirby Hale.*
She should be safe with him.
Unless she isn't.
We'd best split up... keep looking for her.
It'll be night before we know it, and I want to know where she is in case of trouble.
What else do you think could happen?
The man who attacked us... you gave him one helluva case of *lead poisoning.*
Once upon a time, that might have been the end of it...

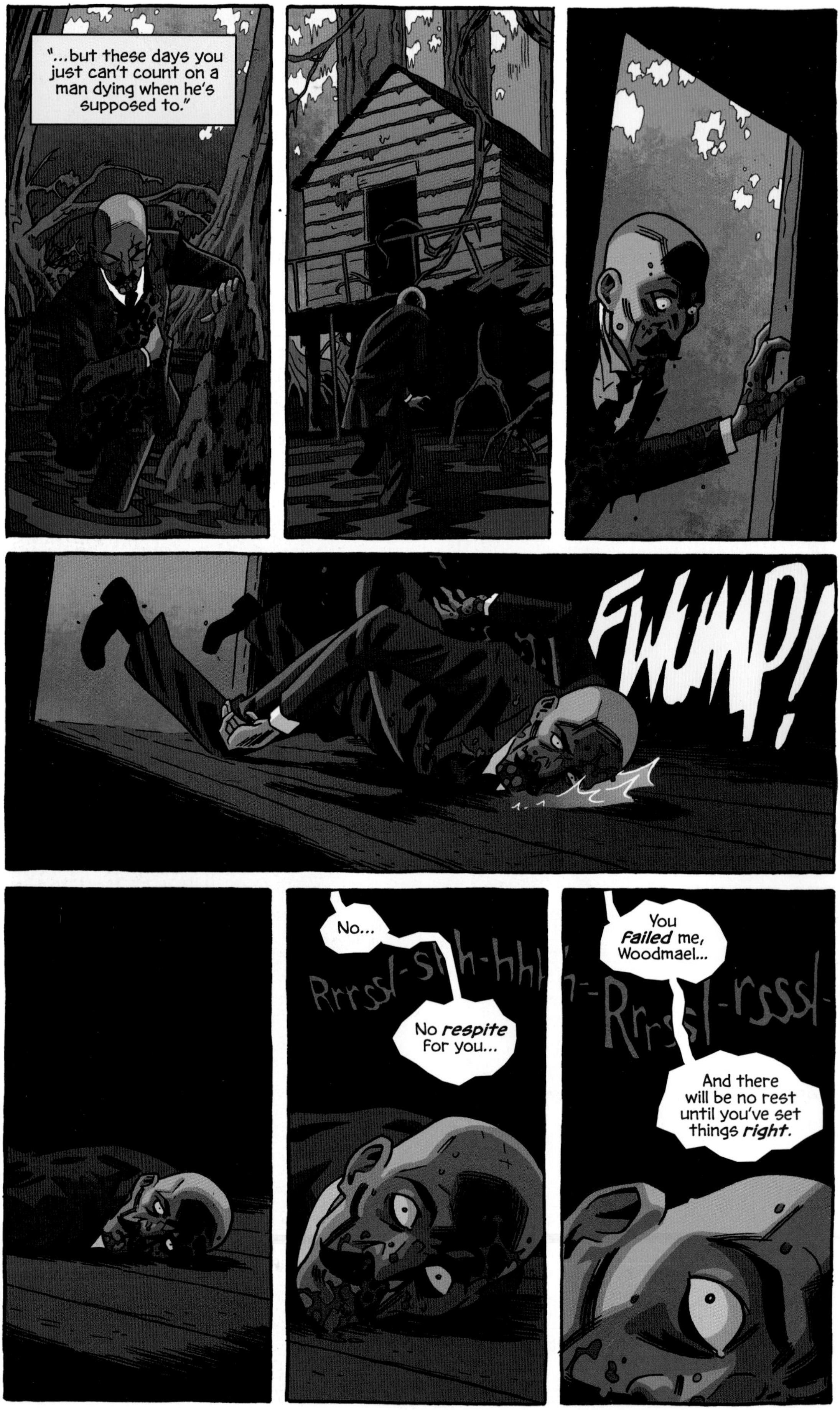

"...but these days you just can't count on a man dying when he's supposed to."
FWUMP!
No...
Rrrssl-sshh-hhhh-
No *respite* for you...
You *failed* me, Woodmael...
Rrrssl-rsssl-
And there will be no rest until you've set things *right*.

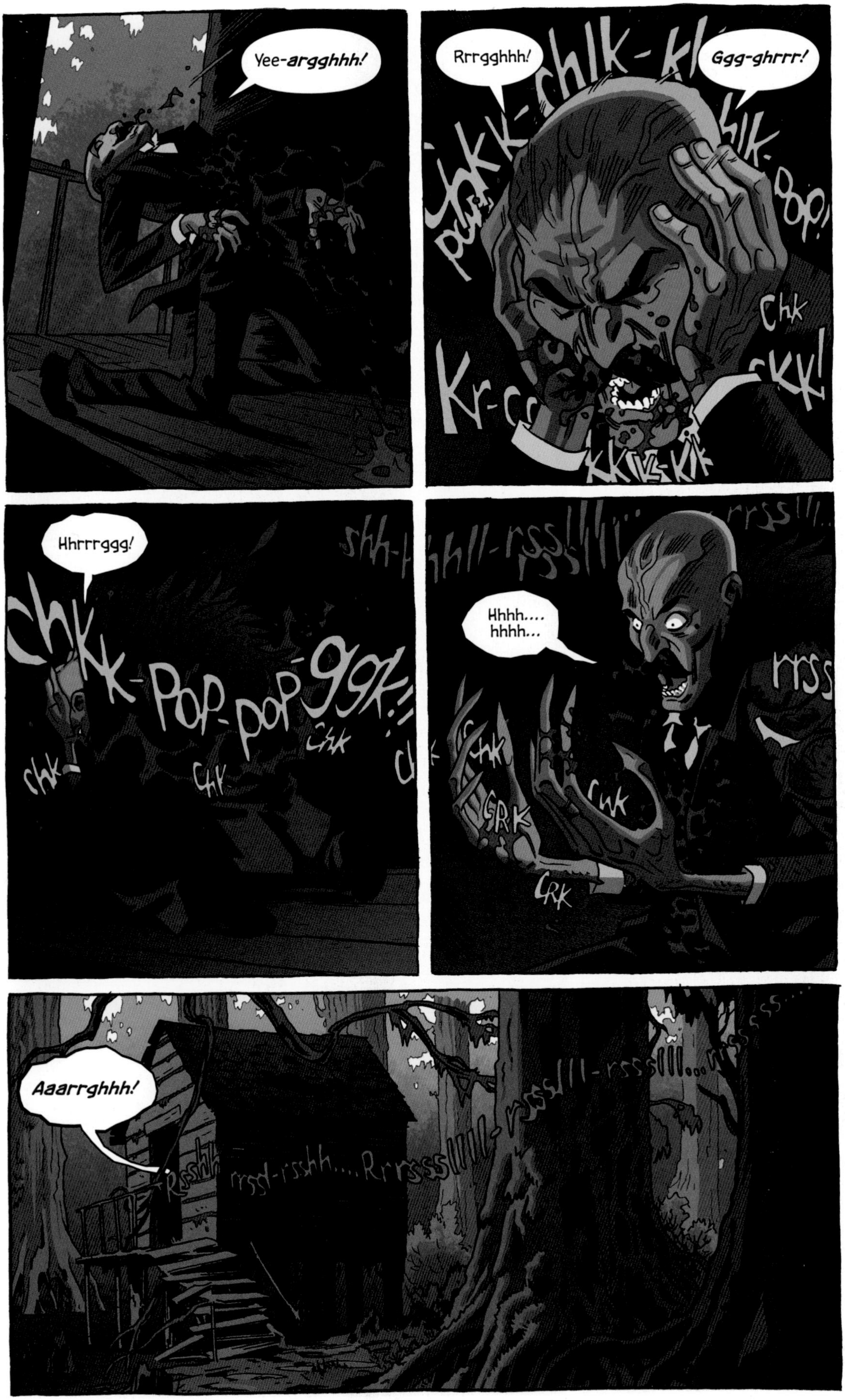
Yee-argghhh!
Rrrgghhh!
Ggg-ghrrr!
Hhrrrggg!
Hhhh....
hhhh...
Aaarrghhh!

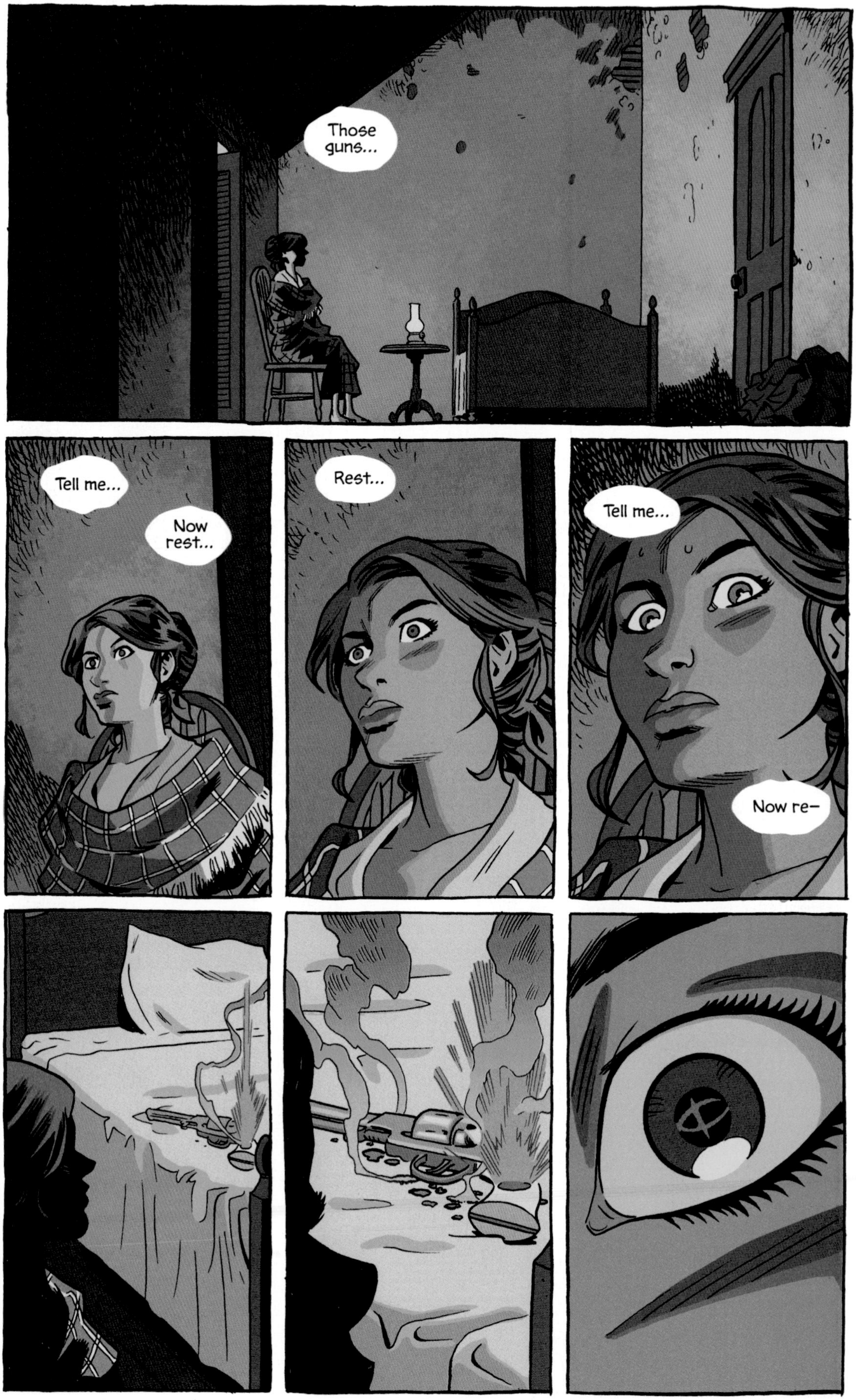
Those guns...
Tell me...
Now rest...
Rest...
Tell me...
Now re-

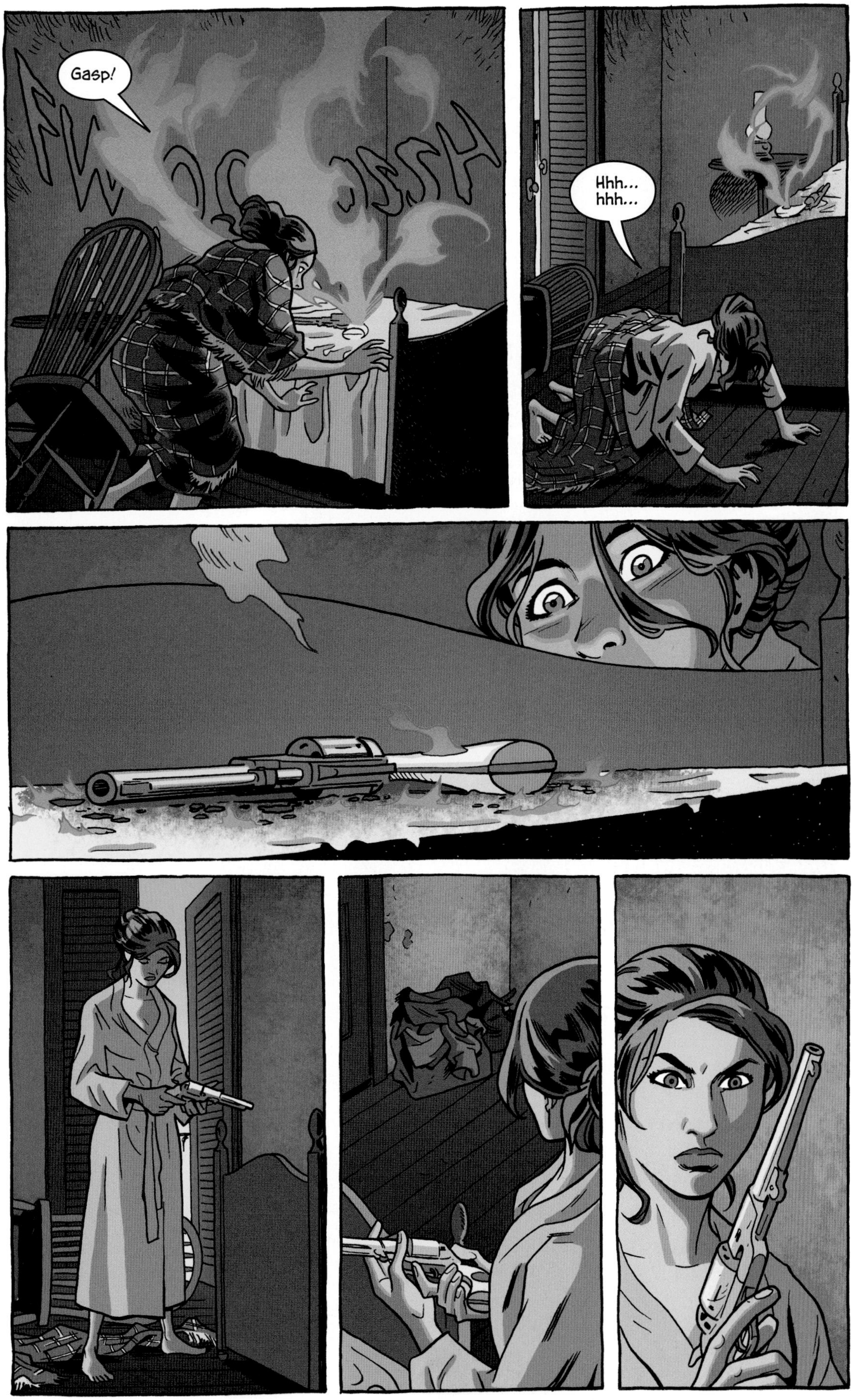
Gasp!
Hhh... hhh...

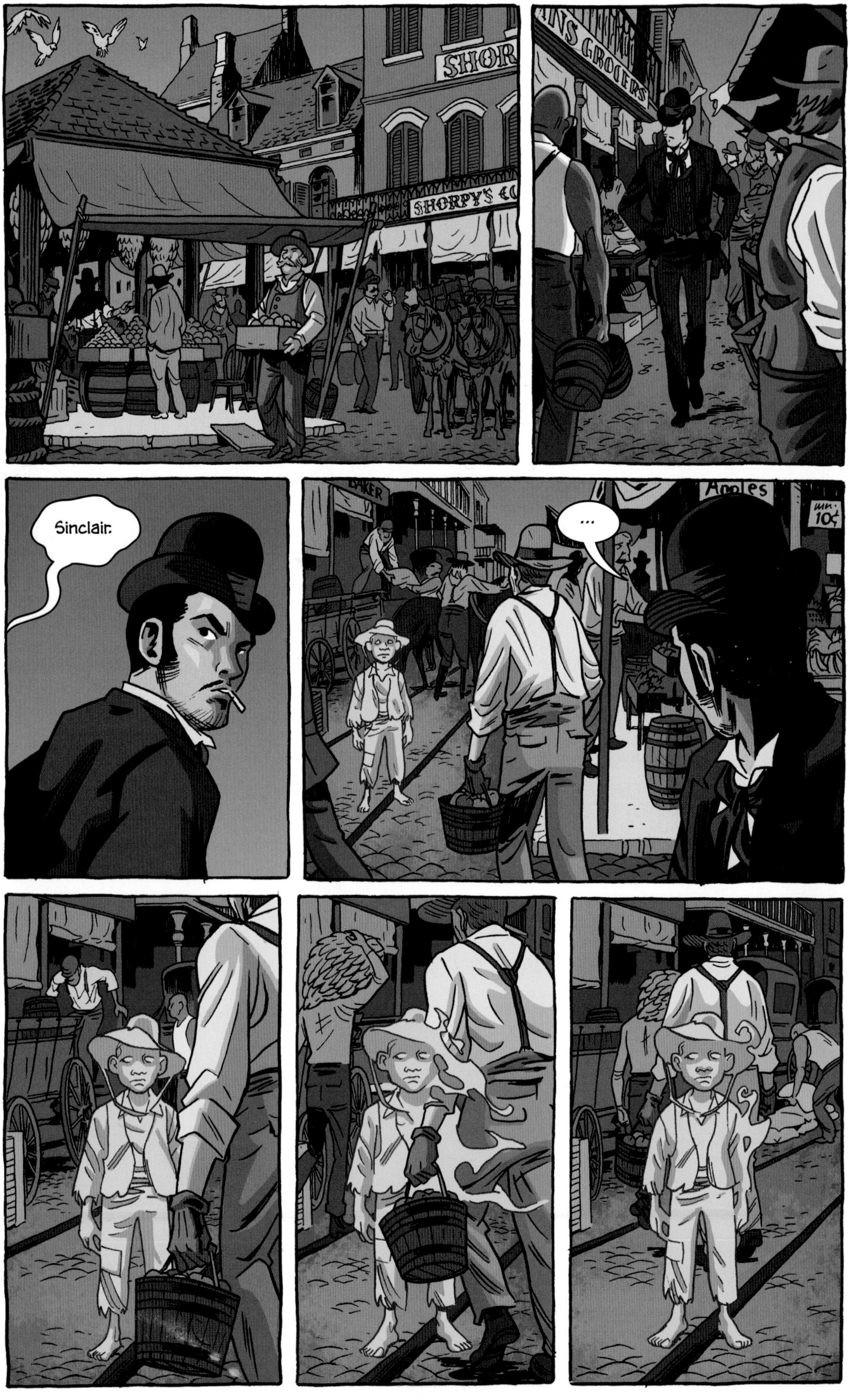
SHOR
SHORPY'S
GROCERS
Sinclair.
BAKER
...
Apples
10¢

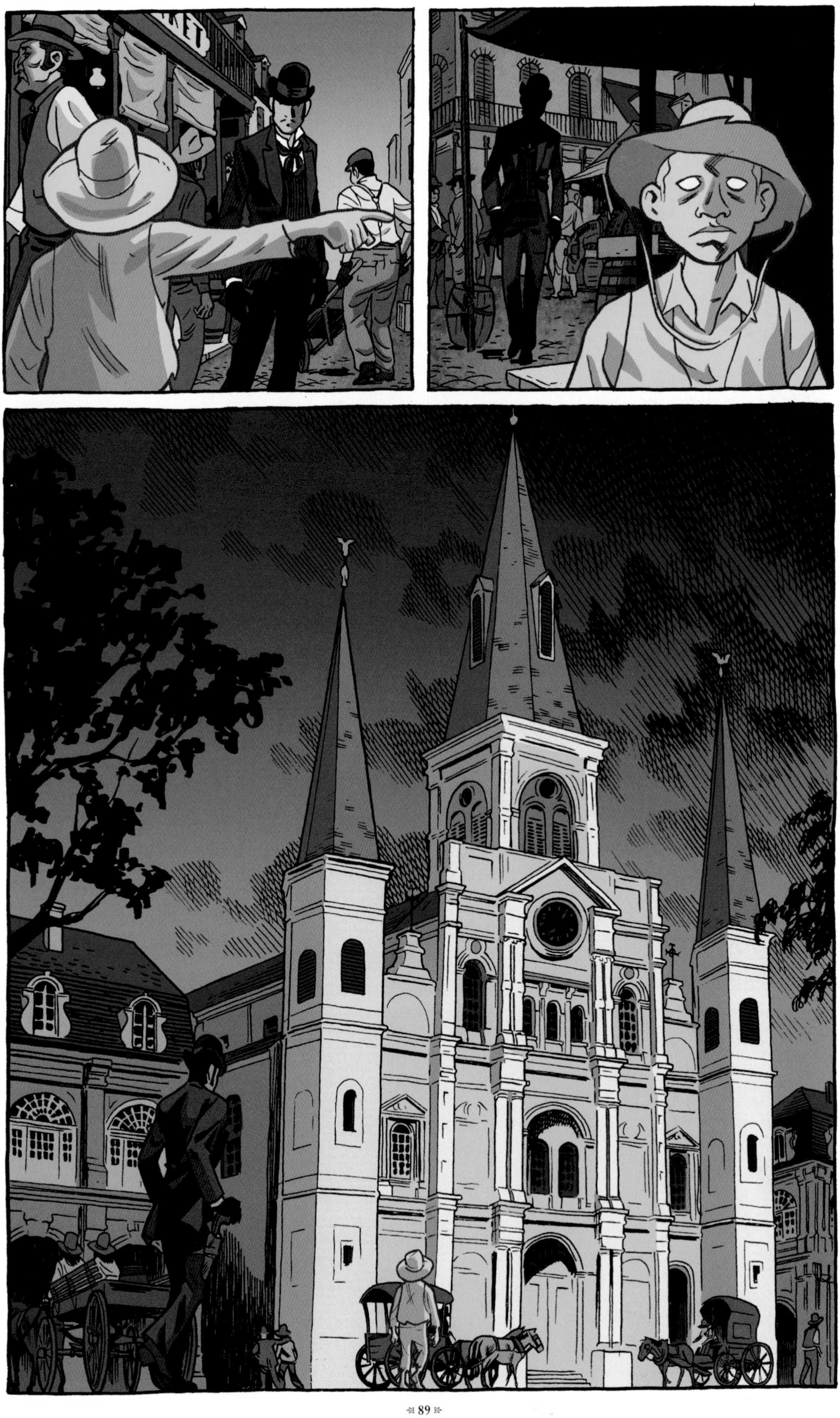

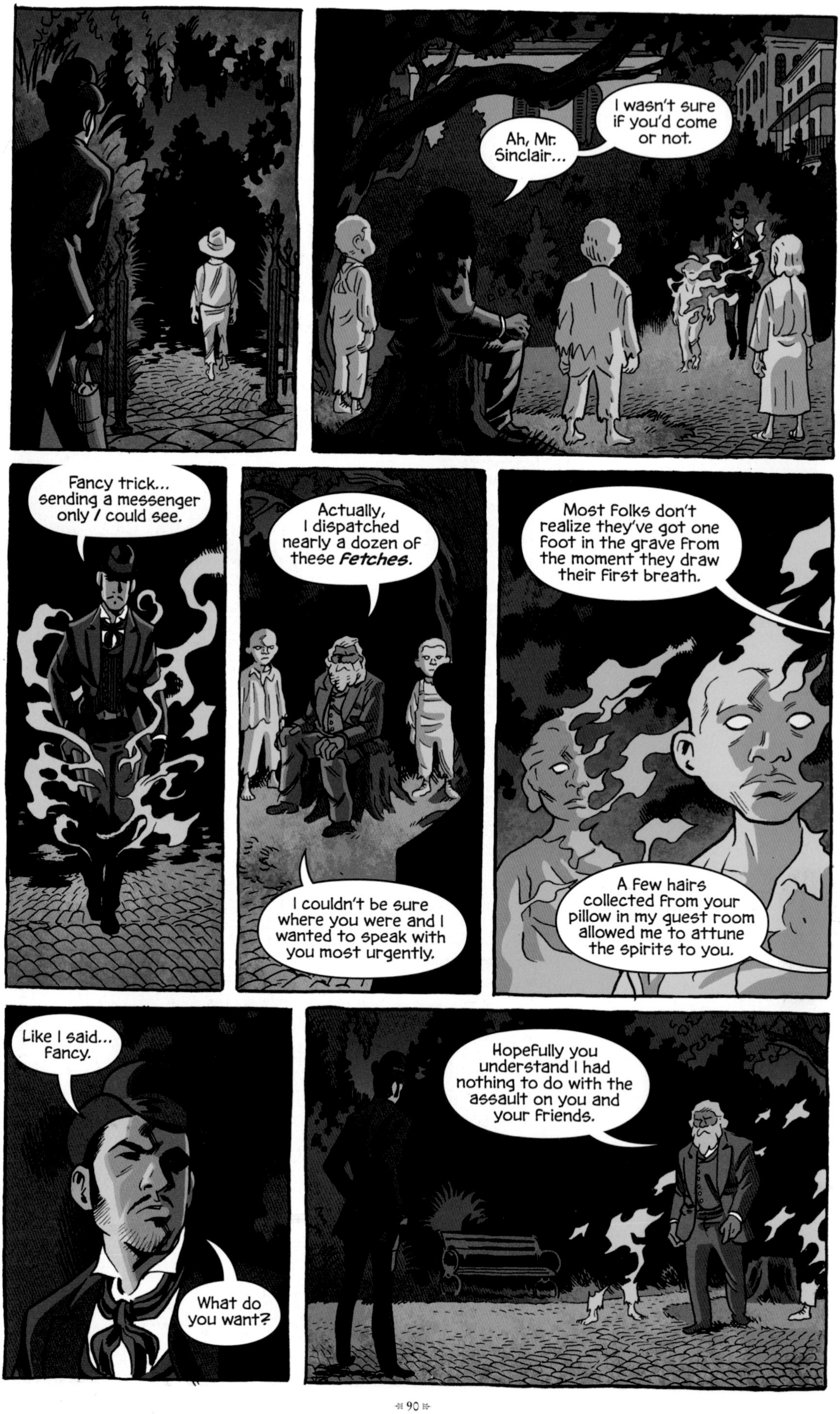
Ah, Mr. Sinclair...
I wasn't sure if you'd come or not.
Fancy trick... sending a messenger only *I* could see.
Actually, I dispatched nearly a dozen of these ***Fetches***.
I couldn't be sure where you were and I wanted to speak with you most urgently.
Most folks don't realize they've got one foot in the grave from the moment they draw their first breath.
A few hairs collected from your pillow in my guest room allowed me to attune the spirits to you.
Like I said... Fancy.
What do you want?
Hopefully you understand I had nothing to do with the assault on you and your friends.

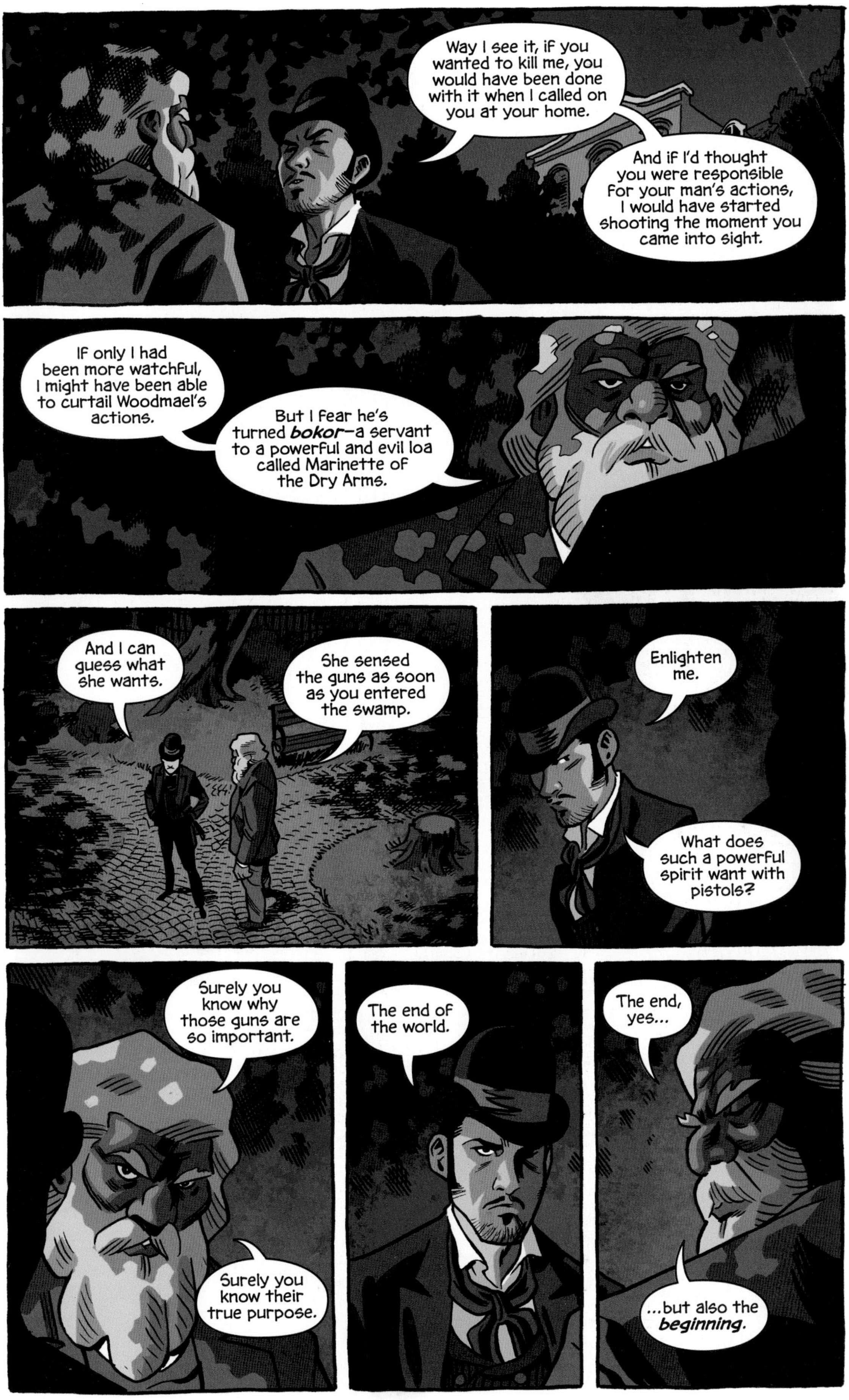

Way I see it, if you wanted to kill me, you would have been done with it when I called on you at your home.
And if I'd thought you were responsible for your man's actions, I would have started shooting the moment you came into sight.
If only I had been more watchful, I might have been able to curtail Woodmael's actions.
But I fear he's turned ***bokor***—a servant to a powerful and evil loa called Marinette of the Dry Arms.
And I can guess what she wants.
She sensed the guns as soon as you entered the swamp.
Enlighten me.
What does such a powerful spirit want with pistols?
Surely you know why those guns are so important.
Surely you know their true purpose.
The end of the world.
The end, yes...
...but also the ***beginning***.

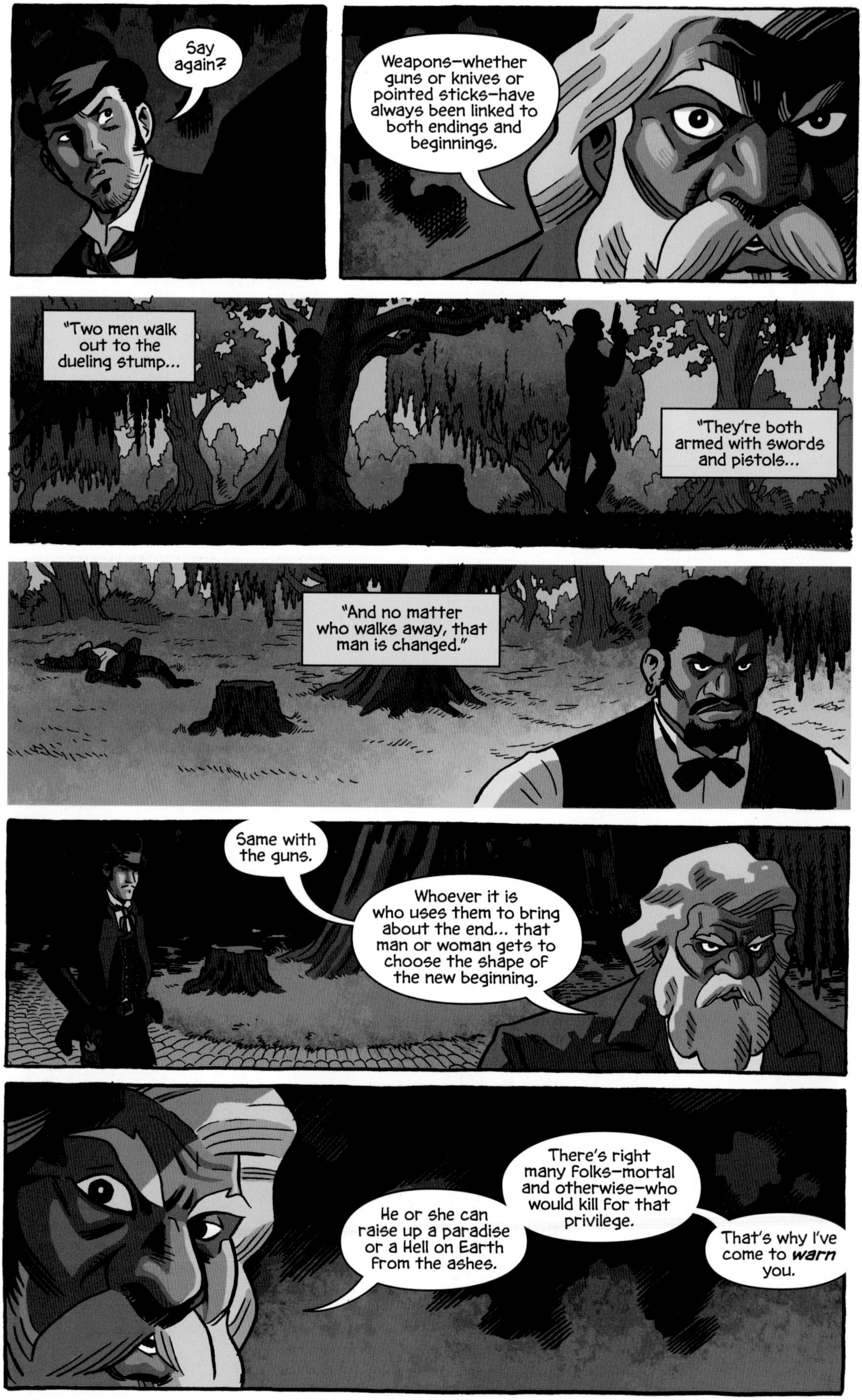
Say again?
Weapons—whether guns or knives or pointed sticks—have always been linked to both endings and beginnings.
"Two men walk out to the dueling stump...
"They're both armed with swords and pistols...
"And no matter who walks away, that man is changed."
Same with the guns.
Whoever it is who uses them to bring about the end... that man or woman gets to choose the shape of the new beginning.
He or she can raise up a paradise or a Hell on Earth from the ashes.
There's right many folks—mortal and otherwise—who would kill for that privilege.
That's why I've come to *warn* you.

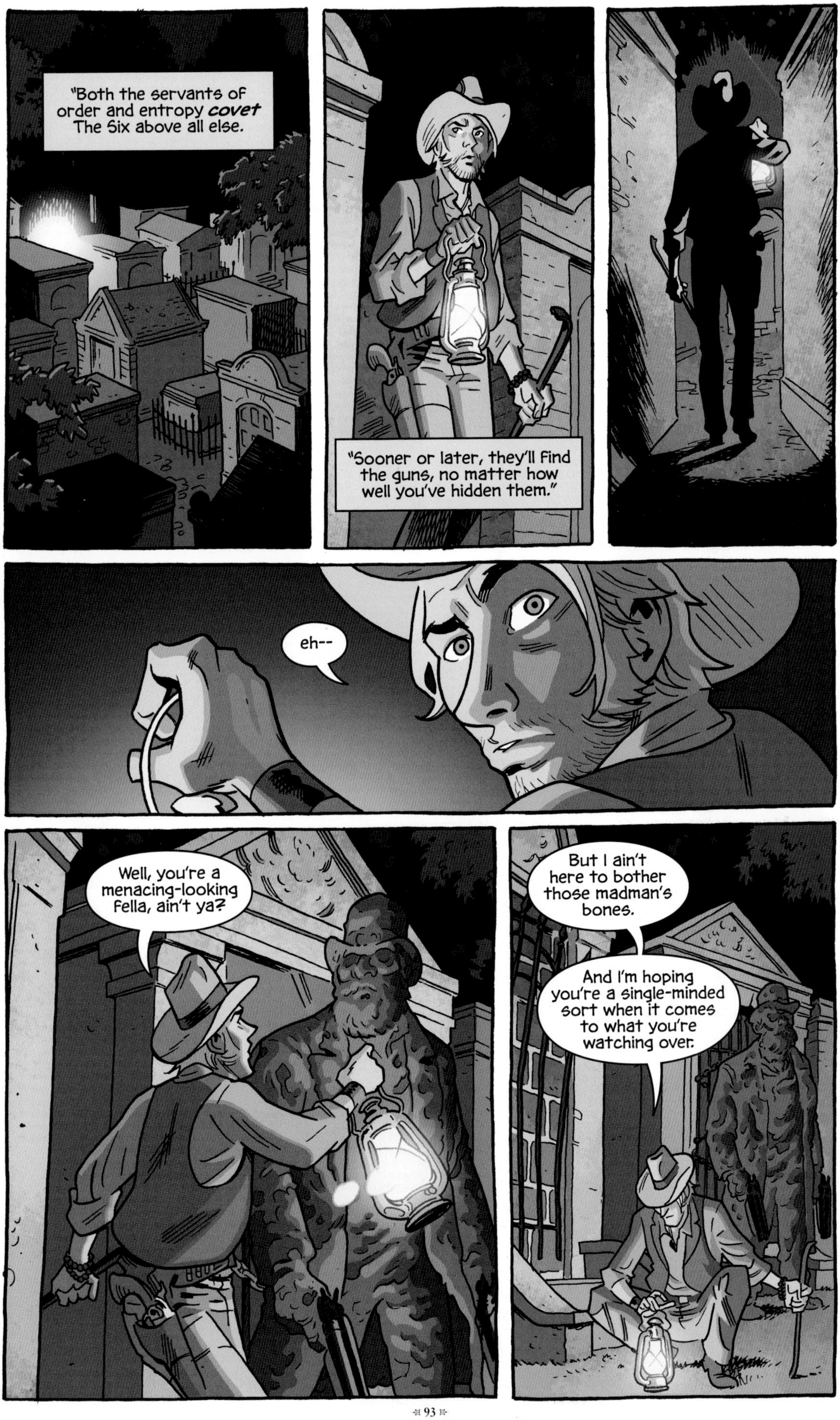
"Both the servants of order and entropy *covet* The Six above all else.
"Sooner or later, they'll find the guns, no matter how well you've hidden them."
eh--
Well, you're a menacing-looking fella, ain't ya?
But I ain't here to bother those madman's bones.
And I'm hoping you're a single-minded sort when it comes to what you're watching over.

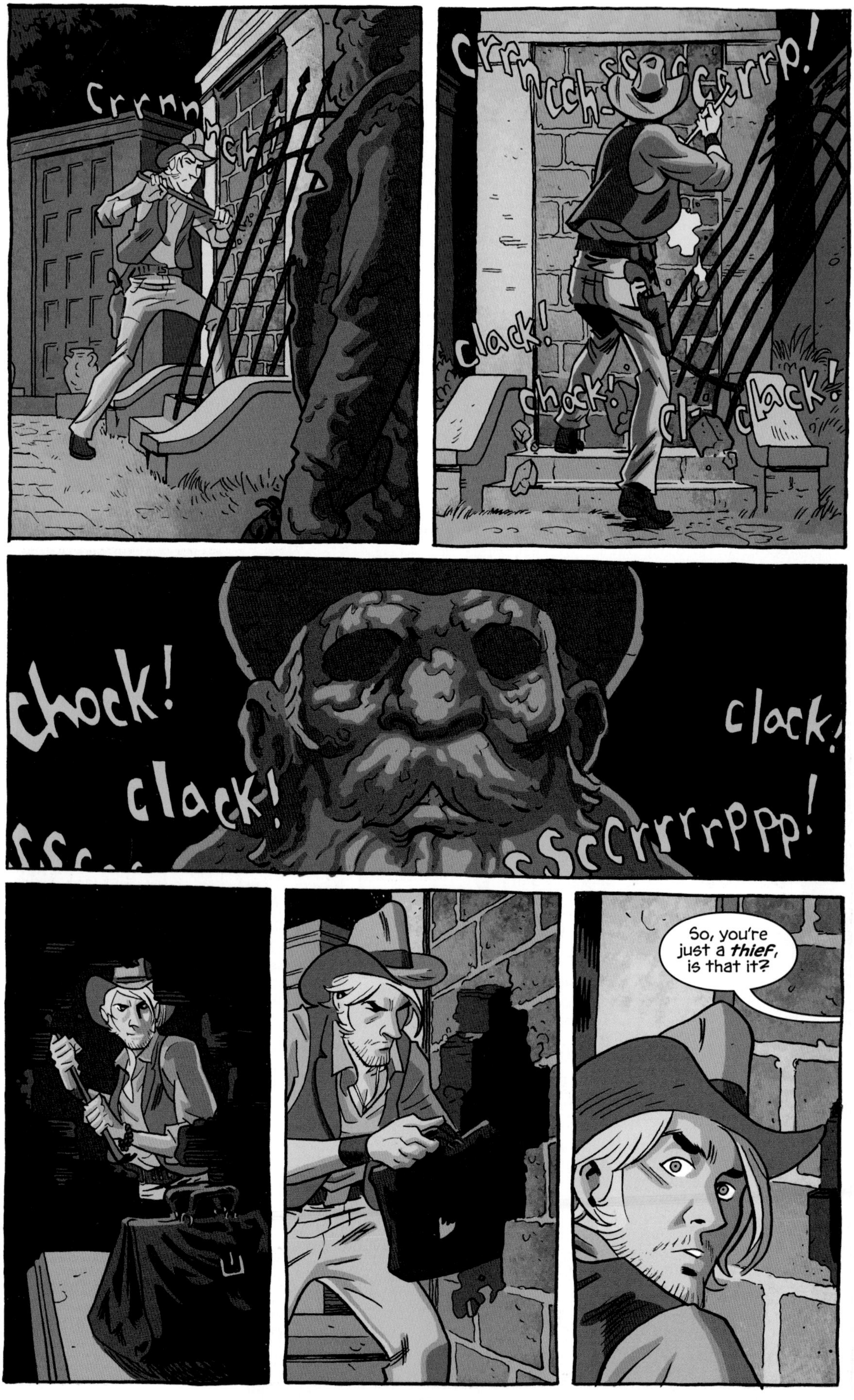
Crrrnnch!
Crrrnnch-ssccccerrrp!
clack!
chock!
cl-clack!
chock!
clack!
clack!
sSccrrrrrppp!
So, you're just a ***thief***, is that it?

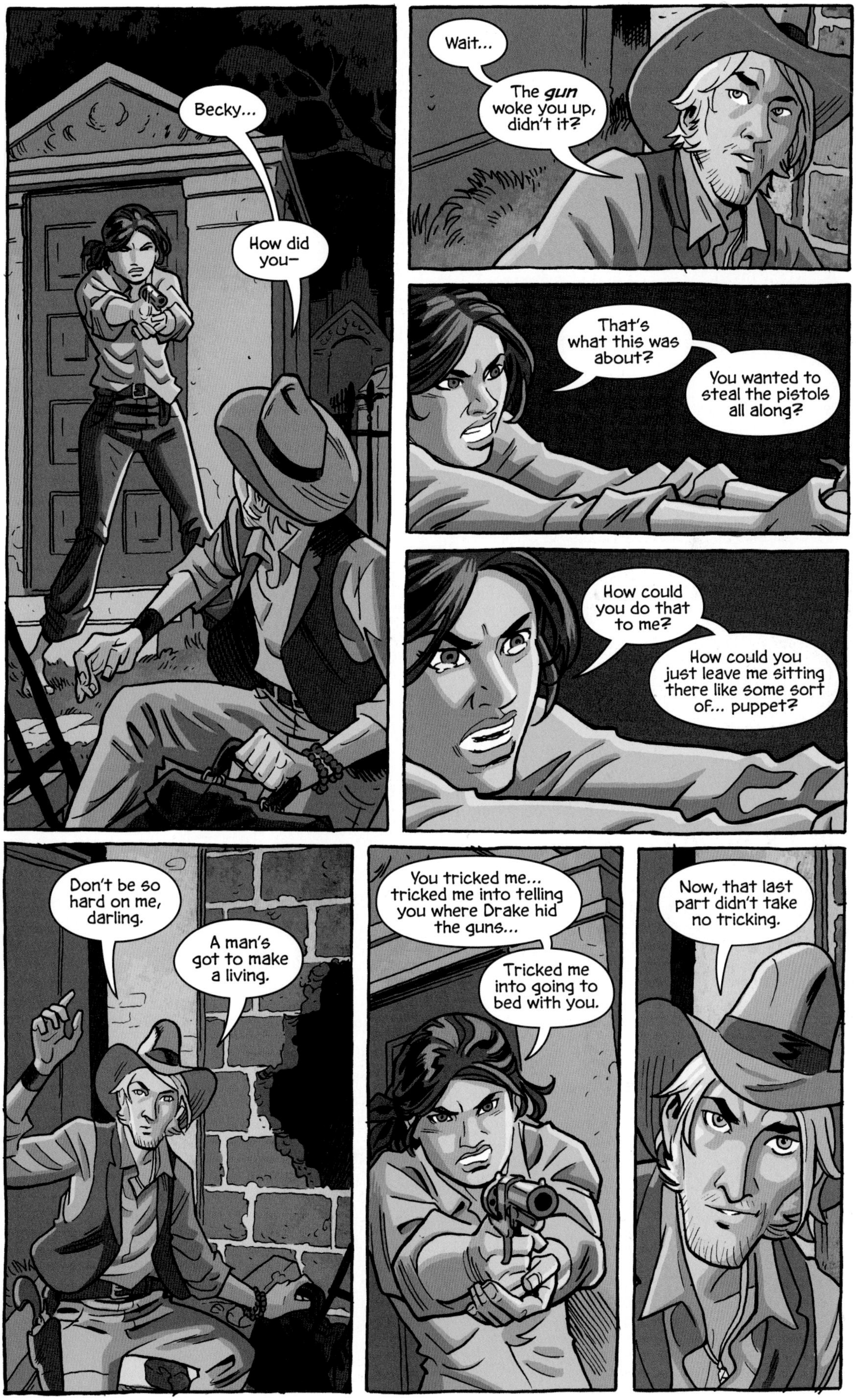
Becky...
How did you–
Wait...
The *gun* woke you up, didn't it?
That's what this was about?
You wanted to steal the pistols all along?
How could you do that to me?
How could you just leave me sitting there like some sort of... puppet?
Don't be so hard on me, darling.
A man's got to make a living.
You tricked me... tricked me into telling you where Drake hid the guns...
Tricked me into going to bed with you.
Now, that last part didn't take no tricking.

You're **not** taking those guns.

You can't use them anyway, unless—

Are you planning on **killing** Drake?

I don't want the guns for myself.

Now, selling them, that's a different story.

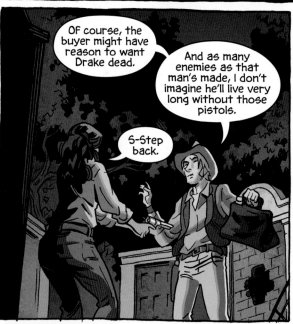

Of course, the buyer might have reason to want Drake dead.

And as many enemies as that man's made, I don't imagine he'll live very long without those pistols.

S-Step back.

You're not going to shoot me, darling. The last thing I want is a fight with you.

I want you to come with me.

Come with you? After what you did?

Have you lost your mind?

Maybe so, but I want you by my side just the same.

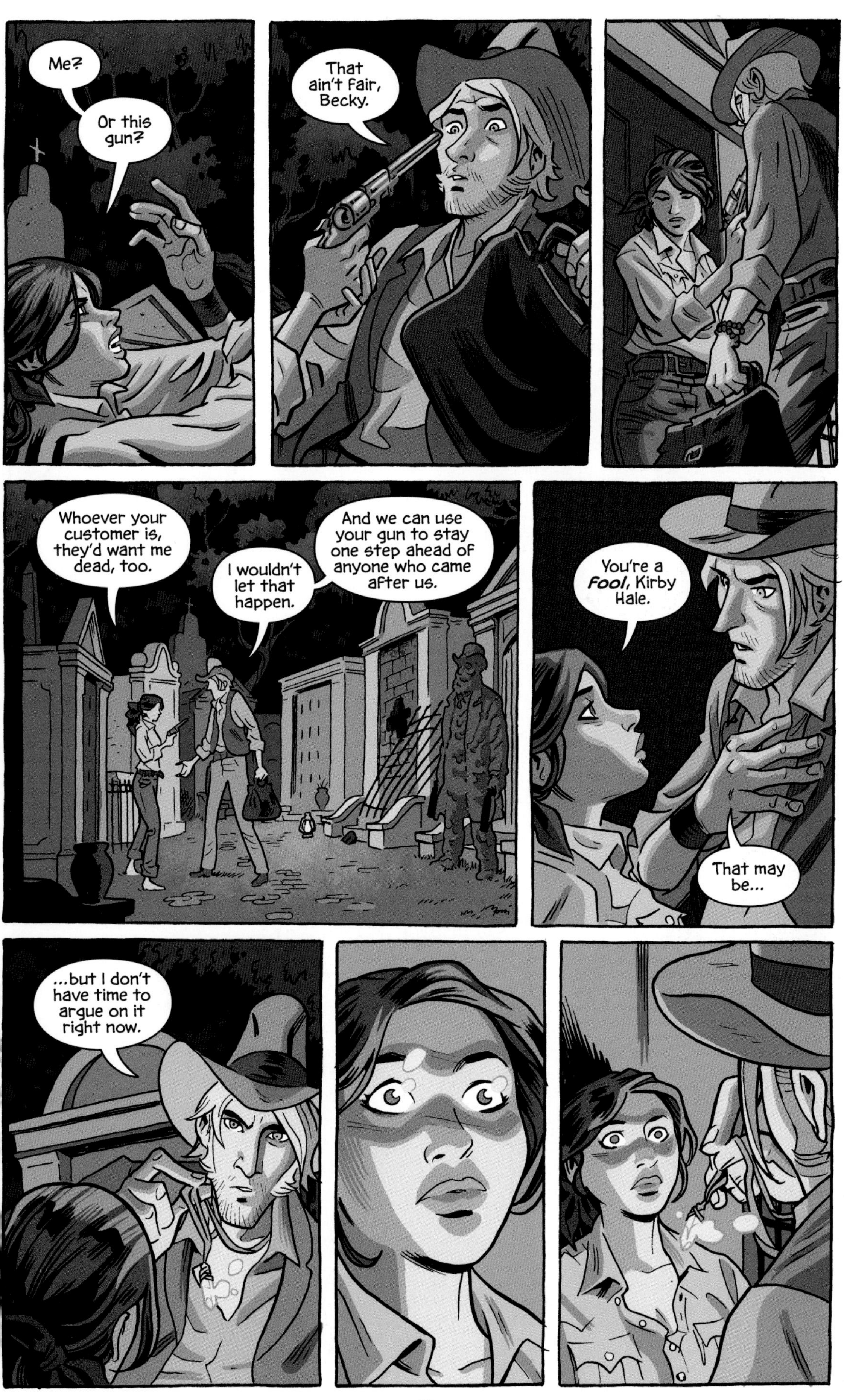
Me?
Or this gun?
That ain't fair, Becky.
Whoever your customer is, they'd want me dead, too.
I wouldn't let that happen.
And we can use your gun to stay one step ahead of anyone who came after us.
You're a **fool**, Kirby Hale.
That may be...
...but I don't have time to argue on it right now.

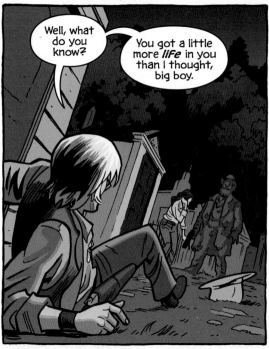

Well, what do you know?

You got a little more *life* in you than I thought, big boy.

But... while I'd love to discuss free will and the location of the soul...

...I'm afraid I've got to be going.

And if you need to shoot me, Becky, you go right ahead.

I won't be shooting back.

That was a foolish thing to do, Miss Montcrief.

And, sadly, to be expected.

The Six can't be trusted in the hands of a farm girl and a common outlaw.

Tonio, Izador, Baltazar—

Retrieve the guns.

See that the thief troubles us no longer.

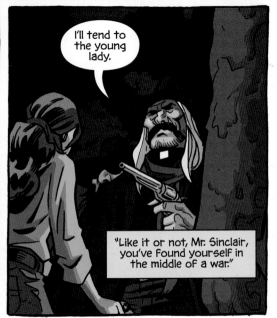

I'll tend to the young lady.

"Like it or not, Mr. Sinclair, you've found yourself in the middle of a war."

I've seen war before.

I'm sure you have.

And I'm sure it *changed* you.

But nothing you've seen thus far will hold a candle to the battle that comes next.

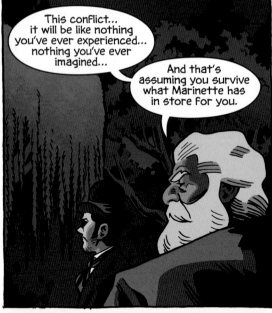

This conflict... it will be like nothing you've ever experienced... nothing you've ever imagined...

And that's assuming you survive what Marinette has in store for you.

I've managed so far.

Thus far, she's struck at you using proxies.

"Next time, I imagine, she'll come for you herself."

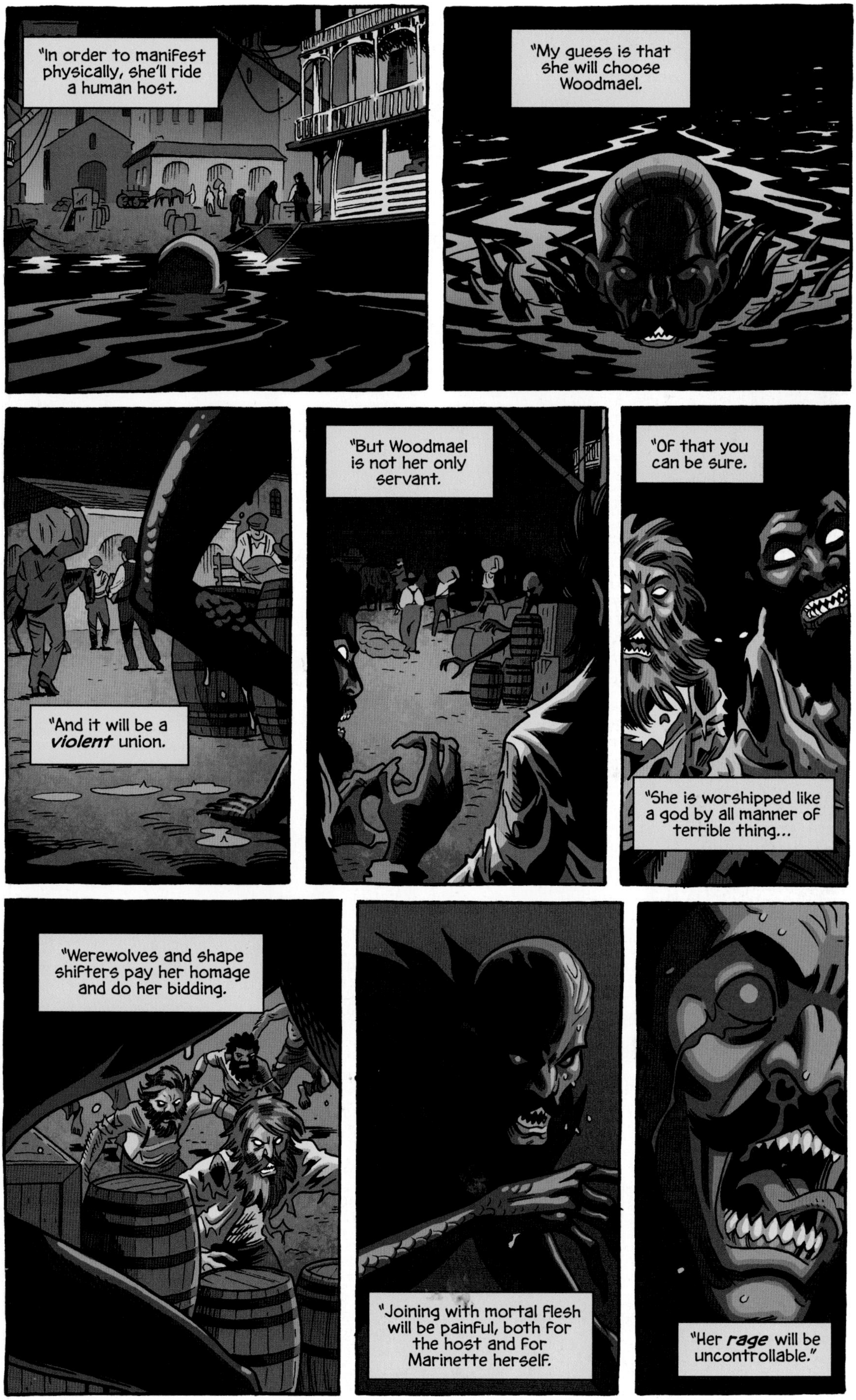
"In order to manifest physically, she'll ride a human host.
"My guess is that she will choose Woodmael.
"And it will be a *violent* union.
"But Woodmael is not her only servant.
"Of that you can be sure.
"She is worshipped like a god by all manner of terrible thing...
"Werewolves and shape shifters pay her homage and do her bidding.
"Joining with mortal flesh will be painful, both for the host and for Marinette herself.
"Her *rage* will be uncontrollable."

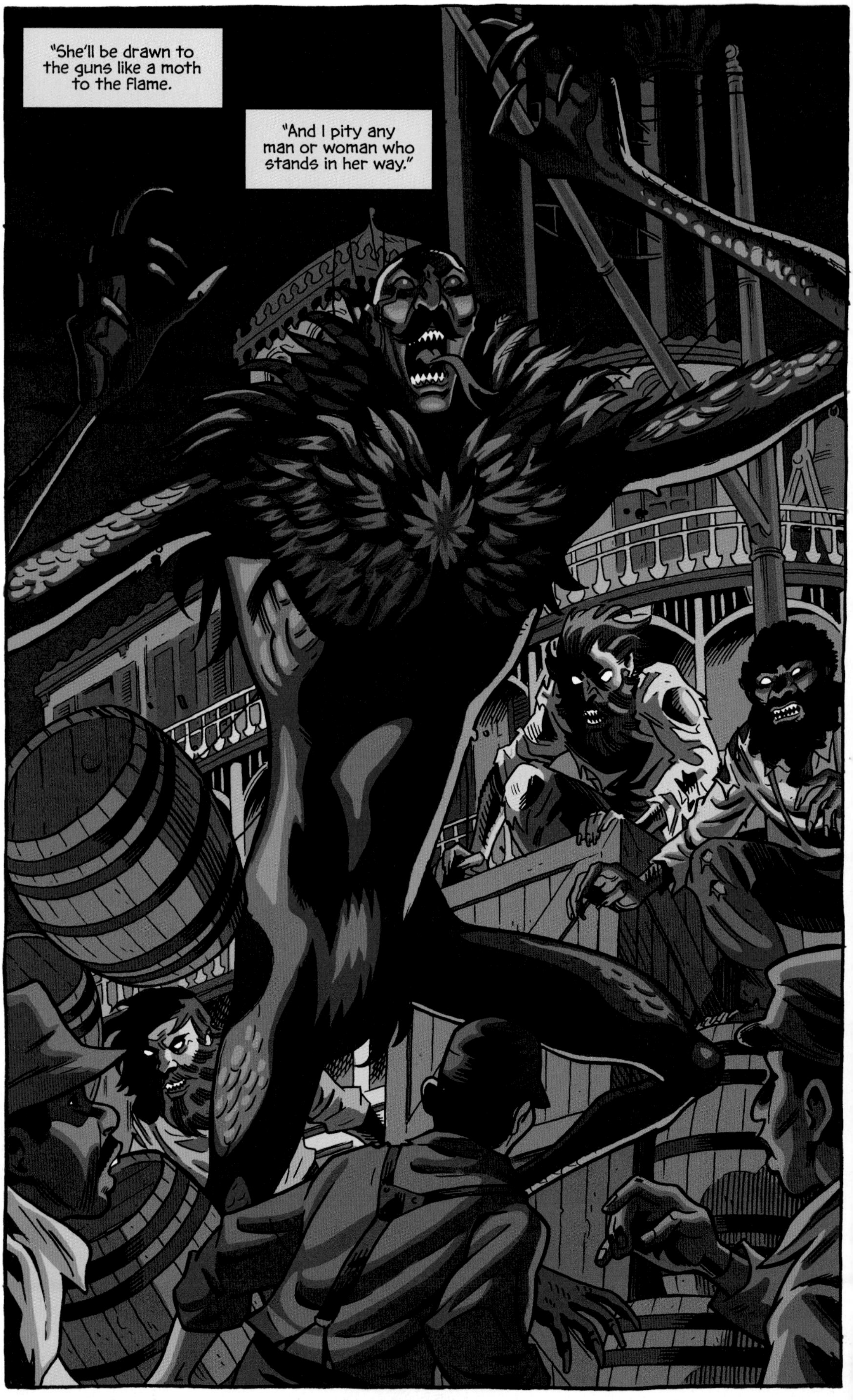
"She'll be drawn to the guns like a moth to the flame.
"And I pity any man or woman who stands in her way."

CHAPTER
FIVE

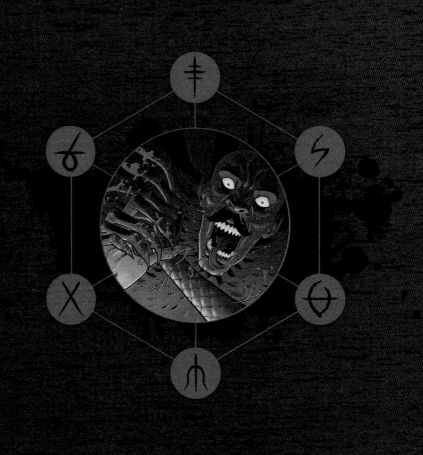

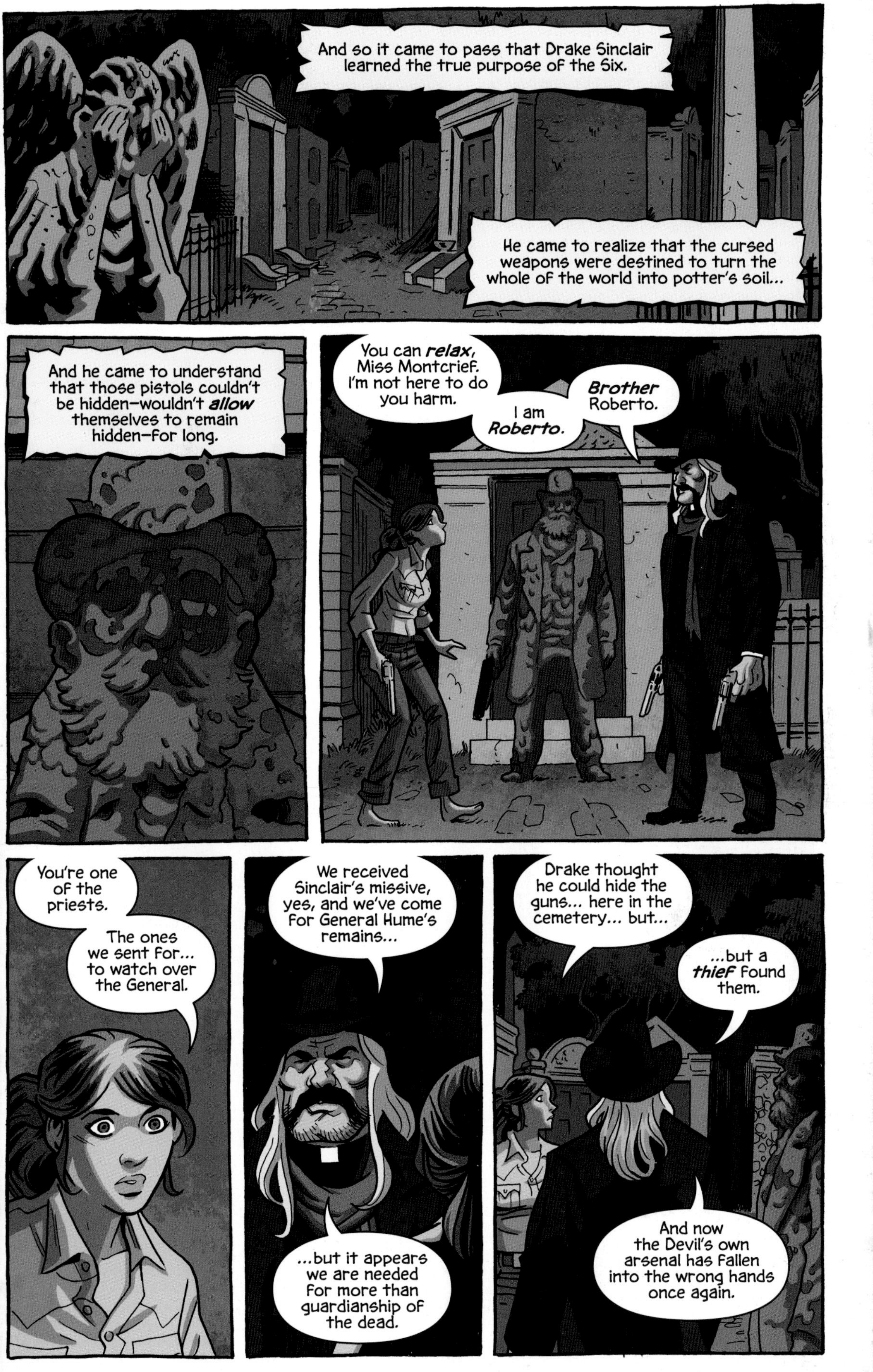
And so it came to pass that Drake Sinclair learned the true purpose of the Six.
He came to realize that the cursed weapons were destined to turn the whole of the world into potter's soil...
And he came to understand that those pistols couldn't be hidden—wouldn't *allow* themselves to remain hidden—for long.
You can *relax*, Miss Montcrief. I'm not here to do you harm.
I am *Roberto.*
Brother Roberto.
You're one of the priests.
The ones we sent for... to watch over the General.
We received Sinclair's missive, yes, and we've come for General Hume's remains...
...but it appears we are needed for more than guardianship of the dead.
Drake thought he could hide the guns... here in the cemetery... but...
...but a *thief* found them.
And now the Devil's own arsenal has fallen into the wrong hands once again.

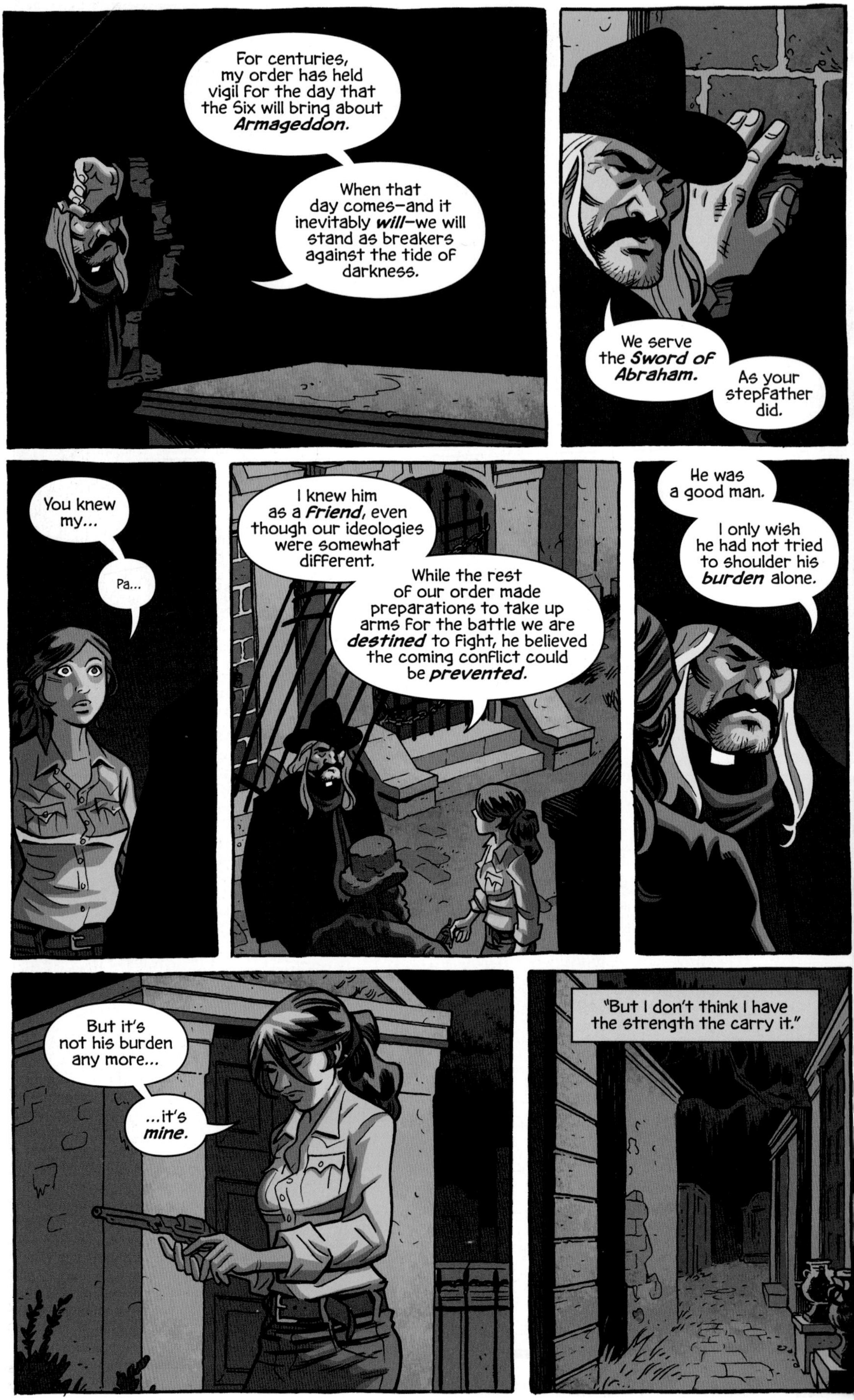
For centuries, my order has held vigil for the day that the Six will bring about *Armageddon*.
When that day comes—and it inevitably *will*—we will stand as breakers against the tide of darkness.
We serve the *Sword of Abraham*.
As your stepfather did.
You knew my...
Pa...
I knew him as a *friend*, even though our ideologies were somewhat different.
While the rest of our order made preparations to take up arms for the battle we are *destined* to fight, he believed the coming conflict could be *prevented*.
He was a good man.
I only wish he had not tried to shoulder his *burden* alone.
But it's not his burden any more...
...it's *mine*.
"But I don't think I have the strength the carry it."

Meanwhile, in another part of the Crescent City, a powerful force tracked the Six...

Relentless... Cruel...

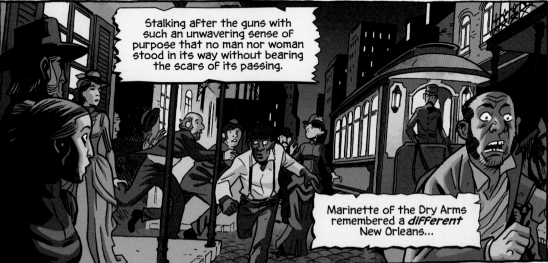

Stalking after the guns with such an unwavering sense of purpose that no man nor woman stood in its way without bearing the scars of its passing.

Marinette of the Dry Arms remembered a *different* New Orleans...

A city crawling with worshippers who trembled at the very utterance of her dreaded name...

She pined for those days of old like a long, lost lover...

FWWW—WWW-FF

FWW

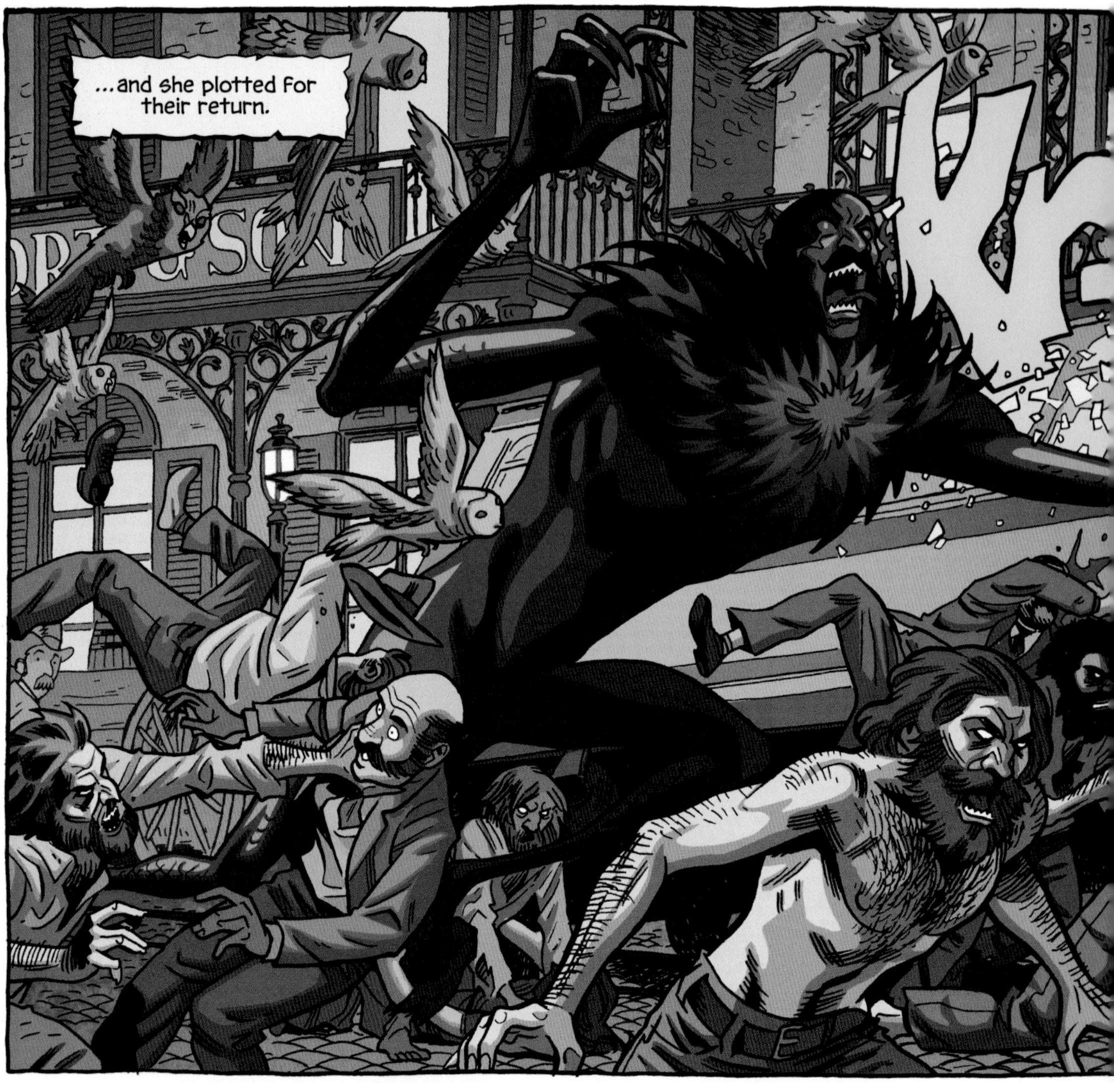
...and she plotted for their return.

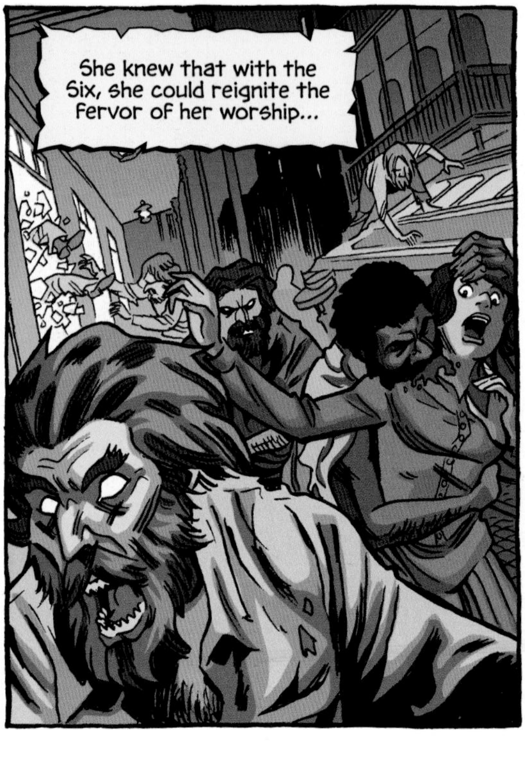
She knew that with the Six, she could reignite the fervor of her worship...

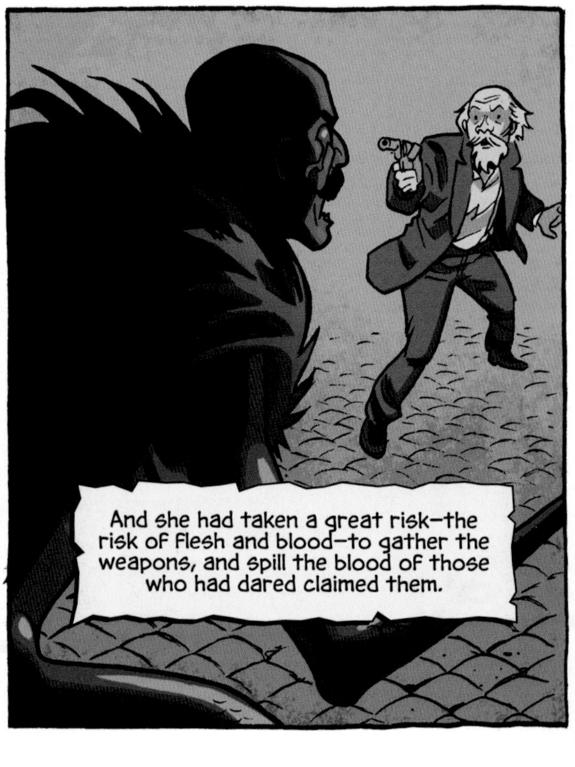
And she had taken a great risk—the risk of flesh and blood—to gather the weapons, and spill the blood of those who had dared claimed them.

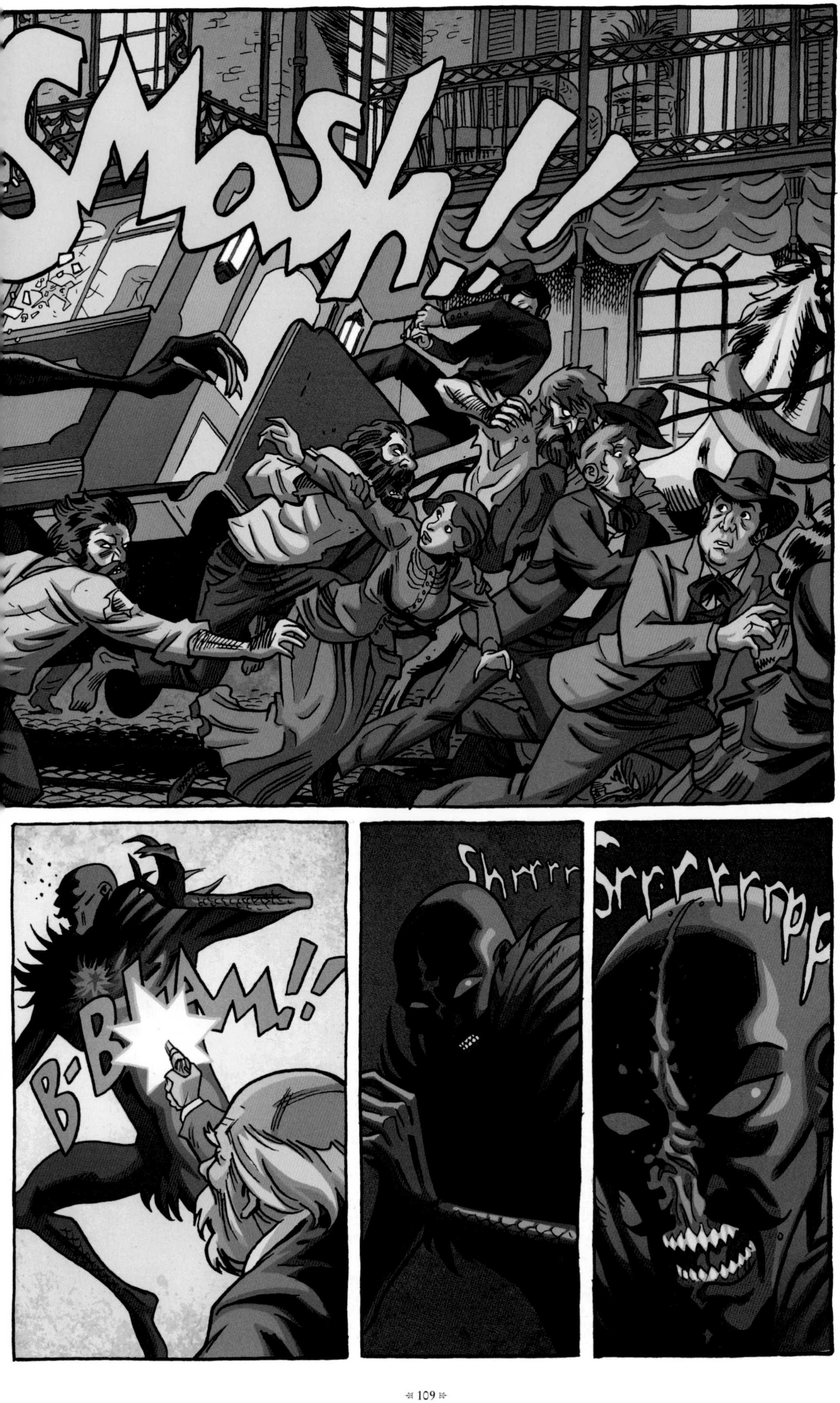
SMASH!!
B-BLAM!!
Shrrr
Srrrrrrpp

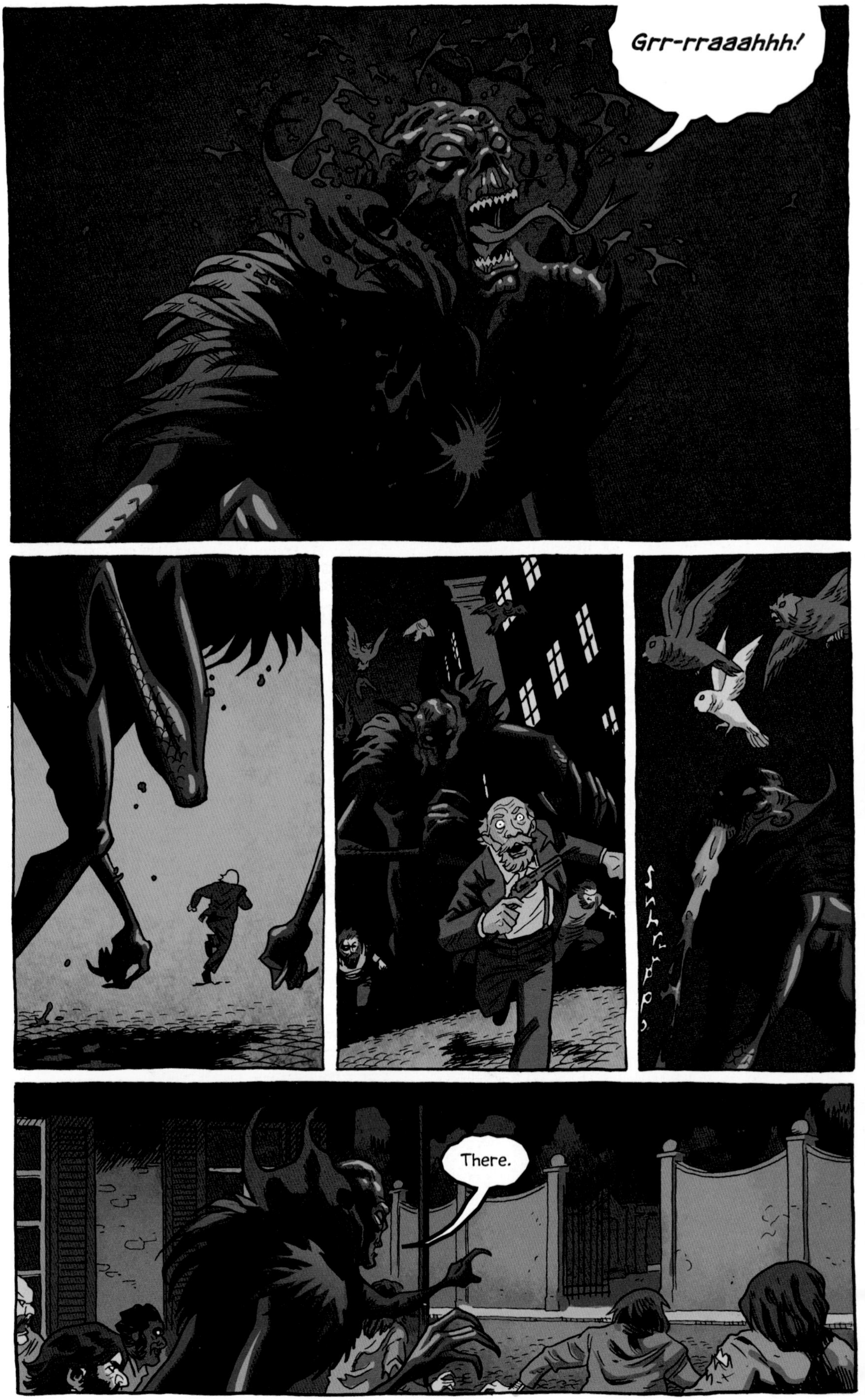
Grr-rraaahhh!
There.

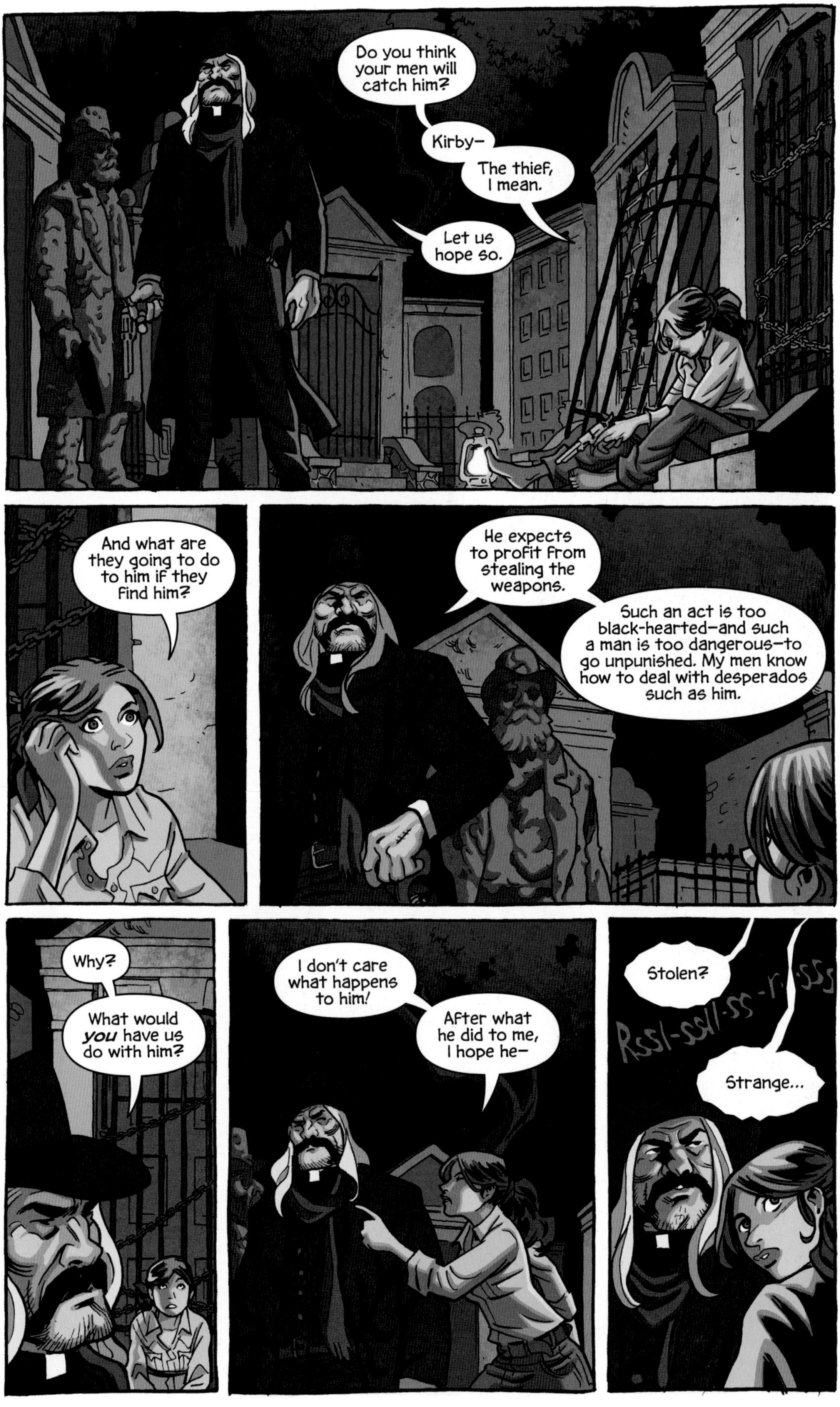
Do you think your men will catch him?
Kirby–
The thief, I mean.
Let us hope so.
And what are they going to do to him if they find him?
He expects to profit from stealing the weapons.
Such an act is too black-hearted–and such a man is too dangerous–to go unpunished. My men know how to deal with desperados such as him.
Why?
What would *you* have us do with him?
I don't care what happens to him!
After what he did to me, I hope he–
Stolen?
Strange...

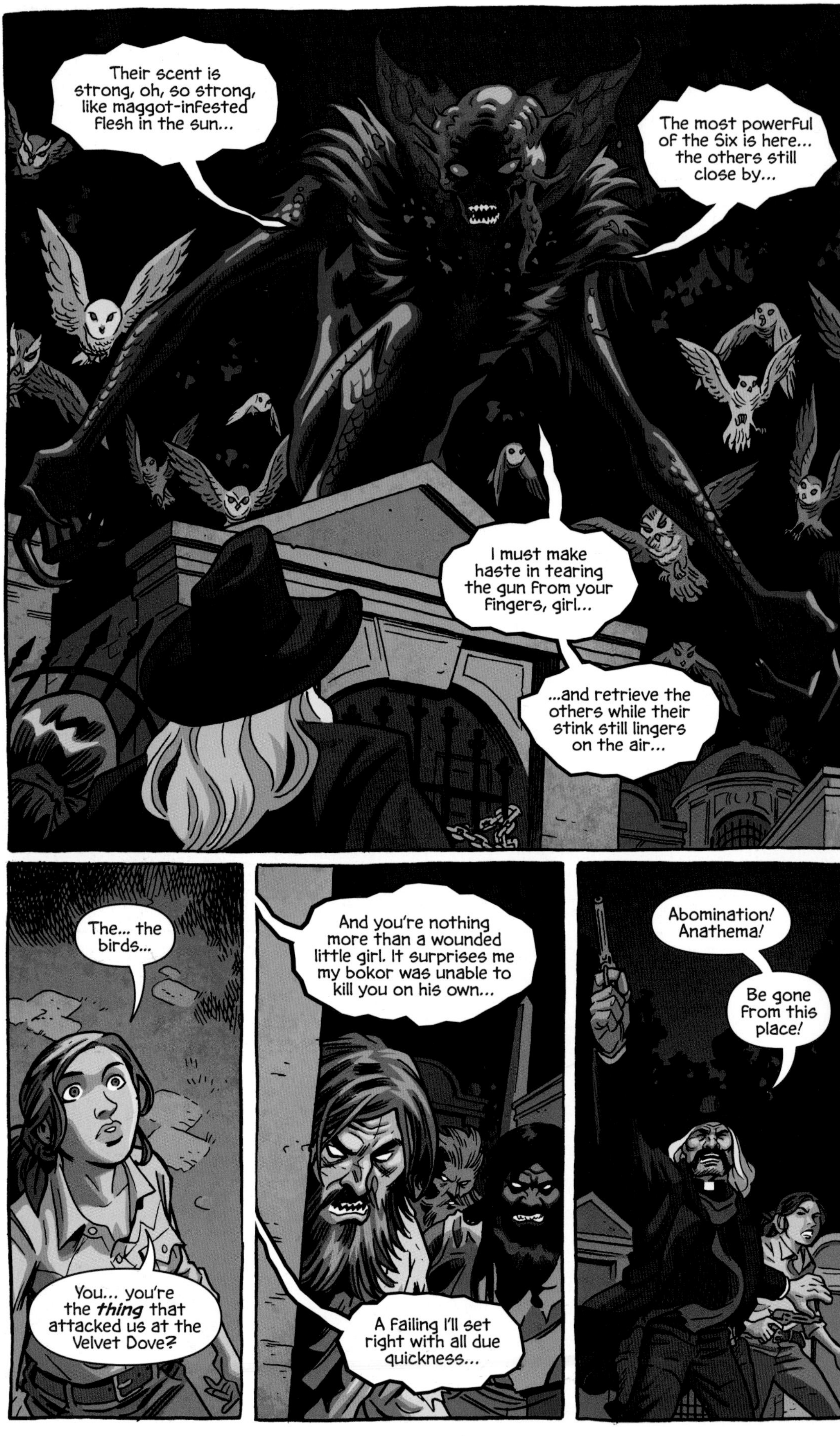
Their scent is strong, oh, so strong, like maggot-infested flesh in the sun...
The most powerful of the Six is here... the others still close by...
I must make haste in tearing the gun from your fingers, girl...
...and retrieve the others while their stink still lingers on the air...
The... the birds...
You... you're the *thing* that attacked us at the Velvet Dove?
And you're nothing more than a wounded little girl. It surprises me my bokor was unable to kill you on his own...
A failing I'll set right with all due quickness...
Abomination! Anathema!
Be gone from this place!

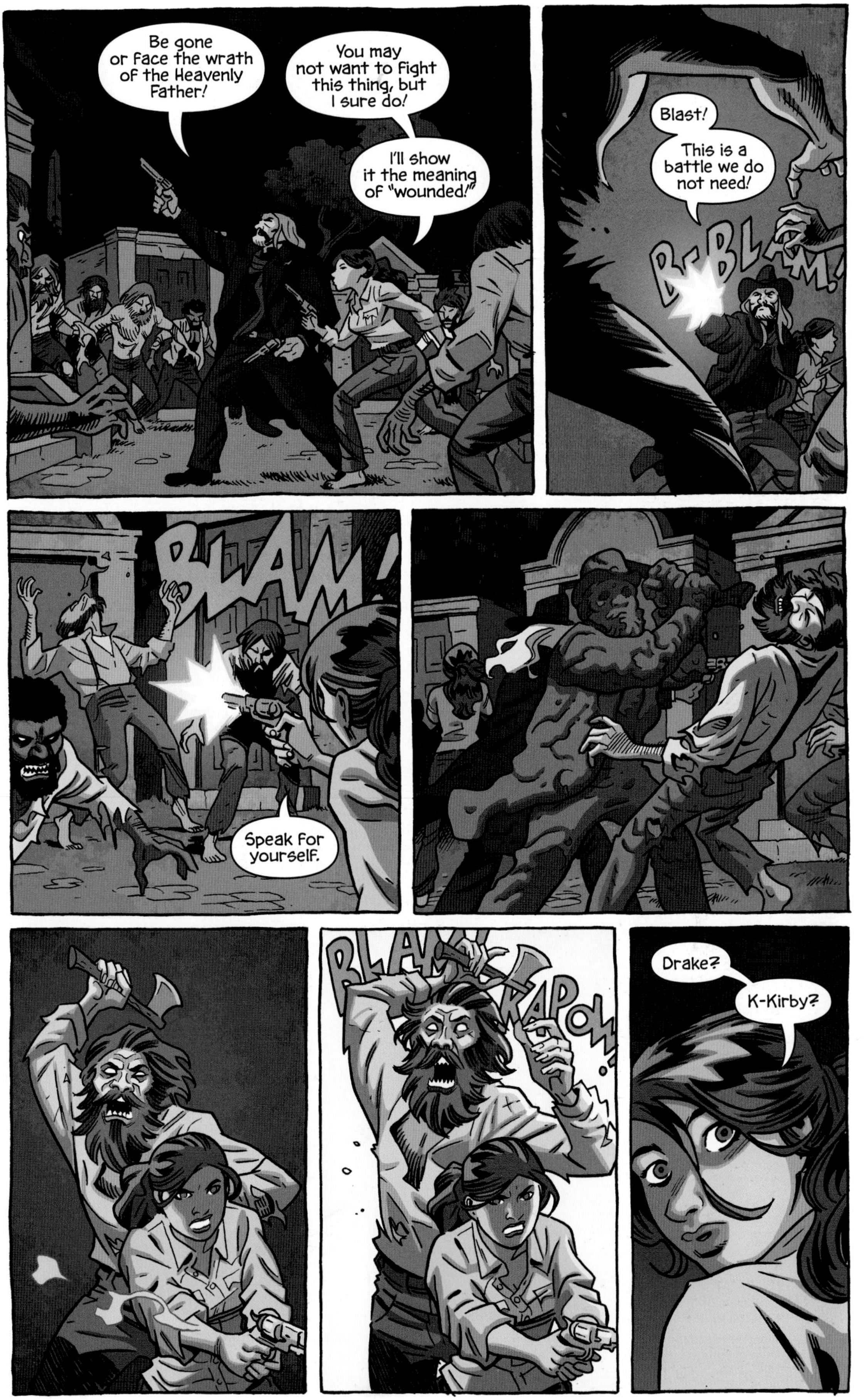
Be gone or face the wrath of the Heavenly Father!
You may not want to fight this thing, but I sure do!
I'll show it the meaning of "wounded!"
Blast!
This is a battle we do not need!
B-BLAM!
BLAM!
Speak for yourself.
BLAM!
KAPOW!
Drake?
K-Kirby?

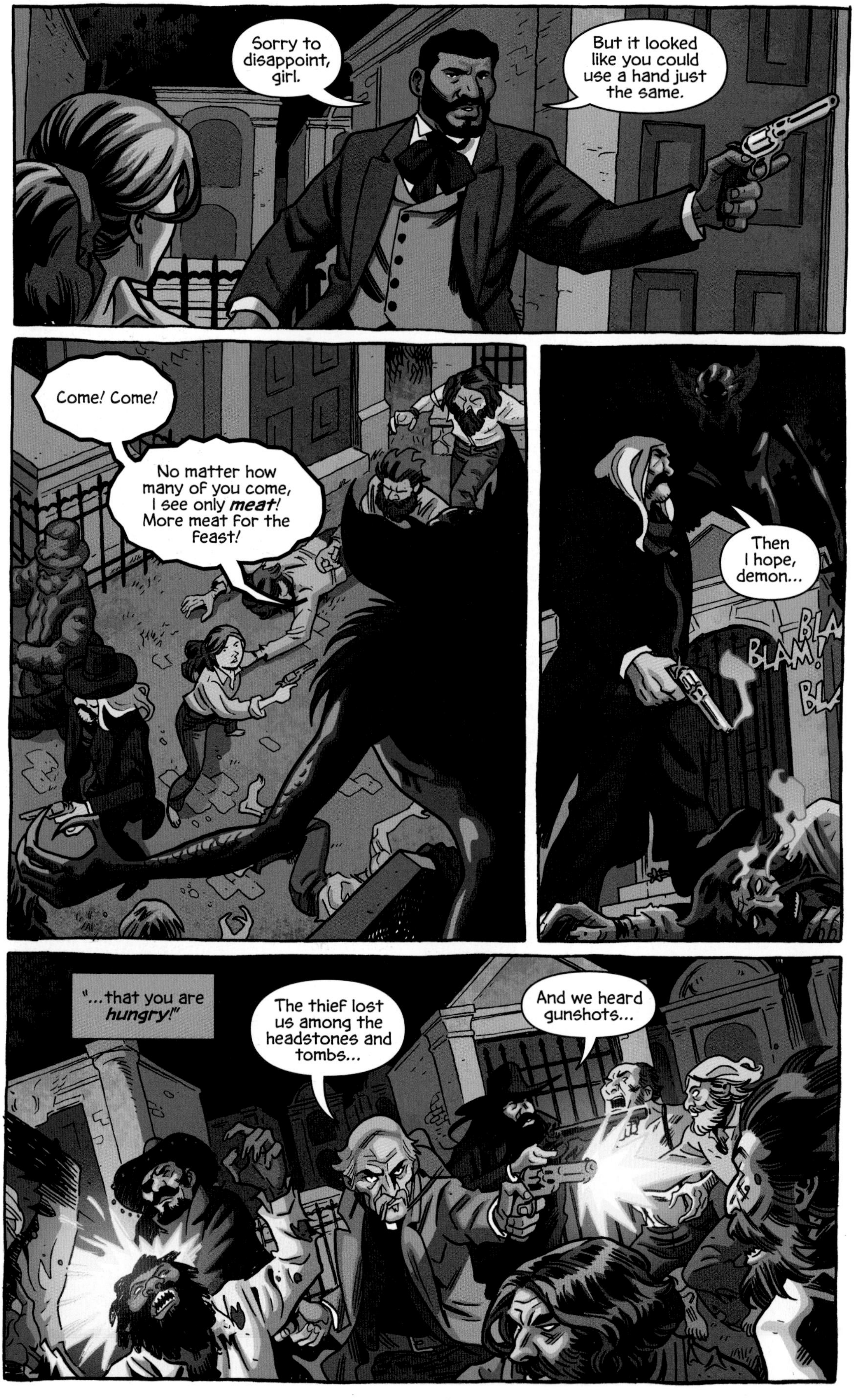
Sorry to disappoint, girl.
But it looked like you could use a hand just the same.
Come! Come!
No matter how many of you come, I see only *meat*! More meat for the feast!
Then I hope, demon...
BLAM!
"...that you are *hungry*!"
The thief lost us among the headstones and tombs...
And we heard gunshots...

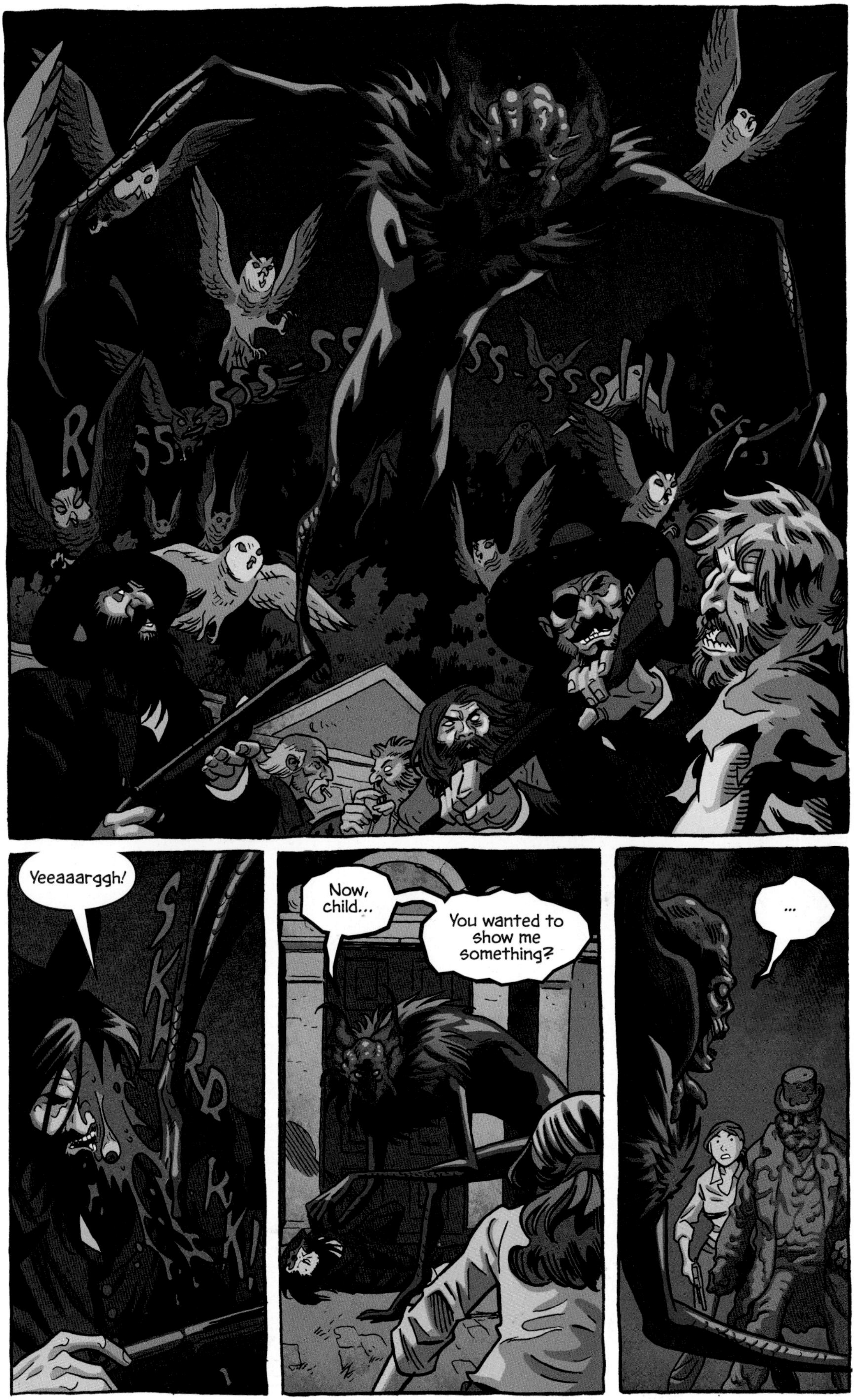
Yeeaaarggh!
Now, child...
You wanted to show me something?
...

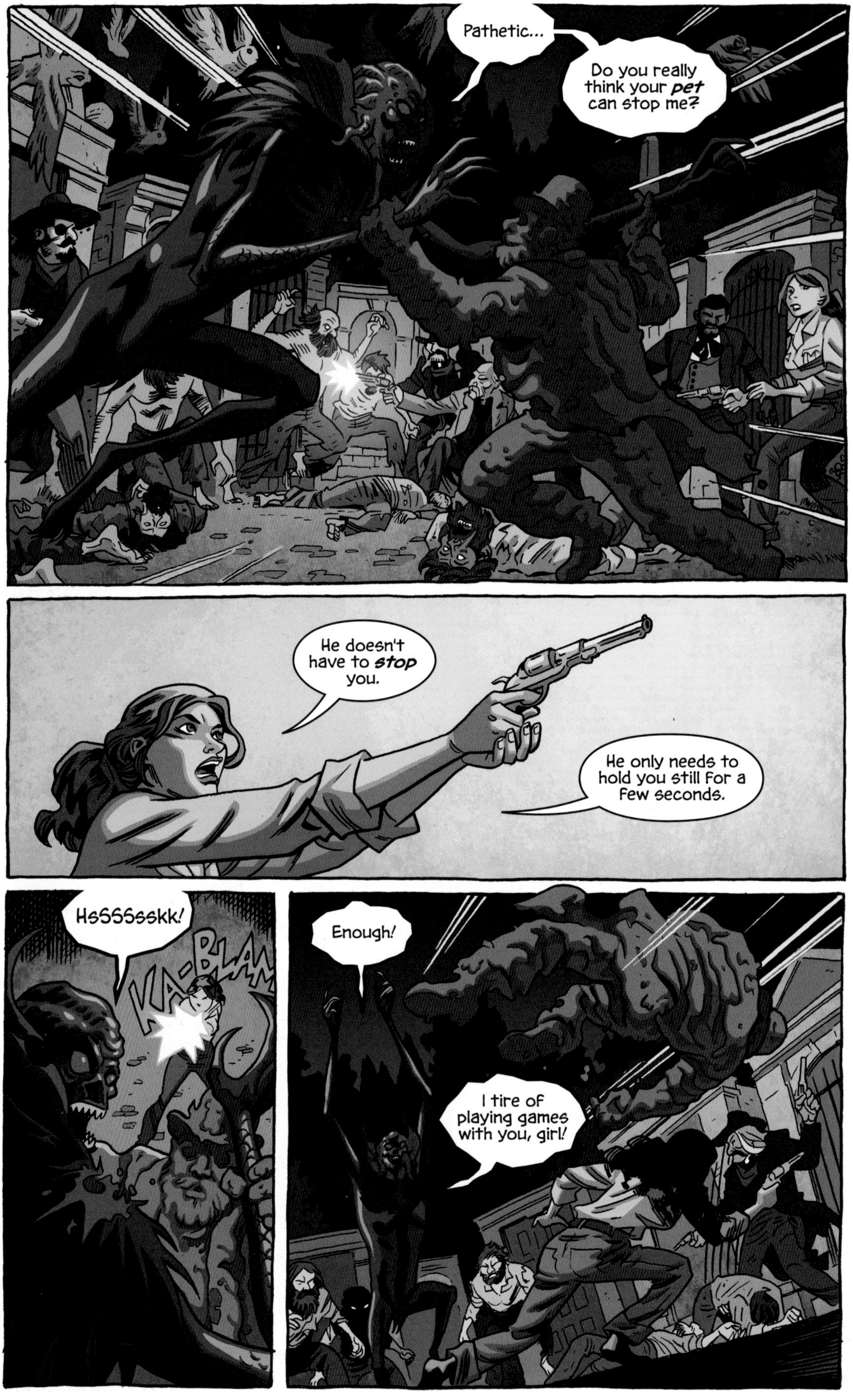
Pathetic...
Do you really think your *pet* can stop me?
He doesn't have to *stop* you.
He only needs to hold you still for a few seconds.
HsSSSsskk!
KA-BLAM
Enough!
I tire of playing games with you, girl!

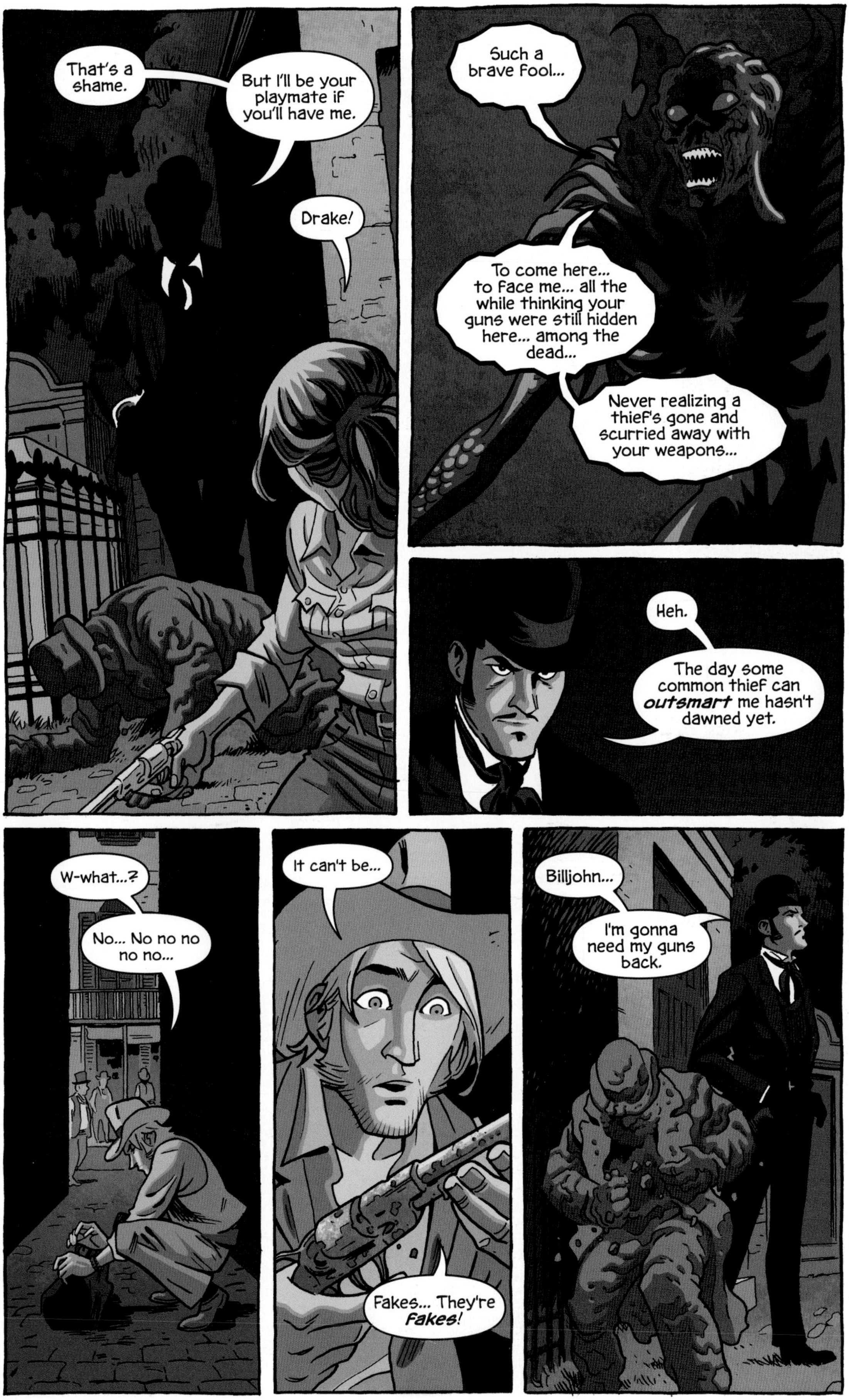
That's a shame.
But I'll be your playmate if you'll have me.
Drake!
Such a brave fool...
To come here... to face me... all the while thinking your guns were still hidden here... among the dead...
Never realizing a thief's gone and scurried away with your weapons...
Heh.
The day some common thief can *outsmart* me hasn't dawned yet.
W-what...?
No... No no no no no...
It can't be...
Fakes... They're *fakes*!
Billjohn...
I'm gonna need my guns back.

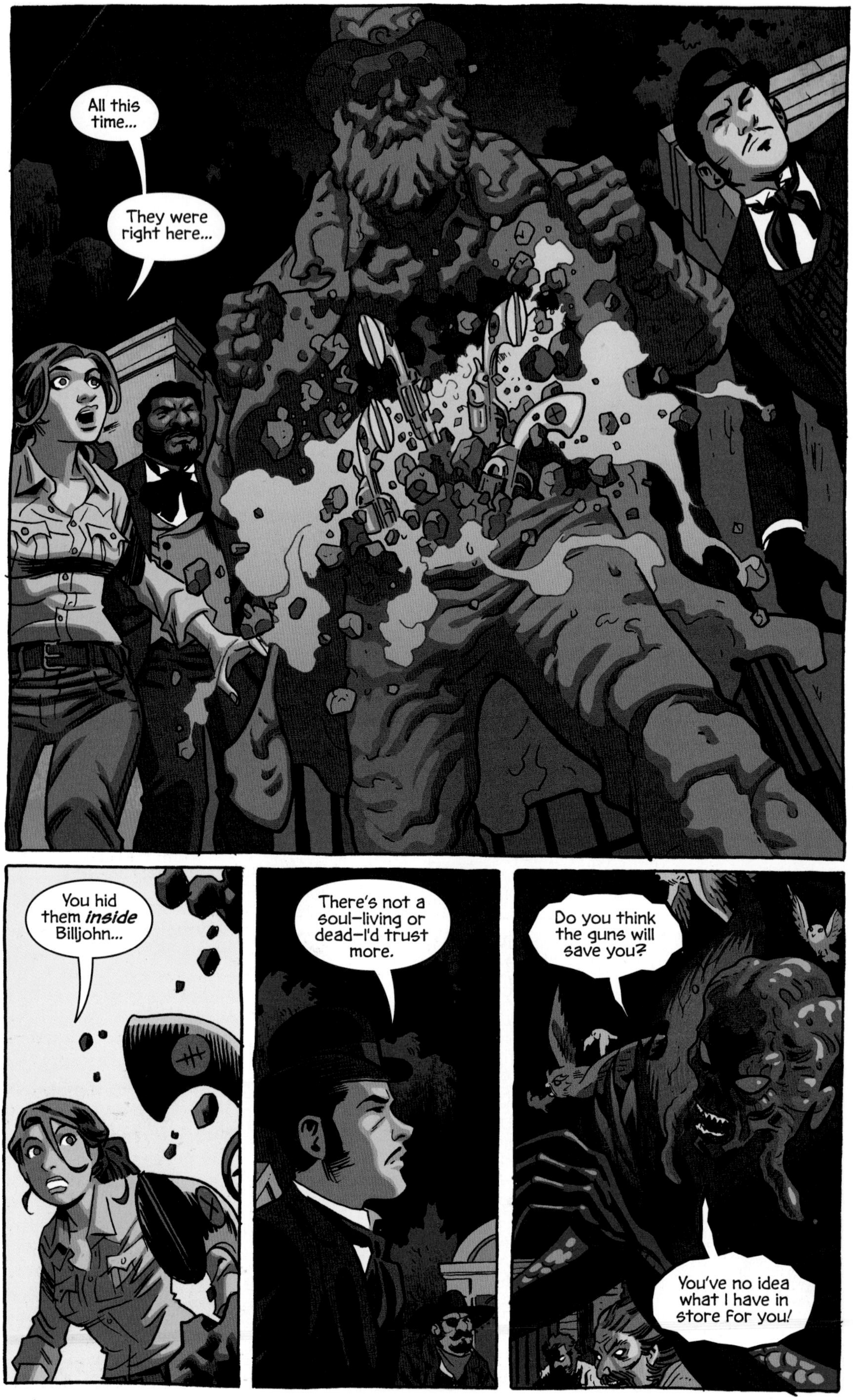
All this time...
They were right here...
You hid them inside Billjohn...
There's not a soul—living or dead—I'd trust more.
Do you think the guns will save you?
You've no idea what I have in store for you!

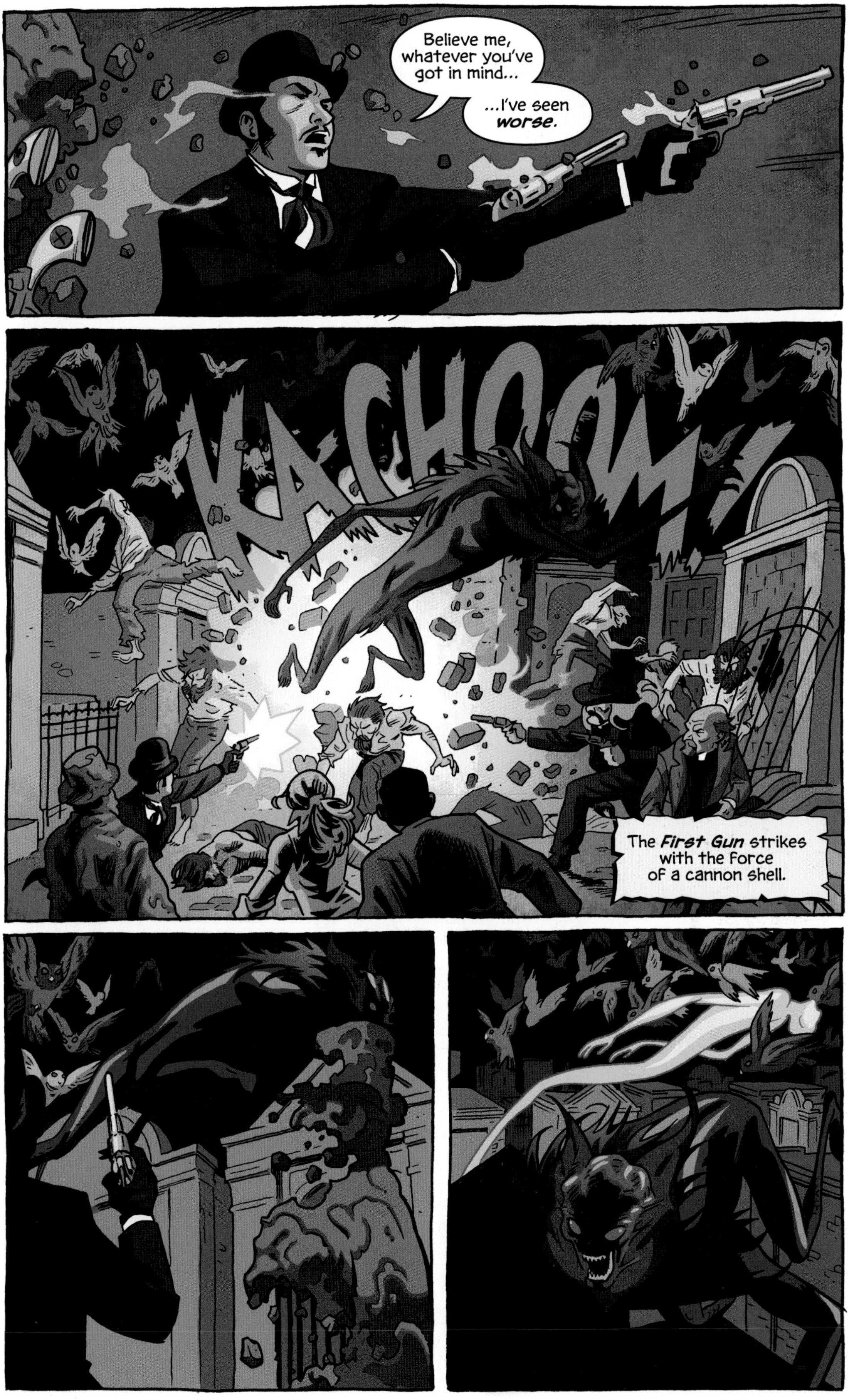
Believe me, whatever you've got in mind...
...I've seen worse.
KA-CHOOM!
The First Gun strikes with the force of a cannon shell.

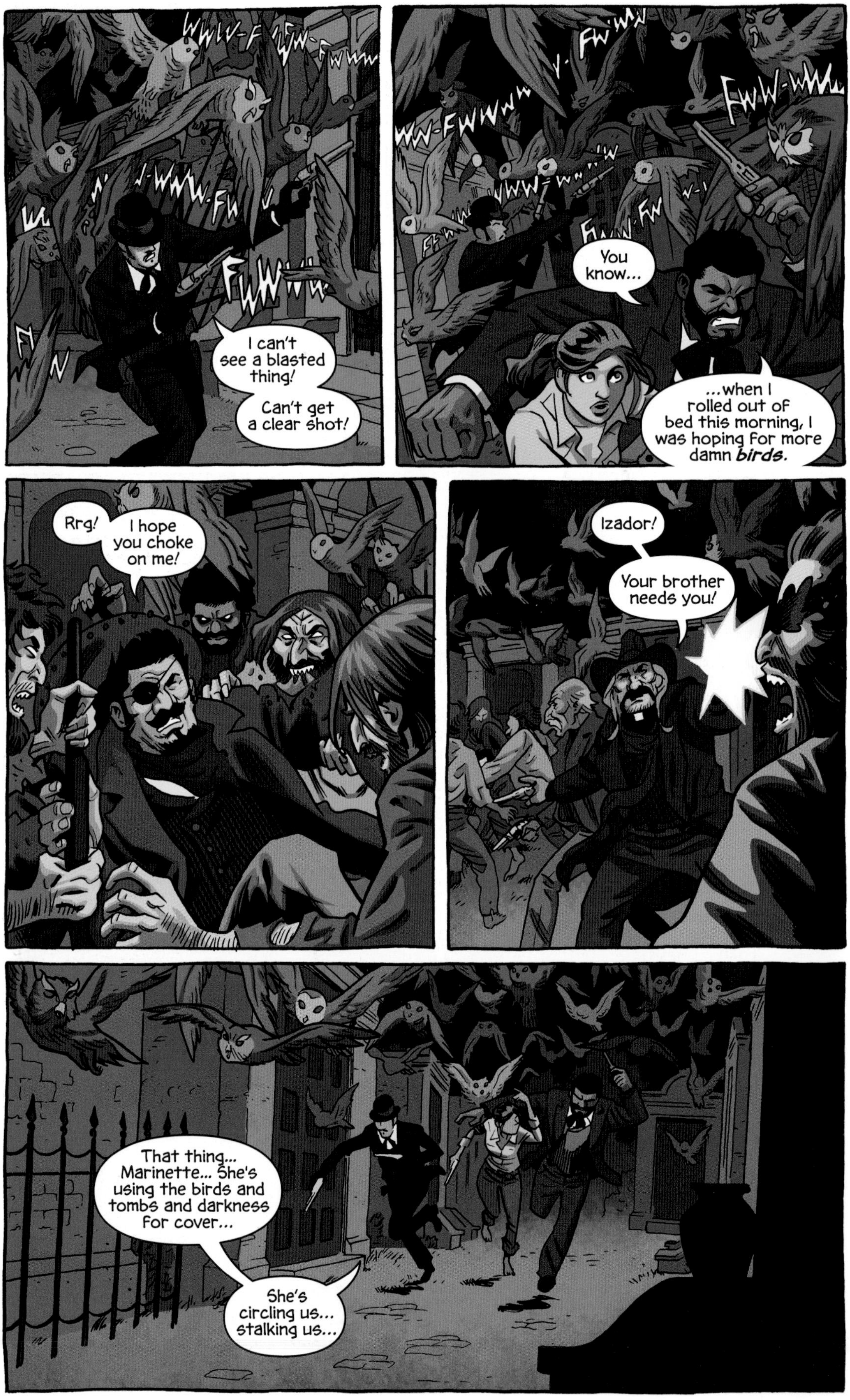
WWLV-FWW-FWWW
WW-JWWW-FW
FWWW
FN
I can't see a blasted thing!
Can't get a clear shot!
FWW-WWL
WN-FWWWW
WWW-WW
FWW-FW
You know...
...when I rolled out of bed this morning, I was hoping for more damn ***birds.***
Rrg!
I hope you choke on me!
Izador!
Your brother needs you!
That thing... Marinette... She's using the birds and tombs and darkness for cover...
She's circling us... stalking us...

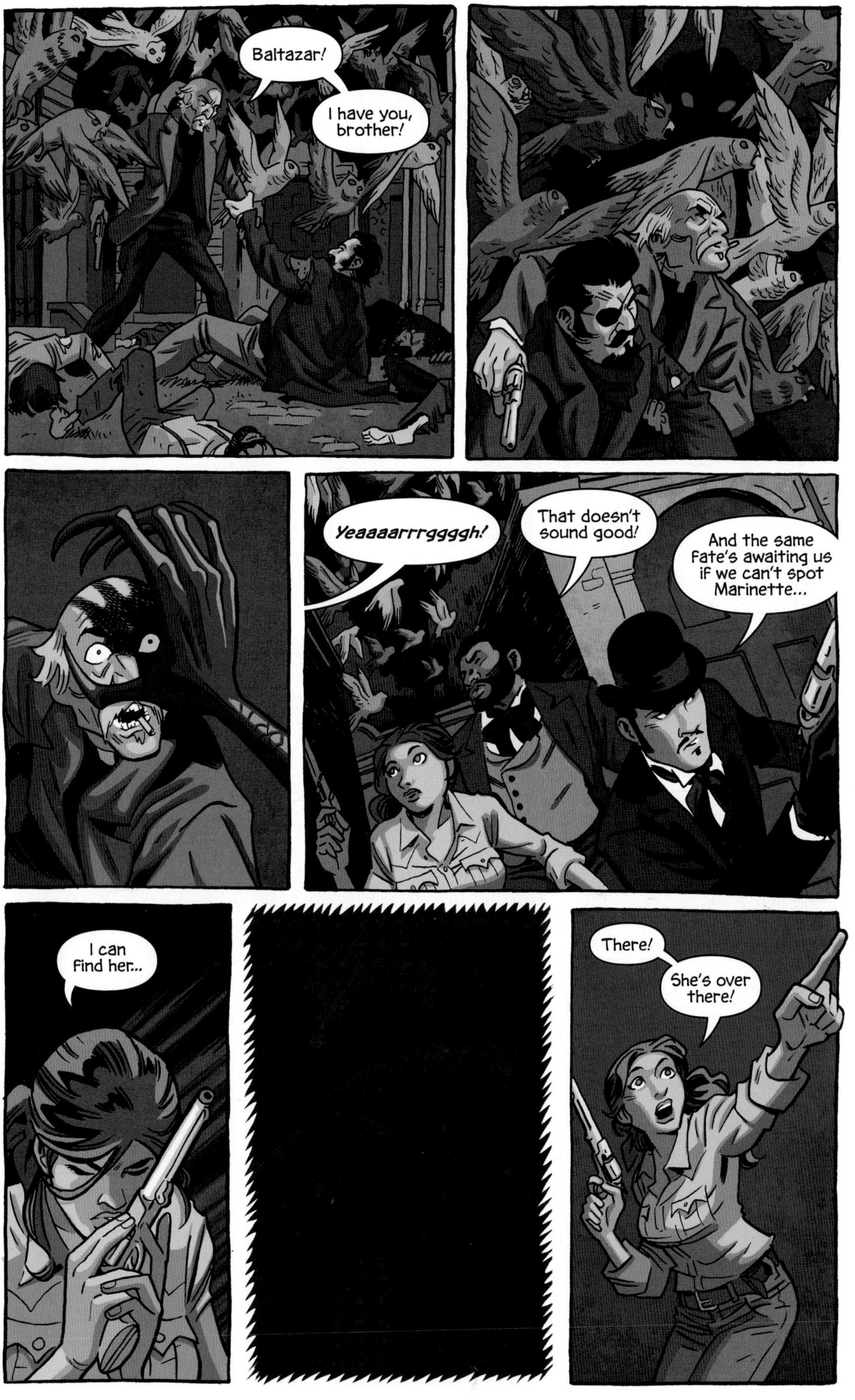

Baltazar!
I have you, brother!
Yeaaaarrrggggh!
That doesn't sound good!
And the same fate's awaiting us if we can't spot Marinette...
I can find her...
There!
She's over there!

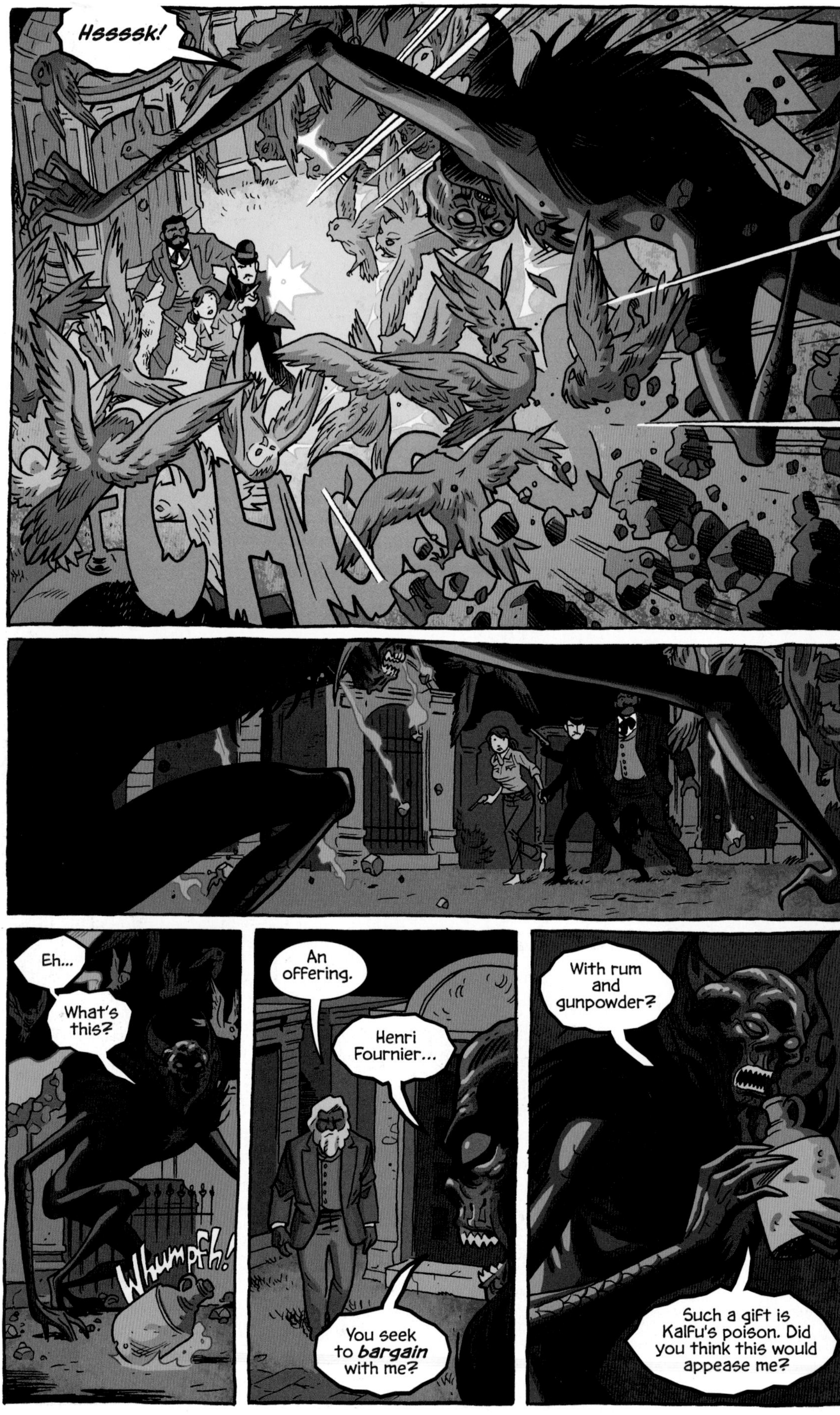
Hssssk!
Eh...
What's this?
Whumpfh!
An offering.
Henri Fournier...
You seek to bargain with me?
With rum and gunpowder?
Such a gift is Kalfu's poison. Did you think this would appease me?

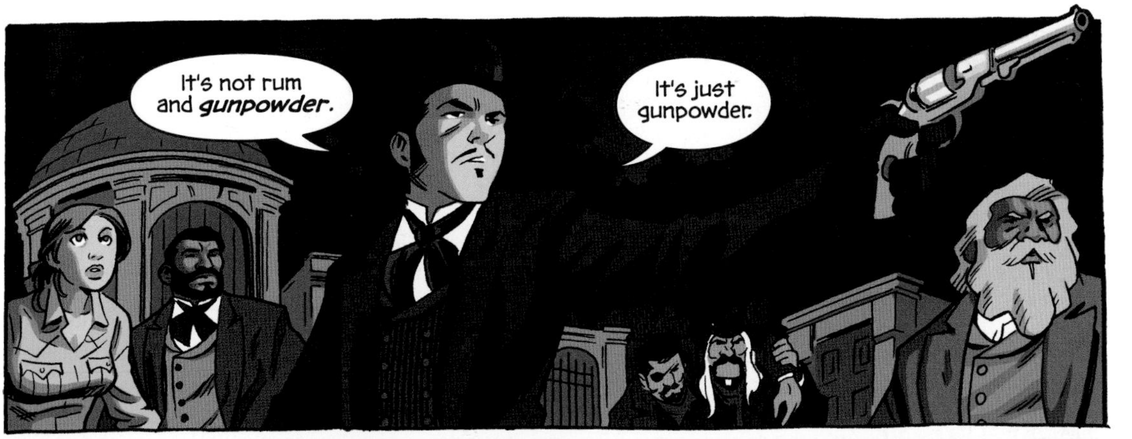
It's not rum and *gunpowder*.
It's just gunpowder.

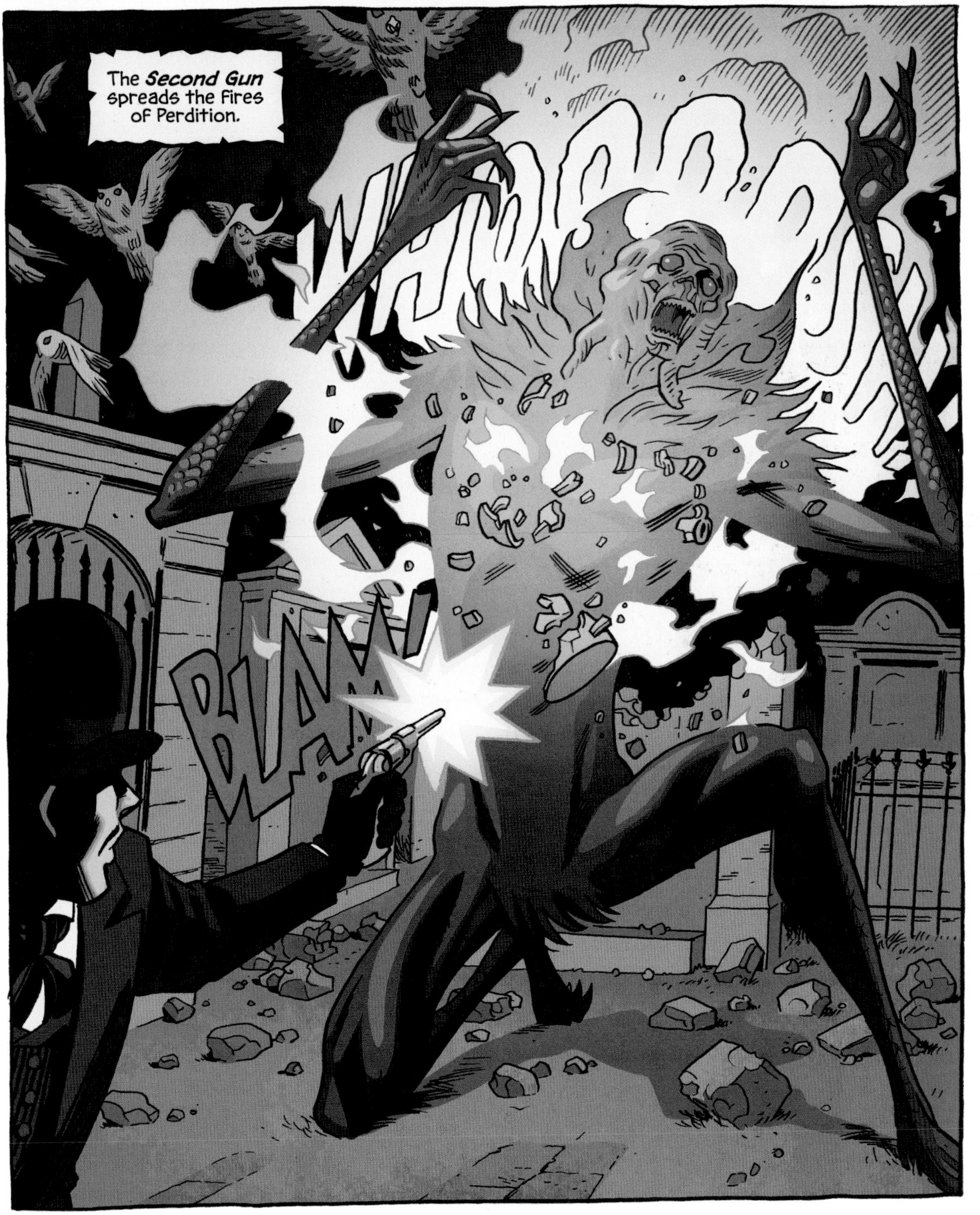
The *Second Gun* spreads the fires of Perdition.
BLAM!

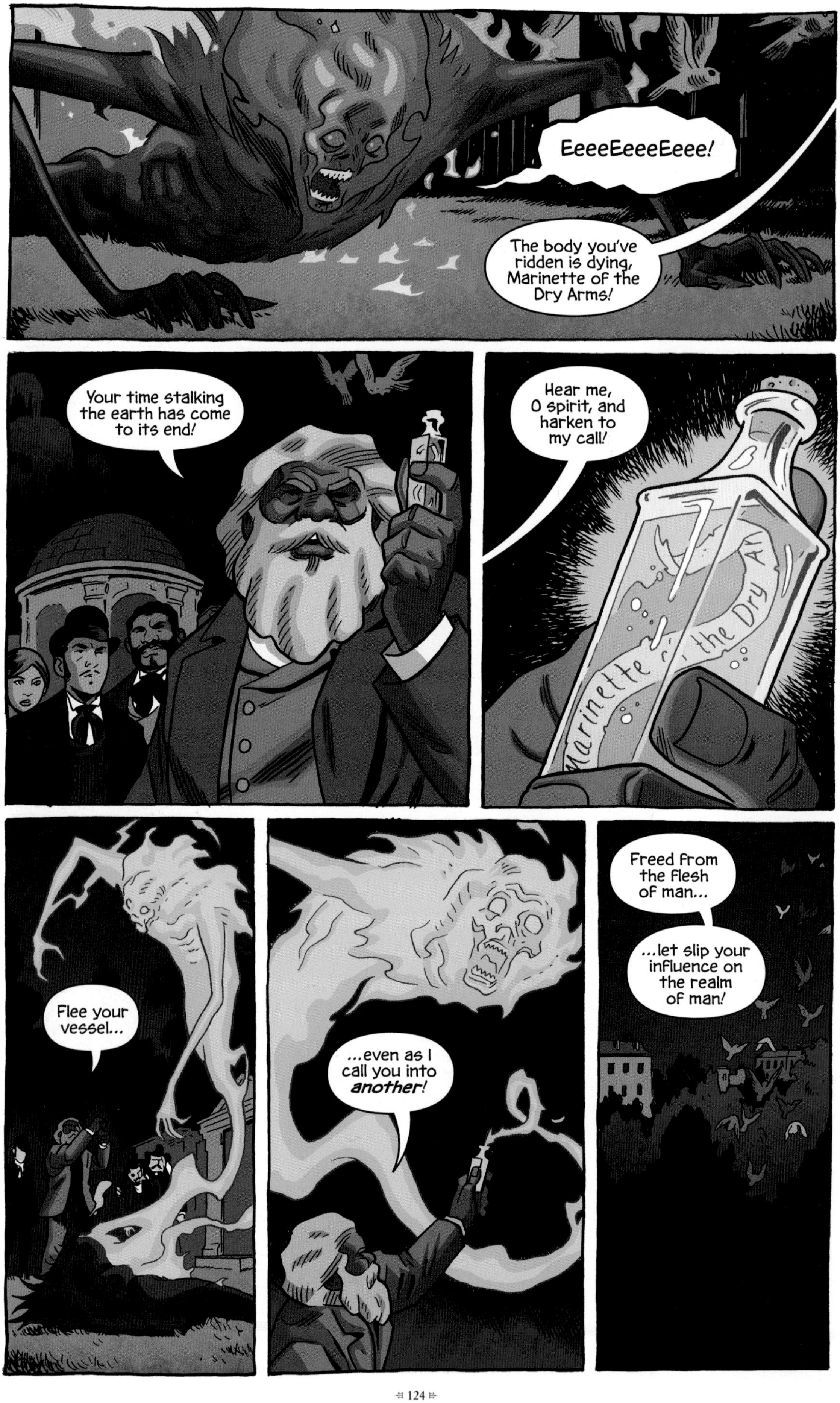
EeeeEeeeEeee!
The body you've ridden is dying, Marinette of the Dry Arms!
Your time stalking the earth has come to its end!
Hear me, O spirit, and harken to my call!
Marinette ... the Dry A
Flee your vessel...
...even as I call you into *another*!
Freed from the flesh of man...
...let slip your influence on the realm of man!

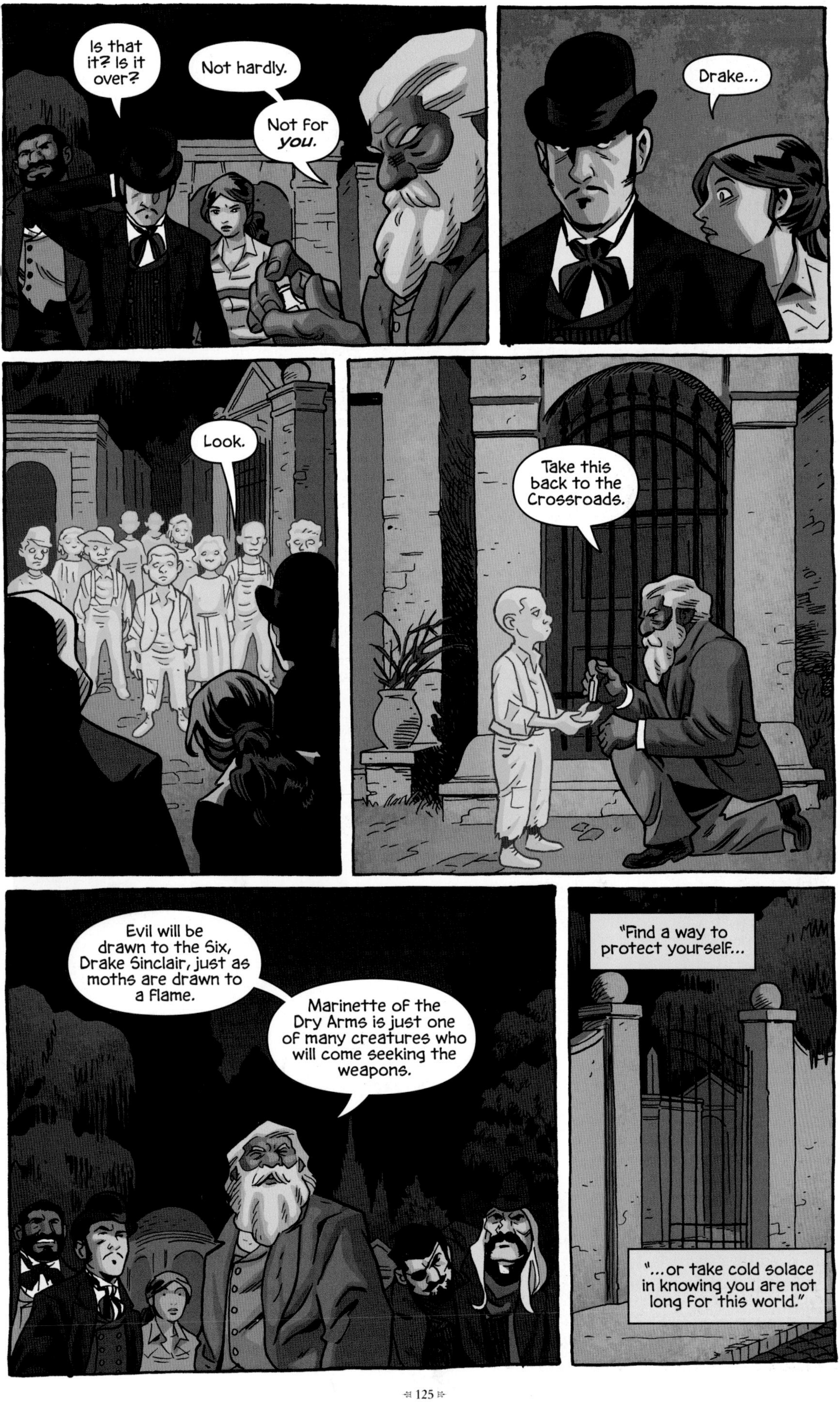
Is that it? Is it over?
Not hardly.
Not for *you.*
Drake...
Look.
Take this back to the Crossroads.
Evil will be drawn to the Six, Drake Sinclair, just as moths are drawn to a flame.
Marinette of the Dry Arms is just one of many creatures who will come seeking the weapons.
"Find a way to protect yourself...
"...or take cold solace in knowing you are not long for this world."

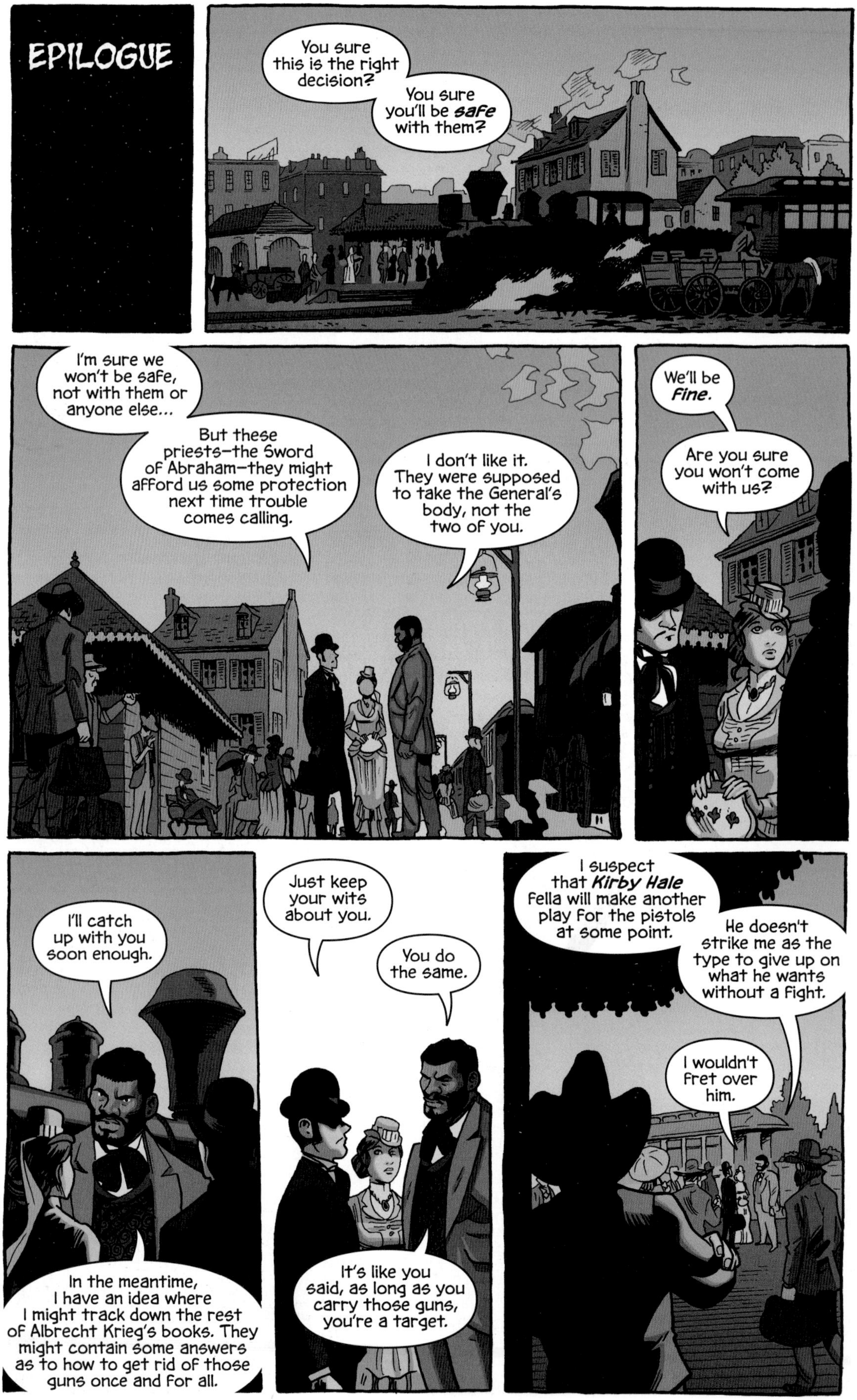
EPILOGUE
You sure this is the right decision?
You sure you'll be *safe* with them?
I'm sure we won't be safe, not with them or anyone else...
But these priests—the Sword of Abraham—they might afford us some protection next time trouble comes calling.
I don't like it. They were supposed to take the General's body, not the two of you.
We'll be *Fine*.
Are you sure you won't come with us?
I'll catch up with you soon enough.
In the meantime, I have an idea where I might track down the rest of Albrecht Krieg's books. They might contain some answers as to how to get rid of those guns once and for all.
Just keep your wits about you.
You do the same.
It's like you said, as long as you carry those guns, you're a target.
I suspect that *Kirby Hale* Fella will make another play for the pistols at some point.
He doesn't strike me as the type to give up on what he wants without a fight.
I wouldn't fret over him.

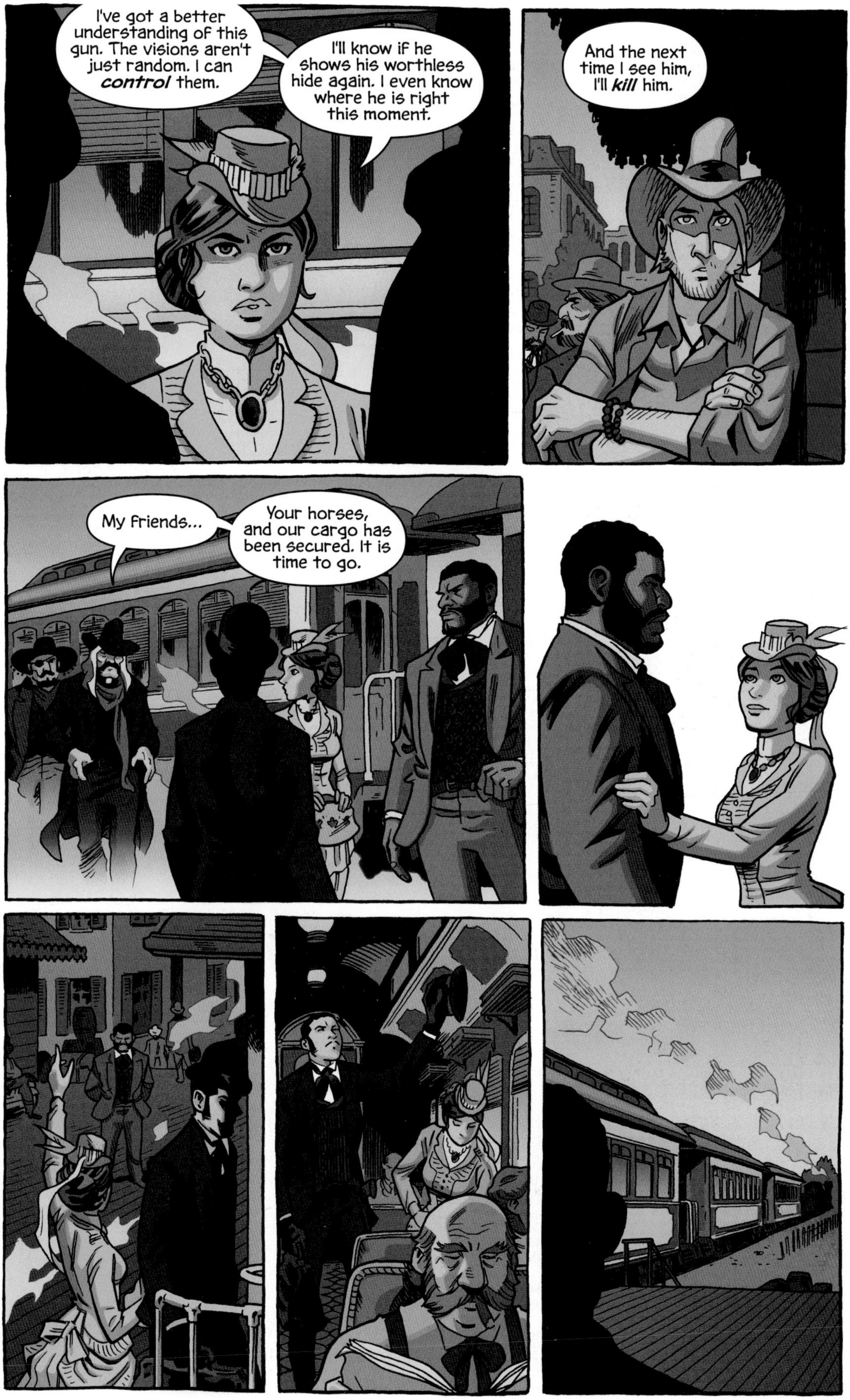
I've got a better understanding of this gun. The visions aren't just random. I can *control* them.
I'll know if he shows his worthless hide again. I even know where he is right this moment.
And the next time I see him, I'll *kill* him.
My friends...
Your horses, and our cargo has been secured. It is time to go.

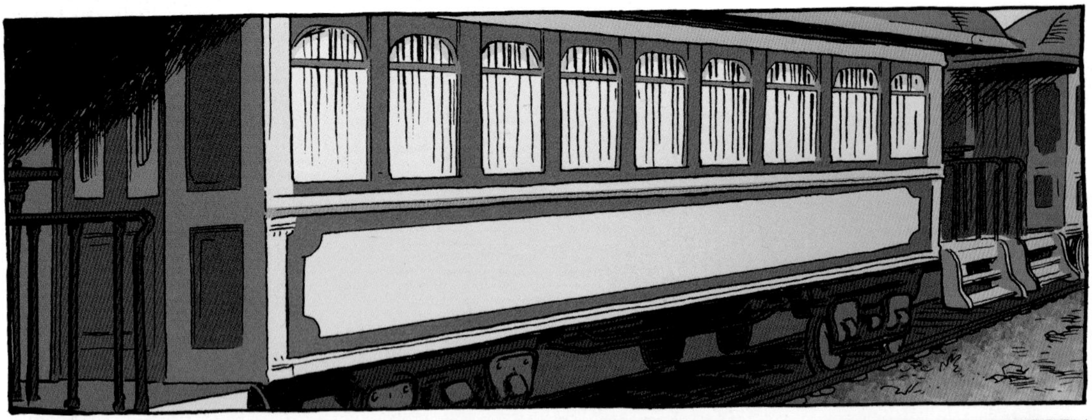

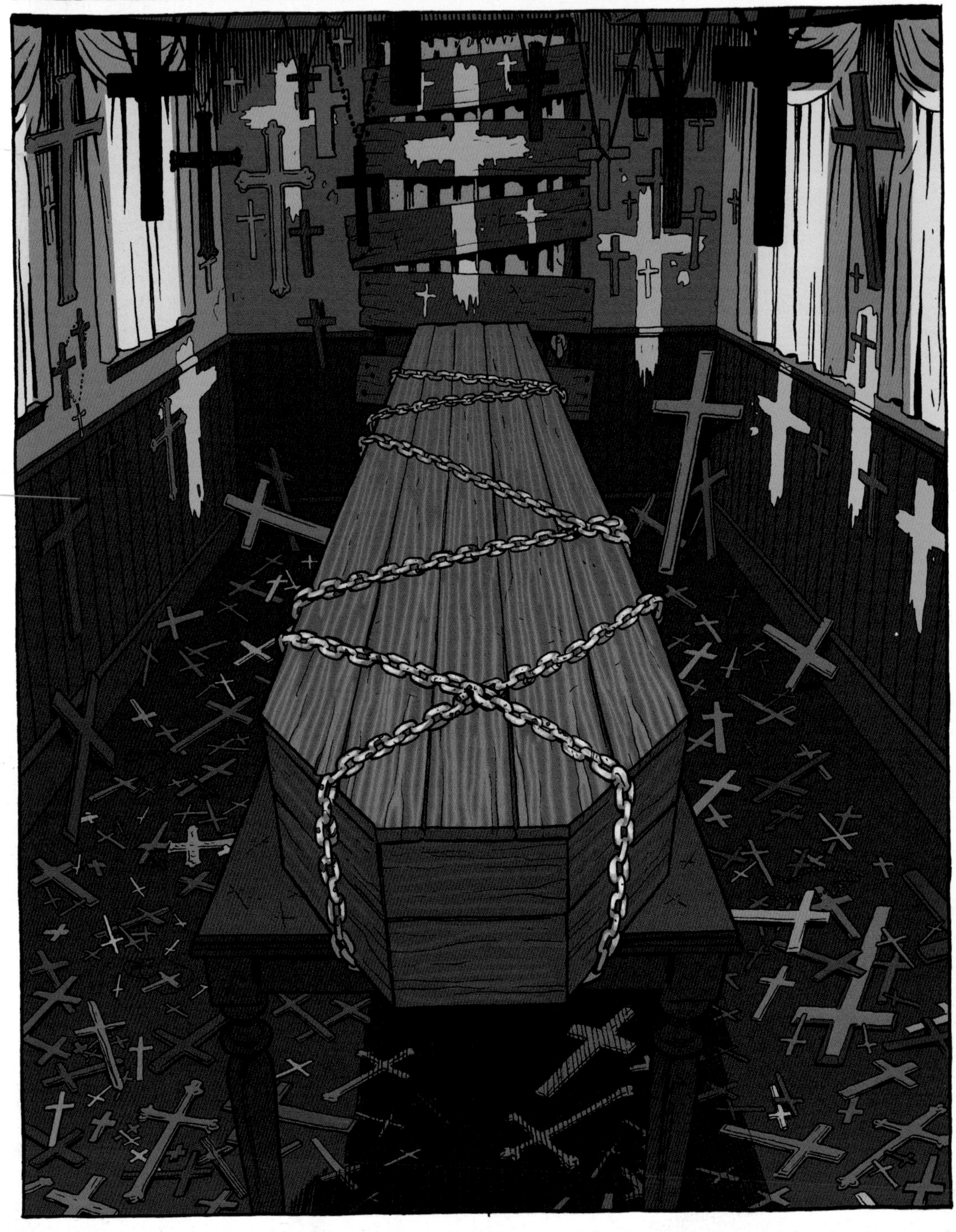

THE SIXTH GUN
ADVENTURE CONTINUES...

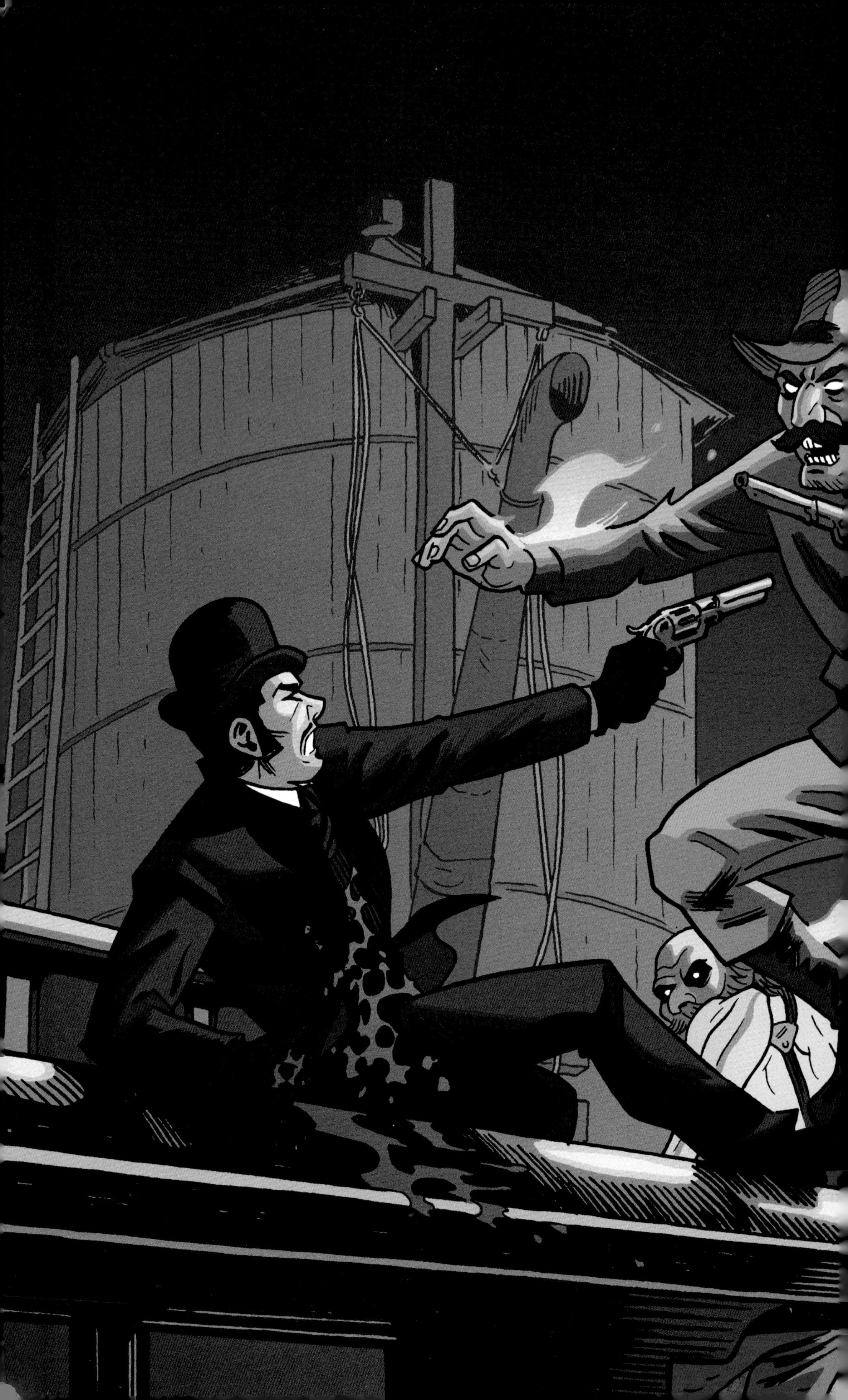

THE ADVENTURE CONTINUES EVERY MONTH!

Marinette of the Dry Arms has been banished into the nether-world, and the rotting remains of General Hume are in the care of the Sword of Abraham. But Drake Sinclair and Becky Montcrief can't rest easy. They're still in possession of five of The Six—a set of cursed pistols they're only just beginning to understand. And the General's widow, Missy, springs a fiendish trap that will change the playing field forever!

Meanwhile, Gord Cantrell embarks on a quest to learn how to destroy The Six once and for all. It's a journey that brings him face to face with his own heartbreaking past... and a man he killed years ago.

Trains! Undead outlaws! Sorcery! Mummies! All have a place in the continuing adventures of Drake Sinclair, Becky Montcrief, Gord Cantrell, and The Six! The Sixth Gun is the critically acclaimed ongoing monthly series from Oni Press! Available at finer comic book shops everywhere!

Cullen Bunn grew up in rural North Carolina, but now lives in the St. Louis area with his wife Cindy and Jackson, his son. His noir/horror comic (and first collaboration with Brian Hurtt), *The Damned*, was published in 2007 by Oni Press. The follow-up, *The Damned: Prodigal Sons*, was released in 2008. In addition to *The Sixth Gun*, his current projects include *The Tooth*, an original graphic novel from Oni Press; *Crooked Hills*, a middle reader horror prose series from Evileye Books; and various work for Marvel and DC. Somewhere along the way, Cullen founded Undaunted Press and edited the critically acclaimed small press horror magazine, *Whispers from the Shattered Forum*.

All writers must pay their dues, and Cullen has worked various odd jobs, including Alien Autopsy Specialist, Rodeo Clown, Professional Wrestler Manager, and Sasquatch Wrangler.

And, yes, he has fought for his life against mountain lions and he did perform on stage as the World's Youngest Hypnotist. Buy him a drink sometime, and he'll tell you all about it.

Visit his website at www.cullenbunn.com.

Brian Hurtt got his start in comics pencilling the second arc of Greg Rucka's *Queen & Country*. This was followed by art duties on several projects including *Queen & Country: Declassified*, *Three Strikes*, and Steve Gerber's critically acclaimed series *Hard Time*.

In 2006, Brian teamed with Cullen Bunn to create the Prohibition-era monster-noir sensation *The Damned*. The two found that their unique tastes and storytelling sensibilities were well-suited to one another and were eager to continue that relationship.

The Sixth Gun is their sophomore endeavor together and the next in what looks to be many years of creative collaboration.

Brian lives in St. Louis where the summers are too hot, the winters too cold, but the rent is just right.

He can be found online at thebrianhurtt.blogspot.com.

X

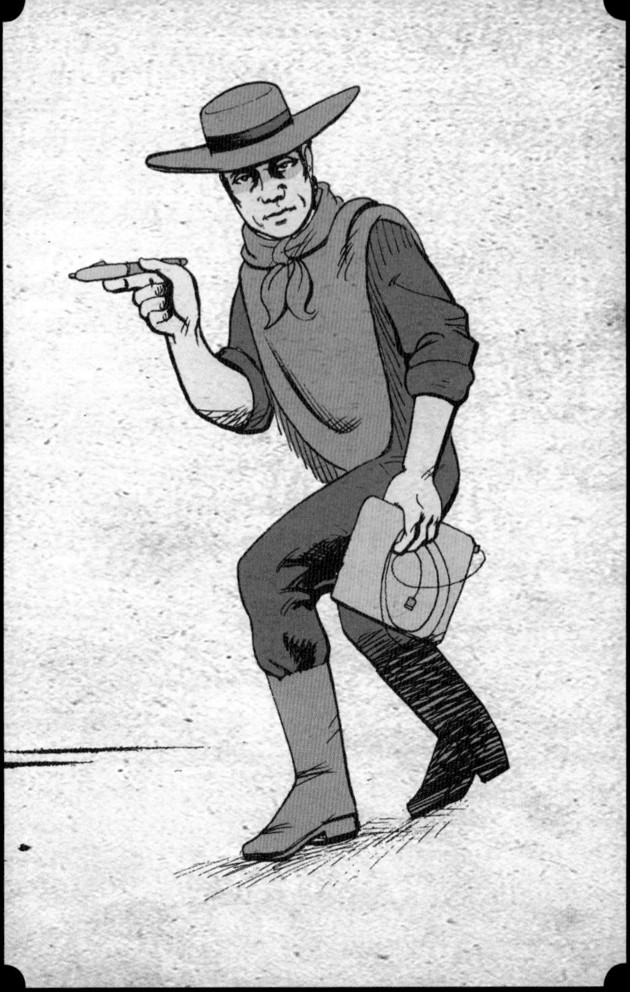

Illustration by Bill Crabtree.

Bill Crabtree's career as a colorist began in 2003 with the launch of Image Comic's *Invincible* and *Firebreather.* He would go on to color the first 50 issues of *Invincible*, which would become a flagship Image Comics title, along with garnering Bill a Harvey Awards nomination.

He continues to color *Firebreather*, which was recently made into a feature film on Cartoon Network, as well as *Godland* and *Jack Staff.*

Perhaps the highlight of his comics career, his role as colorist on *The Sixth Gun* began with issue 6, and has since been described as "like Christmas morning, but with guns."

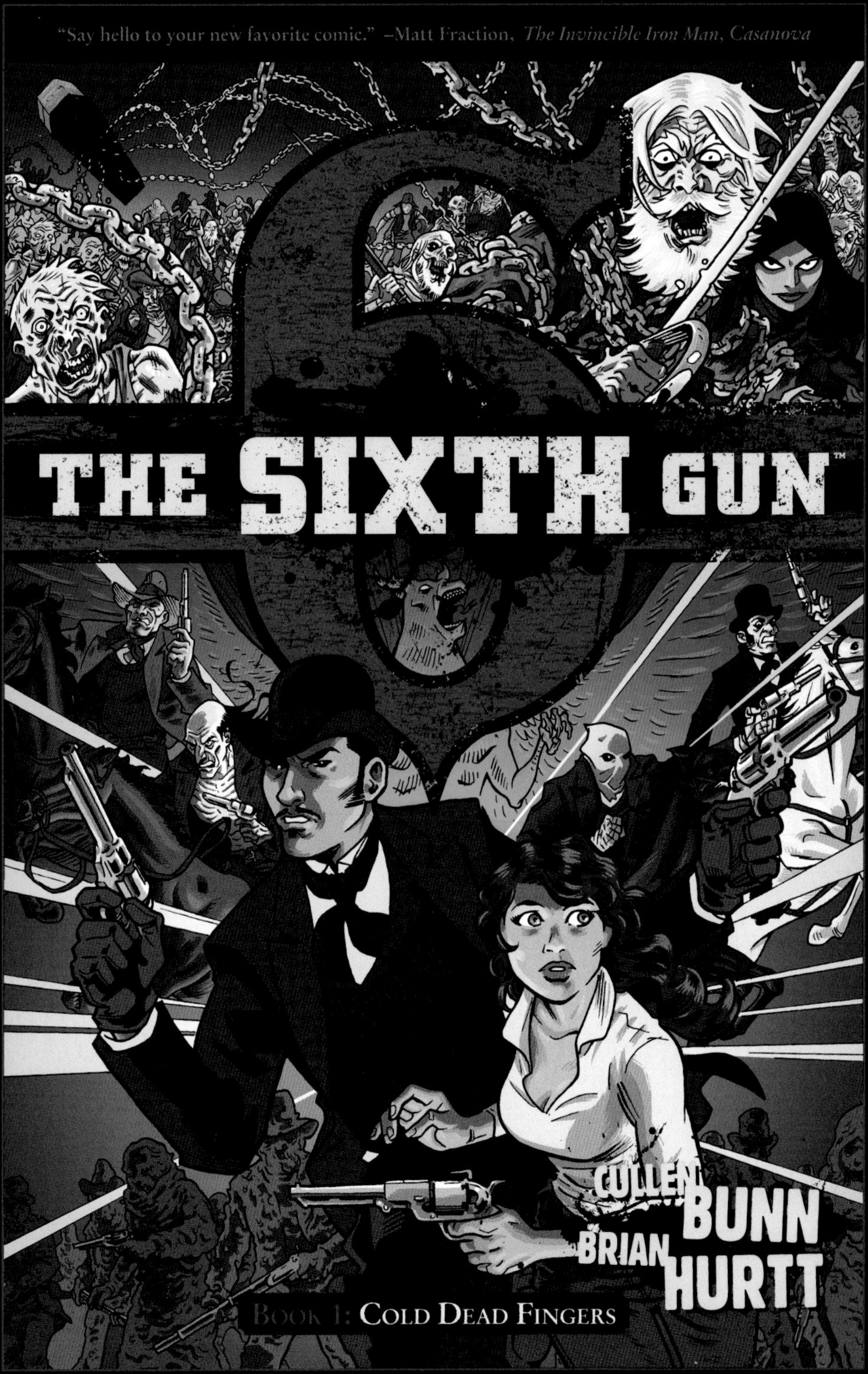
"Say hello to your new favorite comic." –Matt Fraction, *The Invincible Iron Man*, *Casanova*
THE SIXTH GUN™
CULLEN BUNN
BRIAN HURTT
BOOK 1: COLD DEAD FINGERS

From Cullen Bunn, Brian Hurtt & Oni Press...

THE SIXTH GUN, VOLUME 1: COLD DEAD FINGERS
By Cullen Bunn & Brian Hurtt
176 pages • Trade Paperback
Color • $19.99
ISBN 978-1-934964-60-6

THE SIXTH GUN, VOLUME 2: BOUND
By Cullen Bunn & Brian Hurtt
with Tyler Crook
136 pages • Trade Paperback
Color • $19.99
ISBN 978-1-934964-78-1

THE SIXTH GUN, VOLUME 4: A TOWN CALLED PENANCE
By Cullen Bunn & Brian Hurtt
168 pages • Trade Paperback
Color • $19.99
ISBN 978-1-934964-95-8

THE DAMNED: VOLUME 1
By Cullen Bunn & Brian Hurtt
160 pages • 6"x9" • Trade Paperback
Black and White • $14.99 US
ISBN 978-1-932664-6-38

THE TOOTH
By Cullen Bunn, Shawn Lee, and Matt Kindt
184 pages • Hardcover
Color • $24.99
ISBN 978-1-934964-52-1

PETROGRAD
By Philp Gelatt & Tyler Crook
264 pages • 6"x9" Hardcover
2-Color • $29.99
ISBN 978-1-934964-44-6

QUEEN & COUNTRY DEFINITIVE EDITION: VOLUME 1
By Greg Rucka with Steve Rolston, Brian Hurtt, and Leandro Fernandez
366 pages • 6"x9" • Trade Paperback
Black and White • $19.99
ISBN 978-1-932664-87-4

WASTELAND: VOLUME 1
By Antony Johnston & Christopher Mitten
160 pages • Trade Paperback
Black and White • $11.99
ISBN 978-1-932664-59-1

THE SIXTH GUN
CULLEN BUNN
BRIAN HURTT

THE SIXTH GUN
CULLEN BUNN
BRIAN HURTT
TYLER CROOK
BILL CRABTREE

THE SIXTH GUN
CULLEN BUNN
BRIAN HURTT
TYLER CROOK
BILL CRABTREE
A TOWN CALLED PENANCE

DAMNED
VOLUME ONE
"THREE DAYS DEAD"

the Tooth
A New Beginning! The Tooth Unleashed!

PETROGRAD
PHILIP GELATT • TYLER CROOK

GREG RUCKA
QUEEN & COUNTRY
DEFINITIVE EDITION
VOLUME 01

WASTELAND
ANTONY JOHNSTON
CHRISTOPHER MITTEN
BOOK 01
CITIES IN DUST

For more information on these and other fine Oni Press comic books and graphic novels visit www.onipress.com. To find a comic shop specialty store in your area visit www.comicshops.us.

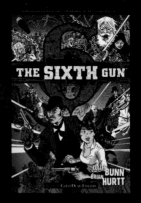

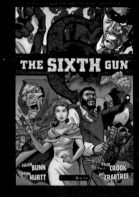

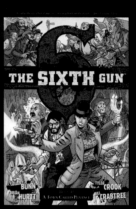

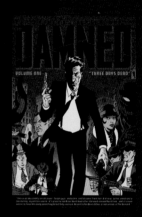

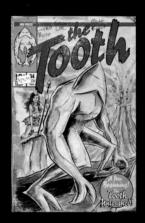

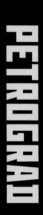

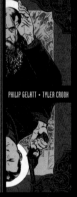

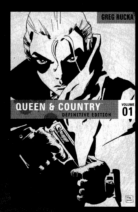

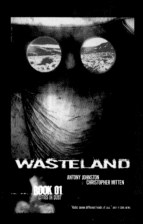

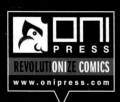